The Early Germans

The Peoples of Europe

General Editors
James Campbell and Barry Cunliffe

This series is about the European tribes and peoples from their origins in prehistory to the present day. Drawing upon a wide range of archaeological and historical evidence, each volume presents a fresh and absorbing account of a group's culture, society and sometimes turbulent history.

Accessible and scholarly, the volumes of 'The Peoples of Europe' will together provide a comprehensive and vivid picture of European society and the peoples who formed it.

Already published

The Mongols
David Morgan

The Basques
Roger Collins

The Franks
Edward James

The Bretons
Patrick Galliou and Michael Jones

The Illyrians
John Wilkes

The Early Germans
Malcolm Todd

In preparation

The Picts
Charles Thomas

The Armenians
Elizabeth Redgate

The Celts
David Dumville

The Gypsies
Angus Fraser

The Normans
Marjorie Chibnall

The Huns
E. A. Thompson

The Spanish
Roger Collins

The Turks
C. J. Heywood

The Sicilians
David Abulafia

The Goths
Peter Heather

The Early English
Sonia Chadwick Hawkes

The Irish
Francis John Byrne and Michael Herity

The Etruscans
Graeme Barker and Thomas Rasmussen

The English
Geoffrey Elton

The Lombards
Neil Christie

The Hungarians
Michael Hurst

The Norsemen
John Haywood

The Early Germans

Malcolm Todd

BLACKWELL
Oxford UK & Cambridge USA

First published 1992
First published in USA 1992

Blackwell Publishers
108 Cowley Road
Oxford OX4 1JF
UK

Three Cambridge Center
Cambridge, Massachusetts 02142
USA

A CIP catalogue record for this book is available from the British Library.

Library of Congress Cataloging-in-Publication Data

Todd, Malcolm, FSA.
The early Germans/Malcolm Todd.
p.   cm.— (The Peoples of Europe)
Includes bibliographical references (p.   ) and index.
ISBN 0–631–16397–2 (acid-free paper)
1.   Germanic tribes—History. I. Title. II. Series.
DD75.T62   1992
909'.043—dc20   91–32493
CIP

Typeset in 11 on 12½pt Sabon
by Photo·graphics, Honiton, Devon
Printed in Great Britain by Biddles Ltd, Guildford

This book is printed on acid-free paper.

To E. A. Thompson

Contents

Illustrations and Maps

Architectonici di Ravenna)

Foreword

The emergence and early history of the Germanic peoples have never been a central concern of British historians. Even those who have written on Anglo-Saxon England have surprisingly rarely sought to relate the Germans who settled in England to the larger family of which they were a small but significant branch. There are, of course, exceptions, among whom Michael Wallace-Hadrill and Edward Thompson immediately come to mind. And a growing school of younger scholars is beginning to provide redress for long neglect. This book is offered as a general introduction to a huge and complex field of study, the literature of which is daunting in its mass. In a single small volume many major subjects can be only briefly touched on, while others have been excluded only for want of space.

Given the nature of the historical evidence, it is clearly impossible to treat the early Germans without close reference to the Roman world and its impact upon them. But there was also significant impact on the Roman world by the Germanic peoples, and not merely after the major migrations. This, too, has been a major concern, though the subject demands attention at far greater length. All books are acts of larceny. Those whose work I have learnt from and converted to my own use are too numerous to receive individual acknowledgement. But my debt to Edward Thompson, which has accumulated over nearly three decades, is too great to be passed over in silence.

Abbreviations

Acta Arch.	*Acta Archaeologica*
Acta Arch. Hung.	*Acta Archaeologica Hungarica*
Arch. Belgica	*Archaeologia Belgica*
Bonner Jahrb.	*Bonner Jahrbücher*
BRGK	*Bericht der Römisch-Germanischen Kommission*
BROB	*Berichten van de Rijksdienst voor het Oudheidkundig Bodemonderzoek*
JRGZM	*Jahrbuch des Römisch-Germanischen Zentralmuseums Mainz*
JRS	*Journal of Roman Studies*
MGH. AA	*Monumenta Germaniae Historica Auctores Antiquissimi*
Oxford Journ. Arch.	*Oxford Journal of Archaeology*
Prähist. Zeitschrift	*Prähistorische Zeitschrift*

Introduction: Rediscovery

The Germani

The peoples known to the Classical Mediterranean world as the Germani were relative latecomers to history. Mediterranean writers knew little of the peoples who inhabited north and central Europe before the second century BC. The earliest surviving references to those peoples make no mention of Germans. In the fifth century BC, the Greek world was conscious of a major barbarian people in west and central Europe; it called them Keltoi (Celts). Herodotus relates that they were the most westerly of European peoples and that the Danube had its source in their territory. He also knew about the nomadic Scythians on the steppes of western Russia, far more indeed than he knew about the Celts. Hekataeus also mentions Celts, in the eastern Alpine region known as Noricum (now mainly occupied by Austria). But neither Herodotus nor Hekataeus refers to Germans, or other major barbarian peoples. A century later, Ephorus named the four great barbarian nations known to him: Celts, Scythians, Persians and Libyans. By the late fourth century BC, knowledge of the remoter parts of Europe was growing. At some date, probably about 320, Pytheas of Marseilles sailed around Britain and along the north European coast, possibly rounding Jutland and entering the western Baltic. His journey was so astonishing an achievement that contemporary and later writers refused to believe his account, and what survives of it amounts only to quotations by others. Much of what Pytheas is said to have recorded is geographically reliable, though it is scanty on the northern European mainland. He is chiefly of interest to us because he may have been the first Mediterranean observer to distinguish Germanoi from Keltoi.

In the two centuries after Pytheas' voyage, remarkably little was added to the canon of information on the northern peoples. The first clear indication of peoples who were distinct from the Celts and who came from far to the north of them was registered late in the second century BC, when a huge and miscellaneous throng of northerners, including Cimbri and Teutones, swept southward and endangered the northern frontiers of the Roman world. At about this time, in his *Histories*, Poseidonius of Apamea distinguished the Germans from the Celts and the Scythians. It is known that Poseidonius visited Gaul and northern Italy, but he clearly had no first-hand knowledge of lands and peoples further north. His sources can only be guessed at, but we should not assume that they were outstandingly well informed. Nor should we assume that what Poseidonius wrote about the Germans had a powerful influence on later writers such as Caesar and Strabo, as many modern scholars have done.[1] That his information was used is certain, but by the first century BC there will have been other sources for the northern peoples. A generation after Poseidonius, Rome was to come into contact with the western Germans, thus inaugurating a long relationship which would lead ultimately to the transformation of Europe.

Roman arms were first carried to the Rhine, and, in two brief campaigns, beyond it by Julius Caesar. His *Commentaries* on his conquests in Gaul provide us with our first sight of material conditions among the Germans. Caesar's sketch of Germanic society and political organization is executed with a few bold strokes.[2] Though it must be accepted as the earliest coherent picture we possess of Germanic society, it is clearly

---

[1] E. Norden, *Die germanische Urgeschichte in Tacitus' Germania* (4th edn; Darmstadt 1959) is still influential in deriving much from the Poseidonian tradition. The case is not without basis, but is overstated.

[2] R. Hachmann, G. Kossack and H. Kuhn, *Völker zwischen Kelten und Germanen* (Neumünster 1962); M. Gelzer, *Caesar: Politician and Statesman* (Cambridge, Mass. 1968).

based upon knowledge of a relatively small part of Germania, that part which Caesar himself saw in the valley of the Rhine and immediately to the east of it. The tribes he mentions are those established at that date in the broken terrain within 100 kilometres of the Rhine (the Suebi, Tencteri, Usipetes) or on the river itself (Ubii, Menapii). No information about the peoples of the interior had reached him and it is difficult to see what sources could have supplied such information at that date. Of the German tribes which Caesar describes the largest and most powerful were the Suebi. For some time before Caesar's arrival in Gaul they had been turning their attentions westward, tending to dominate smaller tribes close to the Rhine. Some adventurous elements from the Suebi, led by Ariovistus, had indeed established themselves west of the Rhine, having been invited in as mercenaries by the Sequani, and it was this German presence in eastern Gaul which gave Caesar a useful pretext for intervening in the affairs of the Gaulish tribes. For this westward drive of the Suebi there is other evidence, both archaeological and philological.[3]

Caesar's picture of the Germans is skilfully drawn. He carefully emphasized the Rhine valley as a divide between the Gauls to the west and the Germans to the east. According to Caesar, these peoples were very different from each other. The Gauls, though tough and warlike, were amenable to the attractions of orderly, civilized life. The Germans on the other hand were primitive, following a life-style which seemed to Romans even more savage than that of other barbarians and one that would never be softened by contact with civilized men. Worse than that, they posed a serious threat to the security of Gaul. The Suebi were poised to cross the Rhine in great strength, following the earlier crossing by an enormous host led by Ariovistus. If this menace was not confronted and beaten off, an invasion of the Roman provinces, perhaps even of Italy itself, could not be prevented. The memory of the invasion of the Cimbri and Teutones had not faded and Caesar could appeal to deep-seated fears in order to justify his own operations in Gaul. Caesar's

---

[3] R. Nierhaus, *Das swebische Gräberfeld von Diersheim* (Berlin 1966) for later German settlement close to the upper Rhine near Strasbourg.

motives have received a great deal of attention. Obviously
his own purposes were to the fore and they did not include
dispassionate ethnographical study. But he may well have been
correct in seeing that the peoples east of the Rhine were likely
to seek land on which to settle in Gaul. The southward thrust
of the Cimbri and others was only one of several major movements of population in central and western Europe in this
period, as competition increased for good land and other natural resources. Before Caesar entered Gaul, migrants had passed
into northern Gaul from across the Rhine, while further east
there were major shifts of population in Noricum and Bohemia.
These movements had been proceeding for some time before
the mid-first century BC. The new component of the scene was
the expansion of Roman power.

Strabo, writing in the reigns of Augustus and Tiberius, not
surprisingly knew more than Caesar about the Germans east
of the Rhine. Like Caesar, he saw the Suebi as the strongest
and most dangerous power and he records that they had already
driven several groups across the river into Gaul. The Cimbri
also interested him, partly no doubt because of their famous
raid a century earlier and also because their gift of a revered
cauldron to Augustus, presumably reciprocated by a Roman
offering, had been recently talked about in Rome. Strabo claims
a fair knowledge of the peoples up to the Elbe, but specifically
says that those areas beyond the Elbe and northwards to the
ocean (the Baltic) were unknown to the Romans. About the
central Germanic regions, in the upper Elbe basin, he is vague.
At the very time that Strabo was writing, however, knowledge
was advancing as Roman arms were advancing to the Elbe and
into Bohemia, and as other contacts with the Germans were
being established.

There is a clear echo of the fear and indeed terror which the
Germans aroused at this time in the writing of Velleius Paterculus, who had served as an officer in the army sent to the
Rhine frontier after the massive defeat of Varus in AD 9. To
Velleius the Germans were inhuman savages, *feri*, resembling
men only in their form and in possessing the power of speech.
Such people could not be governed by laws, much less taught
the civilized arts. This is an extreme view, expressed by someone
who encountered Germans at a time of acute crisis. Yet it is

echoed in other sources at a much later date and reveals not only how dire a threat the Germans were seen to be, but how terrifying these tall, ferocious northerners were, even to soldiers in the best army of the ancient world.

A particularly unfortunate loss to us is that of the *Bella Germaniae* of the elder Pliny, an account of Roman campaigns against the Germans down to the mid-first century AD. Pliny had served on both the lower and the upper Rhine, and his inexhaustible curiosity about every subject undoubtedly would have led him to record much about Germanic life and institutions. It is probable that a number of the statements in Tacitus' *Germania* which seem to be drawn from the life were supplied by Pliny's work; for example the story of the altar dedicated by Ulysses on the Rhine, and the memorial tumuli inscribed in Greek. After Pliny, we know of no work of literature which dealt with the Germans until the publication of Tacitus' *Germania* in AD 98. But during this period primary sources of knowledge about northern Europe increased enormously. Roman commanders frequently produced memoirs of their campaigns, along the line of Caesar's *Commentaries*, and these circulated in Roman literary circles, even if they were never published. Diplomatic exchanges certainly brought some German leaders to Rome and, doubtless, Roman emissaries to barbarian courts. Above all else, traders greatly extended their activities among the barbarians, on occasion with official engagement, and their intelligence about the barbarian world in all its aspects is likely to have been more rounded than that gathered by the military men (below, p. 89). Such reports must have been of particular interest for what they provided about the peoples of the north and the east, with whom official contacts were sparse.

The short monograph by Cornelius Tacitus published in AD 98 and known to us generally as the *Germania* or *On the Origin and Situation of the Germans*, is the most substantial treatment of barbarians to survive from Antiquity. The tradition of ethnographical writing was old and there was much material which could not only be imitated but also copied from earlier sources. The work of Poseidonius early in the first century BC was a late flowering of this tradition and clearly influenced the writers of the next two centuries. But it did not

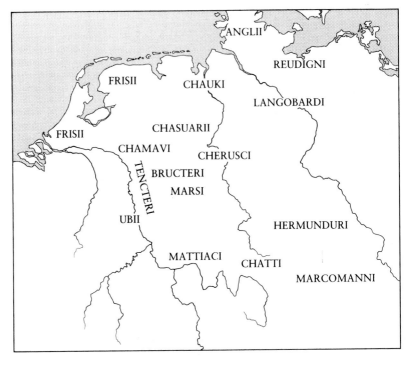

Figure 1 The western Germanic peoples: c.AD 100.

dominate their accounts as completely as some scholars have suggested. Though set within a well defined literary genre, the *Germania* offers an unrivalled account of the peoples of northern and eastern Europe, its contents ranging from the clearly factual to the obviously fabulous. There is much in the ancient descriptions of barbarians that is conventional and this shows in the *Germania*. But there is much more that obviously derives from written sources that were by any standards well informed. The tribal catalogue that makes up nearly half of the monograph is detailed and circumstantial. But the sources which Tacitus used were far from up to date. Most probably a great deal was taken from Pliny's *German Wars*, which itself contained material gathered earlier by merchants and other travellers. Remarkably, the *Germania* says virtually nothing about the Germans in the forty or so years preceding publication. At certain points, this leads to highly misleading statements, as when Tacitus reports that the Marcomanni and Quadi were loyal to Rome. In fact those peoples had decisively turned against the Empire nearly a decade earlier, in 89. The *Germania* must be read with due care, but it is nevertheless an important statement on the barbarian peoples of the North and represents a significant stage in their rediscovery.

After the *Germania*, the sources available to us are neither extensive in range nor impressive in quality. From the middle of the second century we have the *Geography* of Ptolemy, an astronomer–geographer who worked in Alexandria. The *Geography* relied heavily on first-century sources and consists

Figure 2 The eastern Germanic peoples: c.AD 100.

largely of lists of places, geographical features and tribes, lati-
tude and longitude being provided for the places. The status
of the individual sites given by Ptolemy is not always clear.
Some were probably major settlements, others may be market-
centres or river crossings which Roman merchants had had
reason to make note of. Some of his names are garbled and
some places are obviously wrongly positioned, so that an accur-
ate map cannot be reconstructed from the information he
gives. He does, however, record sixty-nine tribes and ninety-five
places, many of them mentioned by no other source, along
with major rivers and other natural features. Inadequate as the
Geography is, it is the only extensive source for the geography
of northern Europe for the centuries between the *Germania* of
Tacitus and the changed world of the fourth century.

From late Antiquity, no extensive study of the Germanic
peoples has survived, if it was ever written. Ammianus Marcellinus is our best witness for the Franks and Alamanni of the
fourth century, but mainly as opponents of Rome.[4] No single
writer treats the migrating peoples in any coherent way and
some on whom our reliance must rest *faute de mieux*, such as
Zosimus and Jordanes, are often infuriating. There are far more
rewarding sources on the later Germanic kingdoms, such as
Cassiodorus on Theoderic's Italy, Hydatius on Spain, Gregory
of Tours on the Franks and Paul the Deacon on the Lombards.
But even these writers leave many subjects untouched and
others in a heavy shadow which we cannot completely disperse.

Origins

Who, then, were the Germani; where and when did they orig-
inate? The first point to be made is that they had no collective
consciousness of themselves as a separate people, nation or
group of tribes. There is no evidence that they called themselves
'Germani' or their land 'Germania'. These were terms applied
by writers in the Mediterranean world and they can be traced

---

[4] J. Matthews, *The Roman Empire of Ammianus Marcellinus* (London
1988), 306–18.

with certainty no further back than the time of Poseidonius. The meaning and origin of the word 'Germanus' are unknown, but it is certain that the term was not in general use among the early Germans themselves. By the time of Julius Caesar in the mid-first century BC, 'Germanus' and its derivatives were well established and Caesar himself clearly thought that no further explanation was required. The tradition which was current when Tacitus collected information for the *Germania* in the late first century AD held that the name was originally borne by a group of people who crossed the Rhine from the East, drove out the Gauls from a region in eastern Belgium and settled there, later becoming known as the Tungri. What had originally been the name of a single tribe became the name by which all the related peoples were known. There is no evidence which goes to support this derivation of the name 'Germani', though there is nothing inherently implausible in Tacitus' account. The Roman name for the Greeks, 'Graeci', comes from the little tribe of the Grai, and the name applied by the French to the Germans, 'Allemands', from a single Germanic group, the Alamanni. The linguistic origins of 'Germani' are also obscure. It is not even clear which language supplied the name. Celtic, Germanic, Latin and Illyrian have all had their supporters. All that is reasonably certain is that a member of a German tribe, when asked about his or her affiliations, would have answered 'Langobard', 'Vandal', 'Frisian' or 'Goth', not 'Germanus'.

Modern approaches to the problem of German origins have to a large extent been governed by shifts in political feeling since the mid-nineteenth century. Origins as far back as human activities could be traced were sought in the glow of German nationalism after 1848. Before the end of the century the idea of an ancient and inviolate *Germanentum* had emerged. The origins of the *Volk* were traced back to the remotest prehistoric periods and subsequent influence from outside was seen as minimal. It was easy for the National–Socialist party to incorporate this view of the German past into its political programme. After 1945 there came an inevitable reaction against such excesses. Both the exclusivity and the antiquity of the Germanic peoples came under scrutiny, at the same time as the ability of archaeological evidence alone to give definition to ethnic blocs was being increasingly called into question. In the early 1960s, Germanic origins came under intense examination from linguists as well as archaeologists.[5] Long-held notions about the separateness of the Germans were seriously challenged. The spread of Germanic peoples from a northern heartland was brought into question and the creation of a Germanic identity was linked with the advance of Roman power to the Rhine and Danube. The reaction against extreme nationalism had gone too far. In the 1980s the pendulum began a backward swing. Once again, arguments which trace the origin of the Germanic peoples to a remote period of European prehistory, to the later Neolithic, are heard.[6] Lothar Kilian in two important studies has presented a strongly argued case, based partly on elements of continuity in archaeological cultures, partly on linguistic evidence. The case does not carry conviction. It is possible to accept that the ancestors of the Germans known to our earliest surviving historical accounts can be traced back to the mid-first millennium BC, the period of the Jastorf culture, on the north German plain between Elbe and Oder, and the Harpstedt culture, in north-west Germany and Holland. To this same period philologists attribute certain sound-changes which were significant in the formation of proto-Germanic. But to what extent the progenitors of these cultures were 'Germanic' or 'proto-Germanic' is much more problematic. It is true that there is a general impression of cultural stability in northern Germany and southern Scandinavia from the late Neolithic onward. But how securely this can be regarded as indicating an ethnic continuum is still, at best, uncertain. The Germans were first certainly distinguished from the other peoples of northern Europe in the early first century BC, or possibly late in the fourth century. It is stretching the evidence to breaking-point to trace their ethnogenesis back more than 2,000 years.

---

[5] R. Hachmann et al., *Völker zwischen Kelten und Germanen*.

[6] L. Kilian, *Zum Ursprung der Indogermanen* (Bonn 1983); *Zum Ursprung der Germanen* (Bonn 1988).

Languages

The languages spoken by the early Germanic peoples formed part of that large group known generally as the Indo-European (earlier Indo-Germanic), which also includes Celtic, Greek, Italic, Illyrian, Hittite, Thracian, Iranian, Sanskrit, Slav and Baltic. An original Indo-European language, spoken by a distinct population living in a definable area, is not now something which all linguistic scholars, or archaeologists, would insist on, but an ancestral language from which many historically attested languages have plainly descended is still a fundamental concept. The original form of that language, however, is accepted to be beyond complete reconstruction. The Indo-European languages that are most fully known are remote from the common ancestor, and those languages belong to very different stages of linguistic development. The earliest written records for individual languages are spaced out over many centuries: Mycenaean Greek from 1200 BC, Sanskrit from 1000 BC, Latin from 300 BC, Celtic and Germanic only from the first centuries AD. The earliest literary tradition for a Germanic language, Gothic, begins only in the fourth century AD and for the other members of the Germanic group, such as Old English and Old High German, in the eighth century. With material like this, it will be clear that we can reconstruct no more than the framework of the early forms of German. About many stages in the development of the various branches there can never be unqualified certainty.

Although we cannot locate the *Urheimat* of Indo-European speakers with any precision,[7] the broad sweep of Europe from the western steppes to the north German plain – a reasonably continuous ecological region – may be plausibly identified as a principal homeland of that population. Archaeology is of no help here, despite many efforts to define cultures which could be termed Indo-European. So far as proto-Germanic is concerned, the most that can be accepted is that this language

[7] For two discussions: C. Renfrew, *Archaeology and Language* (London 1987); J. P. Mallory, *In Search of the Indo-Europeans* (London 1988).

emerged in northern Europe between 2500 and 1000 BC, while further south Celtic, Italic, Venetic and Illyrian were also developing. How unified that language was is not at all clear, and the enormous geographical spread of its speakers must be recognized. It is probably safer to see proto-Germanic as a linguistic complex rather than a unified language existing at one time.

When individual languages are well documented, we find several divisions of Germanic: a northern form, several western dialects, an eastern language which in its principal form was Gothic. The northern branch, not recorded in any detail before the twelfth century, gave rise to the Scandinavian languages in due course, later to be separated by political and cultural circumstances. The western languages, emerging between the Elbe and the Rhine, are of particular interest to us as they included the ancestral form of English, as well as Frisian, Old Saxon and High German. Best known of all the early languages is Gothic, known to us through a number of literary works and fragments, the most important of which is the Gothic translation of the Bible undertaken by the Visigothic bishop Ulfila in the fourth century (below, p. 122), of which several sixth-century manuscripts exist in part. The most important of these is the magnificent *Codex Argenteus* in Uppsala, on purple vellum with silver and gold letters. Of considerable use, though much later in date, are two Gothic alphabets and groups of Gothic words derived from St Luke's Gospel, and parts of a Visigothic calendar from the fourth century when the Visigoths were on the lower Danube. Gothic itself survived as a spoken language in the Crimea for centuries after it disappeared elsewhere; certain words and phrases were brought back from there in the sixteenth century.

Information on the early Germanic languages remains thin until the migration period. The earliest known inscription in a Germanic language occurs on a bronze helmet, one of a group of twenty-four, found at Negau in southern Austria. The date and significance of this unusual cache of helmets have been much discussed, but many uncertainties remain. The inscription reads from right to left HARIXASTITEIVA/// IP (or IL) in a North Italic alphabet which had gone out of use by the beginning of the Christian era and probably before the first century BC. The latest date for the addition of this inscription to the Negau helmet would seem to be the early first century BC, at which time German-speaking auxiliaries might have been drawn into service in the Roman army in the north Italic regions. Many interpretations have been offered as to the meaning of the inscription. The most convincing seems to be that which sees it as an invocation of Teiva, a Germanic god of war, who is given the epithet Harigasti, 'guest of the army'. Others have seen Harigasti as a personal name and the inscription as a whole as a mark of ownership. This ignores the exceptional nature of this prominent inscription on a helmet at this date. An invocation of divine protection for the wearer seems more likely. But unfortunately the Negau inscription reveals little about the Germanic languages in the first century BC and is chiefly notable as the earliest recorded attempt at transmitting German words in writing.

To what extent the early German languages were mutually intelligible is uncertain. Within the three major groups difficulties are unlikely to have been severe. But could a Goth from the Ukraine have understood a Frisian from northern Holland? Except in a general sense, most probably not. The three main divisions of language understandably moved further apart from the migration period onward. One of these, East Germanic, is now extinct. North Germanic spread widely in the Viking centuries and then contracted to its Scandinavian base. The descendants of West Germanic, modern German, English and Dutch, have taken the Germanic languages to every continent of the world.

Part I
Germania

1

Land and People

The land

The heartland of the immense area of northern Europe occupied by the early Germanic peoples was the great expanse of lowland which extends from the Netherlands to western Russia. There are no heights here over 300 metres and most of the land rises no higher than 100 metres. But there is considerable variety in relief and soil conditions. Several areas, like the Lüneburg Heath and the hills of Schleswig-Holstein, are diverse in both relief and landscape. There was until recent times a good deal of marshy ground in the northern parts of the great plain, and a broad belt of coastal marshland girds it on its northern flank. Several major rivers drain the plain, the Ems, Weser and Elbe flowing into the North Sea, the Oder and the Vistula into the Baltic. Their broad valleys offered attractive areas for early settlement, as well as corridors of communication from south to north. The surface deposits on the lowland largely result from successive periods of glaciation. A major influence on relief are the ground moraines, comprising a stiff boulder clay which produces gently undulating plains or a terrain of small, steep-sided hills and hollows, the latter often containing small lakes and marshes, as in the area around Berlin. Other features of the relief are the hills left behind by terminal glacial moraines, the sinuous lakes which are the remains of melt-water, and the embayments created by the sea intruding behind a moraine. Subsequent erosion has significantly modified the glacial relief. The melt-water flowed in the great valleys towards the northern seas, depositing masses of gravel and sand, commonly called *Geest*, over large areas. South of the regions affected by glaciation, huge deposits of gravel were laid down by the rivers, while the wind brought in the light, loamy sand known as loess, which settled on the lower-lying parts of central Europe and provided a fertile, easily worked land for early agriculturists. Blown sand also occupied the floors of the larger valleys and covered extensive areas of eastern Holland and northwestern Germany, again producing soils that were attractive to early settlement. The coastlands from Holland to Schleswig-Holstein are characterized by clay marshland, on which early settlement adopted specialized forms.

To the south, the great plain is bounded by the central European uplands which form plateaus rather than well-defined ranges of hills. The more prominent hills, like the Harz and the Bohemian upland, rise sharply from surrounding high ground. Others, such as the Lysa Gora range in southern Poland, arise more gently and present a rounded profile above the Silesian lowland. The uplands are by no means barren terrain. Most regions could support at least some arable agriculture and all offered opportunities for the raising of stock. The Carpathian mountains to the south-east offered least to early settlers and for long set a boundary to the early Germanic peoples.

To the north of the European plain, the western Baltic lands had much in common with northern Germany. Much of the Danish peninsula is a low plateau, offering mixed soils and an equable climate. Central Jutland was the least attractive area to settlers with its heaths and marshes. Eastern Denmark and the Danish islands were much more amenable. Southern Sweden, outside the region of Skåne with its rich boulder-clay soils, offered a rugged landscape of troughs and steep ravines, though the sediments of Västergötland and Östergötland yielded good land. The Baltic islands of Öland, Gotland and Bornholm were all productive and supported sizeable populations in Antiquity.

The picture which Roman and early medieval writers present of a grim and forbidding land, densely forested and deep in treacherous marshes, is heavily, if understandably, overdrawn. Most of Germania was productive enough to support a substantial population. Large areas, especially the broad river valleys and the loess plains, were very fertile. There was, no doubt, a good deal of woodland, but clearance had made major progress before the first century AD and continued apace thereafter. In some areas, especially in northern Germany and Denmark, there were extensive marshlands which constrained settlement but which did not deter all access to them or use of their resources. The main resources of the land in general were its crops and its animals. There were no large deposits of the precious metals and only limited supplies of the others, with the exception of iron, which was abundant in many areas. Of other desirable commodities, only amber from the Baltic coasts and perhaps furs from the same region seem to have had appeal for the outside world. The human population was the only other major resource, and it was one which won increasing attention from the Roman world. The employment of Germans as slaves, bodyguards and, above all, as soldiers is an important theme in the story of relations between northern Europe and the Mediterranean empire of Rome, and the repercussions for later European history were to be profound.

The eastern regions of the Germanic world merged with the steppelands of western Russia and the Ukraine. The distinction between Germanic peoples who were settled on the land and nomads who roamed over the broad, flat plains north of the Black Sea is still generally emphasized by writers on barbarian Europe. The distinction is misleading. There were steppe-dwellers who were settled agriculturalists, or only partially nomadic. There were Germanic peoples who were either semi-nomadic themselves or associated with nomads for economic purposes. The region between the lower Danube and the Dnieper was occupied by a population which included many nomad groups, some of which had long been accustomed to move south of the Danube into the northern Balkans. The establishment of a Roman frontier on the lower Danube thus set up a barrier which interrupted movement of peoples which had been going on for centuries. Beyond that frontier, the movement westward continued during the period of Roman domination, though record of it is thin. Not until the late fourth century and the irruption of the Huns from deep inside Asia was the Mediter-

ranean world forcibly made aware of the continuing process.
By then, the Roman Empire was ill-equipped to deal with the
consequences.

Germans, Celts and the eastern peoples

The influence of the Celtic world on the material culture of
Germania is evident at several levels. Minor metalwork objects
such as brooches and pins were clearly influenced by the design
and decoration of La Tène metalwork current to the south in
Bohemia and the middle Danube. The techniques of Celtic
craftsmanship, especially in metals and pottery, penetrated as
far east as the area between the Oder and Vistula, and, to the
south-east, to the very edge of the Ukraine. The most spectacular contacts with the world of high Celtic craftsmanship, however, are evident in a number of prestigious items found in
northern Germania, in modern Denmark.[1] The best known of
these is the silver bowl or cauldron found in a peat-bog at
Gundestrup in north Jutland, a work of an eastern Celtic master
based on the lower Danube in the later second or earlier
first century BC. The origins and stylistic affinities of this
extraordinary object are still much debated, but south-east
Europe best satisfies the criteria which define its area of origin.
Whatever its precise significance, this was a cult object, bearing
not only repoussé heads of male and female deities and an
astonishing gallery of divine and totemic animals, some of the
latter showing possible connections with the Hellenistic world,
but also scenes of cultic observance, sacrifice and myth. A silver
cauldron, we are told by Strabo, was the most sacred vessel of
the Cimbri, a fitting gift for the Roman emperor himself, and
the treasure of the Boii contained cauldrons as well as a great
quantity of silver. The Gundestrup vessel belongs to the same
milieu and it presumably arrived in the north as an object of
booty (resulting from the southward thrust of the Cimbri?) or

---

[1] These and their significance are well discussed by O. Klindt-Jensen, *Foreign
Influences in Denmark's Early Iron Age* (Copenhagen 1950), 1; and by J.
Jensen, *The Prehistory of Denmark* (London 1982), 237–40.

of gift-exchange marking high-level contacts between Jutland and the lower Danube region.

There are suggestions of direct links between the North and the western Celtic world in burial ritual. The burial of dismantled carts with the dead at Husby in Schleswig, at Kraghede in Denmark and Langå on Fyn is closely paralleled in the Rhine valley and northern Gaul. The Husby grave is the most fully recorded.[2] The burnt remains of the four-wheeled cart were thrust under a stone cist along with a bronze vessel containing the cremated remains of the dead and the claws of a bear-skin which had been wrapped round his body. The cart itself was of a type well known in the wider Celtic world. The other northern burials of this type also contained cremations and all three probably date from the latter first century BC, a time when alliances between the northern peoples and those nearer the Rhine may well have assumed greater significance in the face of the Roman advance.

Other imports to Denmark further testify to the wide-ranging connections between the Celtic and the northern Germanic worlds in the late pre-Roman Iron Age. A great bronze cauldron, with a capacity of 130 gallons, was found at Brå in Jutland, but had been made in central Europe, perhaps on the middle Danube. Probably from eastern Gaul came two elegant four-wheeled wagons which accompanied a cremation burial in a peat-bog at Dejbjerg in west Jutland. These were superbly constructed vehicles, presumably designed for cult progresses like that described by Tacitus for the fertility-goddess Nerthus, whose shrine lay in this same northern region. The Dejbjerg wagons date from the first century BC or a little later. Celtic war-equipment also found its way to the north. The votive deposit at Hjortspring on the western Baltic island of Als contained many rectangular wooden shields, mail garments and iron spears, along with a substantial wooden boat, the whole assemblage being placed in a peat-bog between 150 and 80 BC.[3] Celtic weaponry, including the long slashing sword, the *spatha*, is represented in Germania by single finds, as are

---

[2] K. Raddatz, *Das Wagengrab der jüngeren vorrömischen Eisenzeit von Husby, Kreis Flensburg* (Neumünster 1967).

[3] G. Rosenberg, 'Hjortspringfundet', *Nordiska Fortidsminder*, 3 (1937).

many lesser items of metalwork such as torques, brooches and other personal ornaments. It is not possible to estimate how regular these contacts with the Celtic world were. The uniformly high quality of the goods imported would readily support the idea that many of them were supplied through the medium of gift-exchange between leaders. But successful military campaigns could also account for the weaponry and the other equipment at Hjortspring, for example.

One of the most fertile areas of contact between Germans and Celts was Bohemia and Moravia. Here, powerful and culturally inventive Celtic peoples had been settled since the middle of the first millennium BC. By 300 BC a major centre of barbarian power had been established in these uplands north of the Danube, aristocratic, aggressive and artistically creative. Even before this, from about 400 BC, Celts had been pushing southward, to the Danube, into northern Italy, through the Carpathians and into the northern Balkans. In 279, a large force of Celts plunged deep into Greece, through Thrace and Macedonia, plundering the treasury at Delphi and threatening cities. These Celts were driven off, but those groups which made for the Danube area were able to create stable kingdoms there, notably the Scordisci about Singidunum (Belgrade) and others on the lower Danube and the Dobrudja plain. The kingdom of Noricum, centred on what is now Austria and north-eastern Italy, emerged as a major power early in the second century BC and quickly attracted the attention of Roman strategists. In the meantime another major tribe, the Boii, had settled in the upper basin of the Elbe, which thenceforward carried their name (*Boiohaemum*: Bohemia) even after they had removed themselves. Further east, the Volcae Tectosages moved into Moravia and the Cotini into Slovakia. These areas of Celtic settlement were to be of particular significance for the Germanic peoples. The development of centres of political power, represented by huge strongholds, or oppida, in these regions led to the exploitation of natural resources on a grand scale and to the concentration of skilled craftsmen under the patronage of strong and wealthy chieftains. This oppidum-based culture flourished in the period from 150 to 50 BC, by which time some of its centres had developed into extensive urban complexes. At Hradisté near Stradonice, craftsmen working in iron, bronze, glass, enamels, gold and pottery were active during the first century BC. Several oppida were carefully planned settlements, with a rectilinear layout of streets reminiscent of Classical cities. The siting of oppida reflected their close control of natural resources. Staré Hradisko, for example, lies close to rich deposits of iron ore. These embryonic urban centres not only produced goods, they also imported. Bronzes, pottery and wine from the Mediterranean world were all brought in, as were amber and other products of northern Europe. This extraordinarily vital culture, which depends almost wholly on archaeology for its reconstruction, lasted for not much more than a century. From the mid-first century BC onward, it was sharply on the wane, partly at least because of the increased pressure of Germanic expansion southward and eastward. The Boii and Scordisci were strong enough to deflect the Cimbri and other northern groups westward in the late second century BC, but more insistent Germanic pressure would shortly afterwards bring about a major reordering of peoples in central Europe. The Boii were pushed eastwards to the middle Danube by the German Marcomanni in the first century BC, there to suffer at the hands of the Dacians, then approaching the summit of their power. The Helvetii of the western Alps were compelled to migrate into Gaul by the encroachment of their northern German neighbours in 58 BC, thereby giving Julius Caesar an excellent pretext for intervention in Gaulish affairs. Already before this, in 71 BC, the Gaulish Arverni and Sequani had invited the Germanic Suebi from east of the Rhine to assist them against their neighbours the Aedui. Once into Gaul, the Suebi were reluctant to return. Thus, against the western Celts German expansion made significant progress in the first century BC.

The power and cultural influence of the eastern Celts was also on the wane in this period. Celtic peoples had crossed the Carpathians early in the third century and moved on to the Dniester valley in the Ukraine. La Tène material in these regions is far from scarce here, especially in the Dniester valley, and later along the Dnieper. Fine war-equipment is to the fore, especially swords and bronze helmets, in princely burials, but humbler objects such as brooches and pins also indicate the widespread influence of Celtic craftsmen. By the first century

BC, this cultural influence appears to have been much diluted, but it had not entirely vanished. By then, however, a clear Celtic identity has been all but lost in the mingling of populations, both mobile and settled, in south-east Europe.

Among the eastern peoples, the Bastarnae seem to have been a much greater force than is often realized. They are mentioned by sources dating from the third century BC to the fourth century AD, usually in relation to the lower Danube basin. They seem to have arrived there during the disturbed third century BC, probably from the Vistula valley. It is far from certain that they were a Germanic people, whatever that may mean at so early a date. The wide range of their operations prompts the suspicion that they were either a nomadic or a semi-nomadic people. Tacitus made mention of their intermarriage with Sarmatian nomads, a sure sign of degeneracy to a Roman writer. They may, however, have included German elements in their composition, especially after their movement south to the Danube. A separate bloc which might represent the Bastarnae cannot be identified in the archaeology of the lower Danube region. This, in itself, might support the idea that their economy was based on pastoral nomadism, their material culture being largely borrowed from other inhabitants of the area.

The peoples who lived to the north-east of the Germans, beyond the Vistula and in the plains of western Russia, were little known to the historians of the ancient world. The people whom Pliny, Tacitus and Ptolemy called the Venedi have often been seen as ancestors of the Slavs, or even early Slavs, though the identification is not wholly convincing. The name Venedi is not itself Slavic, though later Germans used the form *Wends* to mean Slavs. We do not know for certain who the ancient Venedi were. They may have been an Indo-European people who were later submerged in one of the large German groups of eastern Europe, such as the Vandals or the Goths, or they may have formed one of the groups from which the Slavs eventually emerged. The Slavs do not enter the full light of history until the sixth century, when they appear in possession of Slovakia and Moravia. Where and how they had originated and why they had moved westward are questions which are hotly debated. The written evidence says hardly anything.

Archaeological research, notably in Poland and Czechoslovakia, has begun to make its contribution, but there is still a long way to any firm ground.[4]

The eastern Baltic lands between the Vistula and the Gulf of Riga were occupied by the Baltic peoples, a long-lived and active cultural grouping.[5] The Balts, or at least those who lived on the Baltic coast, were known to the Classical world as the Aestii, but there were several other tribes in the interior, extending south to the Masurian lakes and eastward into Russia. Two broad divisions of the Balts existed, the western group having close links with the Germanic tribes and with Rome. The material culture of the western Balts reveals considerable interaction with the Przeworsk and related cultures of the eastern Germans, especially in its metalwork. The Balts were a settled agricultural people, well equipped with iron tools and implements, and the storage of grain is attested in their settlements. Trade connections based on the amber of the Samland peninsula have received most attention, but other commodities were probably exported from the eastern Baltic, notably furs and skins. The Balts were closely associated with the Slavs from the sixth century, but they retained their independence in culture and language and were still an identifiably separate people in the time of Charlemagne. The western Balts were in part the ancestors of the medieval Prussians, the Bruzi or Prusi. But they retained their identity through the medieval centuries and down to the present day.

The relations of the eastern Germanic peoples with the mobile populations of the steppes and pre-steppes are poorly documented in the literary sources and archaeological research has not yet greatly enlarged our knowledge of the matter. It is indeed very difficult to be certain how far to the east the early Germans extended. Both Strabo and Tacitus, our most reliable ancient guides, imply a mingling of populations in the easternmost parts of Europe and this gains some support from the archaeology of these regions. A clear and abrupt distinction between Germanic tribes, settled on the land and more or

[4] Z. Vana, *The World of the Ancient Slavs* (London 1983) provides an excellent summary of work down to the early 1980s.
[5] M. Gimbutas, *The Balts* (London 1973).

less stationary, and nomadic peoples, restlessly following their flocks and herds and living in tents and wagons, is certainly false and is not conveyed by the best of our sources. The broad plains which extend from the lower Danube basin to the Ukraine were ranged over by many peoples who are often seen as nomads, but whose economy was more probably mixed in character and whose culture drew upon a variety of traditions. It is not possible in these lands to draw up the kind of maps which can be constructed further west on the evidence provided by Tacitus and Ptolemy. Here, peoples were on the move, especially from north to south, and the establishment of a Roman frontier on the Danube was to form a relatively short-lived episode in a long history of migration which would continue into modern times.

These south-eastern areas of Europe where Germanic peoples mixed with ancestors of the Slavs, with nomads and with other more shadowy groups, present major archaeological problems, particularly for those who attempt to identify cultures defined by their material equipment with individual peoples. The most extensive archaeological culture is that generally known as Przeworsk.[6] This emerged during the first century BC and flourished for more than five centuries over a huge territory from the upper Dniester to the Tisza valley in Hungary and northward to the middle Vistula and Oder. Essentially, this was an amalgam of a series of localized cultures, most with roots in earlier traditions, altered to varying degrees by contact with the Celtic peoples of the Danube basin and with the Jastorf cultural groups in the Oder and Elbe valleys and the Bell-Grave culture of the Polish plain. The material evidence for the bearers of the Przeworsk culture is largely derived from cemeteries, mainly of cremations with occasional inhumations. Warrier-graves are fairly frequent and a high proportion contain horse-gear and spurs. Several very richly furnished graves are known from the early Roman Iron Age (Leg Piekarski, Goslawice and Kosin) and others from the third and fourth

---

[6] K. Godlowski, *The Chronology of the Late Roman and Early Migration Periods in Central Europe* (Cracow 1970); R. Kenk, 'Studien zum Beginn der jüngeren römischen Kaiserzeit in der Przeworsk-Kultur', *BRGK 58* (1977), 161.

centuries (Sakrau and Bialecin). The pottery and metalwork types reveal great variety in their forms, reflecting the many influences at play, but overall the links with the Germanic cultures to the west are most strongly in evidence. The fact that related material is found as far to the east as the Dniester has, however, led some eastern European scholars to seek early Slavs, or ancestors of the Slavs, behind the Przeworsk culture. The case is weak. It is impossible to believe that a single people lay behind a unified culture which covered so immense a tract of country, while the manifold elements in material equipment are eloquent of the widest range of contacts. The Venedi may have played their part here, but there are other likely contributors: Vandals, Burgundians and even Sarmatians.

Further east in the Ukrainian steppe, another mixed culture developed from the late first millennium BC, the Zarubintsy culture. Celtic influences were also at work here on pottery, ornaments and weapons, and possibly on burial rites. Any direct link with early Slavs is highly unlikely as the material record underwent a profound change in the second century AD, perhaps indicating immigration from the east or the northeast. Equally, it is hard to see this culture as borne by Germans. More problematic is the large culture group to the south-east, stretching from the lower Danube and the Black Sea to the Dnieper plain, the Cjernjakhov culture, named after a cemetery near Kiev first studied in 1900. Many settlement-sites and cemeteries in the river valleys attest the numerous population of this region and the dynamism of its culture. High quality polished black pottery vessels, iron tools produced to impressive standards and fine ornaments in other metals characterize a unified culture over a huge area. Its origins seem to lie in the second century AD and its seed-bed was fairly certainly the Scytho-Sarmatian semi-nomadic population. Imports from the Roman world were common, especially wine, pottery and metal goods, and the technical advances evident in the Cjernjakhov material may well have been stimulated by craftsmen from the Graeco-Roman Black Sea cities. The main debate over Cjernjakhov, however, has centred on its relations with the Gothic advance into this region in the earlier Roman Iron Age. Some features of the material are related to equipment found in the Vistula valley and Pomerania, for which the likeliest agents were Goths. By the later third and the fourth centuries, when the Cjernjakhov culture extended to the lower Danube, a Gothic population must clearly have been embraced by it. Equally clearly, other peoples were also involved, including Sarmatians, Dacians and possibly precursors of the Slavs. In the late fourth century the stable cultural unity of Cjernjakhov was shattered by the violent irruption of the Huns from central Asia. Certain of its pottery traditions survived in the valleys of the Dniester and the Bug, but only as shadows, like the peoples who were now subject to Hun domination.

2

The Social Fabric

The institutions of society

The social organization of the early Germanic peoples is known to us in its broad outline, though much remains debatable. So much is recorded only by Classical writers whose understanding of tribal society was far from complete and who, inevitably, expressed what they had learnt about it in terms which a Mediterranean public would comprehend. When first revealed in our sources, the early Germans were a primitive tribal society. The individual tribes were probably organisms which originated as groups which successfully competed for and then controlled the natural resources of a region, principally the land itself. They thus varied greatly in size and importance, from the numerous and extensive Suebi and Vandili to small peoples like the Ampsivarii and Tencteri. How far back the tribes revealed to us by Caesar and Tacitus traced their history is unknown, but possibly in many cases it was not over a long period. The second and first centuries BC had been a time of considerable turbulence in central and western Europe, within which there had been considerable displacement of populations. It is possible that many of the tribes known to Tacitus had only emerged as distinct entities after these movements had come to an end, or at least abated. What held a tribe together, apart from its command of territory and natural resources, could vary. Strong political or military leadership could play a part, as it did in the case of the Marcomanni under Maroboduus, but there is no indication that such centralized power was at all common in the early German tribes.[1] Some peoples shared a sense of common origin and community which found expression in particular religious cults. This kind of bonding is widely recorded among tribal societies at many dates in many parts of the world. There may be a trace of it in the cult of Nerthus, shared by several of the northern peoples.

The tribe was not a fixed and indissoluble unit.[2] Several of the major peoples of the earlier Roman Iron Age were very large groupings, covering large areas of territory. The tribal bounds could change as a result of the fortunes of war and of migration. Parts of a tribe could break away from the parent body, as occurred with several groups of the Suebi early in the Roman period. Smaller peoples could be absorbed by larger and lose their identity, as happened to many of the lesser peoples close to the Rhine from the second century AD onward. The larger peoples mentioned by Tacitus and Ptolemy were in reality confederacies of smaller units, held together by bonds that were far from permanent. Within a large tribe there might be internal competition by factions that could seriously weaken it or even bring it to destruction, as seems to have happened to the Cherusci in the earlier Roman period. New groupings could be summoned into existence by successful warfare or the setting of new military targets, as occurred from the early third century onward. The maps that are compiled by modern scholars on the basis of the information given by Tacitus and Ptolemy are records of the tribal geography of Germania in the later first century AD. A century later, the map had significantly changed and a few decades later was largely transformed.

The literary sources speak of tribal assemblies as governing the affairs of peoples and this form of organization continues to be referred to down to the early medieval period. The assembly of free men generally did not initiate action, but considered plans and proposals put to it by kings or other leaders. It either accepted or rejected what was put to it, without elaborate discussion. This, at least, is the impression gained from the few recorded occasions of a tribal assembly at

---

[1] E. A. Thompson, *The Early Germans* (Oxford 1965), 32–8.
[2] R. Wenskus, *Stammesbildung und Verfassung* (Cologne / Graz 1961) is the fullest modern study of Germanic tribal structure.

work. In practice, the assembly can scarcely have been an effective arm of government. Its ability to frame policy independently of strong tribal leaders was very restricted, if it existed at all. The assembly of a large tribe like the Langobardi or Vandili must have been difficult to organize, except at fixed times of the year or when the free warriors were already brought together for war. It is easier to believe that assemblies were limited to a few meetings on an annual cycle, perhaps in connection with religious festivals. The Marcomanni in 180 were ordered by the emperor Commodus to meet together not more than once a month, but this was in a period of warfare and extreme difficulty for the tribe, when the fighting men were in any case in assembly. Perhaps closer to normality was the single annual meeting of the Saxons at the river Weser recorded in the eighth century. The rising power of military leaders must have seriously curtailed whatever power the tribal assembly had enjoyed in earlier days. When Maroboduus, or Arminius or Civilis wanted to pursue a course of action, he might consult with his leading warriors. The assembly of the tribe was rarely involved, except in the most formal manner, if at all.

A far more significant power in society was the retinue, the *comitatus* of Roman writers, which attached itself to chiefs and war-leaders. This is clearly defined in Tacitus' description of Germanic society and it was still familiar to the audience of the *Beowulf* poem in the eighth century. The retinue of a chieftain consisted of leading warriors, bound to him by bonds of loyalty, expressed by service on the battlefield and rewarded by gifts resulting from successful exploits there. Such an institution is widespread within tribal societies which are geared for warfare and it served as a remarkably stable and stabilizing factor in such societies. It did, however, cut across the bounds of the tribe and the family. The retinue of a successful leader could be drawn from several tribes and its military objectives were those of its leader, not of a tribe. The appeal for ambitious young warriors was obvious and potent. They found a focus for loyalty which most young men seek and an outlet for that warlike energy which was their only hope of material gain. For the organization of the tribe, of course, the retinues were destructive. Young warriors were devoted to the cause of a leader, not the well-being of their tribe. If their chieftain won glory, the retinue was enlarged. If he failed, his followers abandoned him and attached themselves to a warrior who seemed to promise better fortune. A successful retinue could break away entirely from its tribe of origin and form a new grouping. This may have been the origin of the Batavi, who broke away from the Chatti and migrated to the lower Rhine. Later, the development of the confederacies of the third century probably owed much to powerful retinues which increased their military reputation in campaigns against the Roman frontier provinces.

The significance of the individual household in Germanic society is evident not only in the written sources but also in the archaeology of settlements, in which the long-houses may be seen as foci for nuclear families. Society was clearly patriarchal, the father of a household having authority over all its members, including slaves. Polygamy is mentioned by a number of our sources, in the version known as resource polygamy: those who could afford it could have more than one wife. Slavery was far from common. Most slaves were taken as prisoners of war and normally belonged to a particular household, providing certain goods and services to the master. They were also used as agricultural workers or sold off to slave traders based in the Roman provinces. Within the family unit, an individual was closely bound to his mother's family as well as to that of his father. Thus, the system of inheritance, in cases where there were no children, allowed possessions to pass first to brothers, then paternal uncles, and finally maternal uncles. The ties between a man and his maternal uncles were significant in other primitive societies and there are echoes of them in later Europe. While the family was a central feature of Germanic society, the kindred or clan appears to have had relatively little real significance by the time the northern peoples enter history. Much has been made of the supposed importance of the clan or kindred in the functioning of society, without there being much sound evidence for it.[3] Outside the immediate family, the most powerful principle imposed on members of a

---

[3] A. C. Murray, *Germanic Kinship Structure* (Toronto 1983).

kindred was to participate in the feuds which involved members of one's own kin, which might extend to between twenty and fifty households. The feud was a regulating device of great import in this and other primitive societies. It alone provided the accepted means of righting a perceived wrong in a social order which prized personal valour above all things. It defused disputes which might otherwise subsist below the surface and undermine communities. So important was the feud that it may have defined the bounds of kinship as nothing else did. It set the rules by which men dealt with their conflicts, but did nothing to promote the unity of the tribe. Like the retinue, the institution of the feud ran like a fault-line across the Germanic tribe, ever-present and unpredictable in its effects.

The origins and nature of early Germanic kingship are obscure.[4] The earliest sources, from Poseidonius to Julius Caesar, report scarcely anything on the subject, while the information contained in the *Germania* of Tacitus, welcome as it is, is couched in a form which would be comprehensible to a Roman audience of the late first century AD, without necessarily conveying all the nuances of a complex institution. The kings whom Tacitus and his informants had heard about were those of peoples who lay close to the Roman frontiers and who had had hostile or diplomatic contact with Rome. About the remoter Germanic peoples even Tacitus had little to say. But Tacitus did know that the tribal society of the early Germans was not dominated by kings. The Germans chose their kings from those of noble blood, their war-leaders (*duces*) from those who had demonstrated their martial prowess. This did not mean that a king could not be a war-leader, only that the position of a king had a quite different basis from that of a war-leader. The *dux* owed his position to his ability as a leader of warriors and he could only maintain it by a record of success. As Tacitus remarked (*Germania* 14), 'It is impossible to maintain a large following of warriors except by violence and warfare.' A leader's authority lasted only as long as his success in war. His family connections would not save him if he proved

[4] J. M. Wallace-Hadrill, *Early Germanic Kingship in England and on the Continent* (Oxford 1971), 1–20.

a failure. The warriors who listened to the deeds of Hrothgar and Beowulf centuries after the *Germania* was written recognized this as a fact of life. This is why the German leaders we hear most about were the great war-leaders. Most of the kings have disappeared without mention, or are no more than names.

The greatest of the Germanic war-leaders whose careers are recorded for us are, of course, those who opposed the extension of Roman power into northern Europe. The authority of most of these rulers extended over more than one people and it was so impressive to the Romans that its holders could only be called *reges*, however they had come to power. Ariovistus, Julius Caesar's opponent in eastern Gaul, had built up a large following among several German peoples and his military reputation was well known to the peoples west of the Rhine. His origins are unknown and we thus do not know whether or not he came from a *stirps regia*. He was, however, recognizably a king of the Germans to Romans and won that official title from the Senate. Maroboduus was another leader who drew his followers from many peoples. He too was called *rex* by Rome and he invited obloquy from his own people by encouraging use of the term. Although his great following was rapidly dispersed after his fall, a *stirps regia* continued to exist after his period of dominance, for we later hear of Marcomannic kings who were of royal blood. Maroboduus' conqueror Arminius was careful not to use the term *rex* of himself, not wishing to arouse the passions which had worked to unseat Maroboduus.[5] But even if Arminius and his warriors were reluctant to use the term, the Romans were not. He exercised the power of a king and thus must be called a *rex*.

These men were giants among early Germanic leaders. Normally, *rex* and *dux* alike had no coercive power over his following or his tribe. Maroboduus, however, for some time enforced a tyranny upon his people and Arminius aimed to do the same. Ariovistus, we are told by an unfriendly witness, behaved like an autocrat in Gaul and clearly had power of coercion over a large following east of the Rhine. Had he not come up against a commander with Caesar's abilities and

[5] D. Timpe, *Arminius-Studien* (Heidelberg 1970).

ambition, he might have established a lasting power base on both sides of the upper Rhine. It is not a coincidence that the weakening of the old tribal system and the concentration of military power in the hands of individual leaders dates from the beginning of the period of exposure of Germanic society to Roman influence, an influence felt most profoundly by the peoples who had direct military and diplomatic contact with Rome. Nor is it coincidence that the Germans who aimed at and achieved supreme power among their own people had served with the Roman army and learnt in the Empire vastly different ideas of command in war from those current among German warriors. Both Maroboduus and Arminius had learnt their military craft during service with Rome and they had absorbed their lessons well. Both knew that the conditions of inter-tribal warfare could not sustain operations against Roman forces. To have any hope of success against Rome, a German army had to be strictly disciplined, trenchantly commanded, and held together longer than barbarian forces had ever been in the past. Maroboduus, in particular, placed great emphasis upon tactics, training and equipment. The achievements of Arminius and Maroboduus were in the short term impressive. Few barbarians could ever claim to match Arminius' defeat of the Romans east of the Rhine. But the style of autocratic leadership which they were compelled to adopt could not be maintained for long in a society of warrior-nobles who pursued their own paths to glory. In the end, both men fell to treachery generated by the jealousy of their own followers.

Indications of an elevated social group may be reasonably looked for in the archaeology of the early Roman Iron Age. In the north German plain, between the Weser and the Vistula, and extending into the west Baltic islands, a group of richly furnished burials is found, in date reaching from the late first century BC to the mid-second century AD.[6] These graves are distinguished from the mass of burials of the period in a variety of ways. They are mostly inhumations, whereas the prevailing manner of burial at the time was cremation. They lie in small

---

[6] H. -J. Eggers, 'Lübsow, ein germanischer Furstensitz der älteren Kaiserzeit', *Prähist. Zeitzchrift*, 34–5 (1950), 58.

groups away from large cemeteries, in some cases under mounds. And their grave furniture is vastly more elaborate and extensive than in the mass of burials. Roman imports of silver, bronze and glass abound, the silver vessels in particular including some costly pieces, like the two figured cups from the Hoby grave. These burials, often referred to as the Lübsow burials after a group found at that site in Poland (now Lubieszewo), plainly were the graves of major figures in early German society: if not tribal leaders, then their principal followers. The presence of fine Roman silverware might also indicate that these men (for these are mainly male burials) have been the targets of Roman diplomacy or at least of friendly overtures, and have achieved recognition of their leading status in their own tribes by the neighbouring great power.

Social distinctions are also in evidence in certain settlements of the Roman Iron Age, most clearly at Feddersen Wierde (below, p. 64–5), where the residence of a leading family or local chieftain is identifiable in the plan. Large isolated houses like those at Fochteloo and Peelo in Holland are also highly suggestive of the presence of substantial families who preferred to live at some distance from their dependants and retainers.

Armament and warfare

Germanic society was a warrior society, a society geared to waging war, within tribes, between different peoples and against external enemies. How this was done was largely determined by the character of Germanic society itself.

The Germanic hosts which swept into southern Europe in the late second century BC were mainly foot-soldiers. A century later the warriors who formed the armies of Maroboduus and Arminius also fought largely on foot. The migrating peoples who passed into the Roman provinces depended overwhelmingly upon their infantry troops, relying for the most part on massed ranks of men. The use of mounted troops among most Germanic peoples was limited, the main exceptions being certain tribes settled near the Rhine, such as the Tencteri, and some of the eastern peoples who had connections with the horsemen of the steppes. Julius Caesar employed German horsemen in his armies in Gaul, though on occasion he had to provide them with Roman mounts, their own horses being too small. The lack of suitably large and fast horses in northern Europe imposed serious limitations on the development of cavalry warfare. The use of the chariot so favoured by the western Celtic peoples was not taken up by the early Germans. There was a further restriction on the use of horsed warriors: the cost of maintaining a mount. But above and beyond such considerations, the size, physical strength and warlike energy of the Germans were most effectively deployed in infantry formations. Long after Germanic peoples had settled in the Roman world, their military strength still resided in their infantry. The cavalrymen who appear in the historical and archaeological record were mainly chiefs and their immediate retinues. A richly furnished series of graves found in Denmark, northern Germany and Poland, containing spurs and other items of horse-gear, makes the point very well. The high quality of this equipment, especially the silver-inlaid spurs, points to a high social status for these warriors.

The equipment of the massed infantry changed relatively little during the early Roman period. Tacitus' remarks on German armament at this time are fully supported by the archaeological record:[7]

Only very few have swords or spears. The lances they carry – *frameae* is the native word – have short and narrow heads, but are so sharp and easy to handle that the same weapon serves for fighting hand-to-hand or at a distance. The horseman demands no more than this shield or spear, but the infantryman also has javelins for throwing, several to each man, and he can hurl them to a great distance.

Finds of Germanic weaponry in graves and votive deposits, and sculpted scenes of combat involving Germans on Imperial reliefs, present the same general picture. The barbarian forces which took the field against Roman armies in the first and second centuries were largely equipped with javelins, lances,

[7] *Germania*, 6.

shields and, to a notably lesser extent, with swords.[8] Swords
do not figure prominently in the record before the third century
AD. So valuable were they to their owners that they were
probably consigned to burials and votive deposits much less
commonly than other weapons. The rank and file probably
rarely possessed swords. Even in the later Roman period, spearmen greatly outnumbered warriors wielding the sword. Virtually the only defensive arm for the vast majority of warriors
was the shield, long and oval or rectangular earlier, smaller
and circular later on. The shield-boss, often, though not
invariably, of iron, was frequently prominent enough to be
used as an offensive weapon, to be thrust at the face of an
opponent. Both wickerwork and wooden shields are reported,
some of the latter being covered with leather and bound with

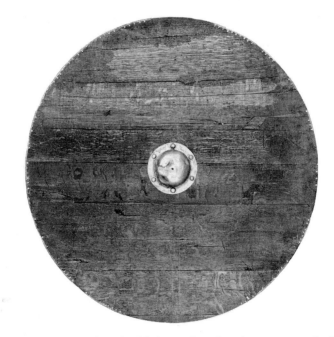

Figure 3 Wooden shield from the Thorsbjerg votive find.

[8] K. Raddatz, 'Die germanische Bewaffnung der vorrömischen Eisenzeit',
Nachrichten Akademie der Wissenschaften Göttingen, Phil.-Hist. Klasse
(1966), 427.

bronze strips at the edges. Body armour was virtually unknown among the German peoples in their early contests with Rome, and indeed for centuries after that. The votive deposit at Hjortspring, on the island of Als in the western Baltic, contained about twenty tunics of mail, but these were obvious imports from the Celtic world of central or western Europe, probably early in the first century BC. Most of the rank-and-file warriors went into battle wearing their customary everyday garments. Some made it a point to fight entirely naked, trusting to divine powers for their protection. Throughout several centuries of warfare against well armoured Roman armies, body armour was not worn by German fighting men. Roman stone reliefs and figurines invariably show German opponents fighting naked or clad only in breeches and cloak. The upper body and the head were usually unprotected, so that the number of casualties in set-piece battles with fully protected legionaries, equipped with a variety of thrusting and throwing weapons, must often have been horrific. And yet this elementary deficiency was not made good, even long after widespread Germanic settlement within the Roman provinces.

This slowness to adapt to changed military circumstances is a marked feature of early Germanic warfare. External influences did, however, work on the swords used in the Germanic world. Before the first century AD, short, one-edged swords were current, usable only at close quarters, especially in single combat. Longer two-edged weapons, based on the Celtic *spatha*, were introduced from central Europe, and these did offer a wider range of fighting modes. Short-bladed knives or *Kampfmesser* were also in widespread use, underlining the frequency of hand-to-hand combat. Roman influence on the swords used in northern Europe was effective by the early second century AD, if not earlier. In southern Scandinavia, for example, a workshop was producing imitations of the legionary *gladius* by that date, while in the Elbe basin versions of a light, slashing sword based on Roman models were current about the same time. In this same period, Roman swords with a ring at the end of the hilt (*Ringknaufschwerter*) appeared in the Elbe valley and in Jutland, some of them arriving with other booty, others perhaps as objects of illicit trade. Although such imports may have provided models for Germanic smiths to follow, there are

*Figure 4 German captives on a Roman statue-base from Mainz:
probably first century AD.*

few signs of widespread imitation of Roman swords at this
time. Nor is there any indication that swords formed a more
dominant element in German armament. Those warriors who
possessed such weapons still seem to have been the *nobiles* and
their followings.

The long wars with Roman armies in the later second century saw the beginning of a period in which change to armament and fighting methods was effected, without fundamentally transforming the character of Germanic warfare.[9]

Helmets and body armour remained rare throughout the period of migration; only chieftains and their leading warriors were able to acquire them. The Franks who fought against the Byzantine commander Narses in sixth-century Italy did so without protection for their bodies. The common warriors were naked to the waist, their lower bodies clad in leather or linen trousers and their legs bound with leather or cloth puttees. Body armour of any kind appears extremely rare in even the most aristocratic burials. The Frankish laws assessed the value of a mail-coat as two horses or six oxen, that of a helmet as equal to a horse. The richest warrior burials of the sixth and seventh centuries may contain helmets: rarely do they contain a garment of mail or any other form of armour. From the fifth century onward, the helmet generally known as the *Spangenhelm* was widely distributed among warriors of the chieftainly class. This was ultimately derived from sources in western Asia, probably reaching the Mediterranean world as a result of warfare between the late Roman and Persian forces. The type was imitated in Byzantine workshops and was later produced by craftsmen working for Ostrogothic patrons in northern Italy. The *Spangenhelm* was conical, the cap being composed of several plates of iron or bronze attached to an iron framework riveted to a headband. Hinged cheek-pieces and a nose-guard were often provided, while a mail curtain might cover the neck. The plates of the cap and the cheek-pieces were often decorated, with gilding and precious inlays in the richer pieces. Such helmets, though they were certainly worn in battle and often have the scars to prove it, were obviously treasured possessions and were handed on to succeeding generations. Several found in burials were of some antiquity when consigned to the ground.

Given the nature of Germanic equipment and organization

---

[9] K. Raddatz, 'Die Bewaffnung der Germanen in der jüngeren römischen Kaiserzeit', *Nachrichten Akademie der Wissenschaften Göttingen, Phil.-Hist. Klasse* (1967), 1.

for war, it is scarcely surprising that siege operations played little part in the warfare between Roman and German until a late date. The invaders of the Empire in the third and fourth centuries were generally not much interested in investing walled towns and cities. Rarely do we hear of organized attempts to break into a well defended circuit of walls using siege engines. When we do, German success was usually limited and due to the incompetence or treachery of the defenders. The construction and deployment of siege machinery by the Goths at Thessalonica in 269 and at Side about the same date met with no success at either city, chiefly because the defenders came up with well planned counter-measures. The German invaders of Gaul and Spain in the third century were able to take many towns and cities, mainly because so few had adequate defences, or any defences at all. After these devastating inroads, the systematic walling of western cities was carried out as a matter of urgency. Normally, barbarian attacks on walled cities were doomed to failure. It was not only that the required engineering skill was lacking. Barbarian forces could not be kept together long enough to complete an investment which might last for weeks or months, and then yield little in the way of plunder. There were easier targets in the Roman provinces and the German rank and file were not easily persuaded that a siege was worth the effort and danger when open settlements beckoned. Even in the large-scale invasions of the late fourth and fifth centuries, German leaders were reluctant to commit their armies to long sieges, except when there was a major political prize at stake, or when a demoralized citizenry might be cowed into submission by a simple blockade. Fritigern of the Visigoths put it concisely when he said that he was at peace with walls. The Alamanni who besieged the emperor Julian in the Gallic town of Sens for thirty days before glumly withdrawing came to the same conclusion about how foolish it was to attempt sieges. And yet the Germans who entered the Roman provinces to stay clearly had no option but to seize control of the centres of Roman wealth and power. With remarkably few exceptions, among which must be ranked the Vandal success in reducing so many cities in north Africa, German expertise in the capture of walled places showed little advance over centuries.

Change to Germanic weapons and warfare is evident from the later third century onward, but this did not by any means affect all aspects of armament. Cavalry continued to play a relatively minor role. It is true that on occasion horsemen made a major intervention in a battle. The Ostrogothic cavalry did so in AD 378 at Adrianople in that crushing defeat for Roman arms, but the credit for the victory must go to the Gothic infantry. Above all, tactics seem to have remained at an elementary level, reliance still being mainly placed on the physical strength and fighting qualities of the German warrior. But there were certain changes in response to the changing character of warfare, especially between Germans and Roman armies. In weaponry, there was increased use of arms which could be used at a distance. Axes become more common in warrior graves, especially the throwing-axe, which was to become one of the favoured weapons of migration period Germans. The bow and arrow, hitherto little used in war, now makes an appearance, in the form of longbows and bundles of arrows in the votive deposit at Nydam. Javelins and long spears retained their significance, so that German warriors were reasonably well equipped for offensive operations against well armoured enemies. Their main weakness still lay in defence. The shield remained the only major item of protection and it had altered very little over the preceding three centuries. The weapon in which significant change was registered was the sword. This is more in evidence in graves and votive finds from the third century onward and the range of types represented is notably wider. The long slashing sword is the most common form, though shorter weapons are also present. The acquisition of Roman swords, and other weapons, clearly became more common, either as a result of increasing success against Roman armies in battle or because Roman weapons were reaching German warriors through channels of trade. Such trade may have been expressly forbidden, but a ban would have been impossible to enforce with total success (below, p. 95). Apart from the two-edged slashing sword, a rapier-like blade was also current in Germania, a weapon particularly useful for its power of penetration. Roman imports reveal themselves in the blades which bear makers' stamps and in those which were produced by the technique of pattern-welding or damascening.

Figure 5 Bows, arrows, spearheads and swords from the votive finds at Nydam and Thorsbjerg.

In this type of sword, the core of the weapon was fashioned from twisted strips and wires of iron which were hammered flat and then fitted with hard steel edges. The faces of the blade were polished so that the pattern resulting from the forging process was clearly visible. This technique of manufacture seems to have been developed in Roman military workshops in the late second or early third centuries. The impact of these swords in northern Europe was very great. The pattern-welded technique was to produce the outstanding swords of the Frankish world and later those of Viking armies.

Although swords became more common in the later Roman Iron Age and the migration period, their significance should not be overestimated. In the votive deposits of the fourth century, swords are uniformly outnumbered by spears and javelins by a considerable margin. In the well excavated deposit at Ejsbøl North in Jutland, an unusually homogeneous find, there were 60 swords, 60 belts and 62 knives, as against 200 javelins, 190 spears and 160 shields.[10] If this represents the equipment of about 200 warriors, then spearmen outnumbered swordsmen by at least three to one.

Body armour is only a little more in evidence in the late Roman period. Mail garments found in peat-bogs at Thorsbjerg and Vimose are most probably Roman imports. So, too, were the helmets from Thorsbjerg and Hagenow, both of them parade pieces of limited use in warfare. Their wearers may have seen them as marks of rank rather than serious items of war-gear. Not for centuries to come were helmets and body armour worn by rank-and-file warriors.

Long contact with the nomadic peoples of the western steppes stimulated the development of cavalry among the Goths and their associates. By the later fourth century, horsed warriors using the long lance or *contus* were playing an increasingly important role in warfare among the eastern Germans. A century later, the armies of Theoderic were primarily horsemen. Heavy armour was now worn by many of the wealthier warriors, supplied by arms workshops in northern Italy, and the

---

[10] M. Orsnes, 'The weapon find in Ejsbøl Moss at Haderslev', *Acta Arch.* 34 (1963), 232.

sword became a much commoner weapon, both for cavalry and infantry troops. The stirrup had, however, still not reached Europe and the Mediterranean world, so that a charge of cavalry against cavalry often ended up as a bloody mêlée fought half on foot. The use of the bow from horseback, employed to devastating effect by the Huns and Alans, made progress among the German peoples, but it was not to become one of their strongest arms. The tactics used by Gothic cavalry, about which we hear most, were simple, being based on the lightning strike from concealed positions, often with the aim of outflanking the enemy infantry. Having made the assault, the horsemen swiftly retired to the cover of their own forces, there to regroup for another strike. The tactic was often successful, the opposing infantry being reduced to panic by the sudden onrush of screaming horsemen. Gothic cavalry were employed by the armies of the eastern Roman Empire, including those of Belisarius and Narses, and served with considerable success under Roman generals. With better training and leadership, Germanic horsemen might have made their mark much earlier than they did.

3

The Germans and the
Advance of Rome

Early encounters

The first clash between Germanic peoples and Rome was both
sudden and dramatic. From the 120s BC, Rome had been
establishing a secure frontier zone in the sub-Alpine borderland
between northern Italy and southern Gaul. Her political intervention in Gaul took on more purposeful shape after the foundation of a colonia at Narbonne (Narbo Martius) in 118 and
the creation of a province shortly afterwards. On the north-
eastern frontier of Italy lay the kingdom of Noricum (largely
covered by modern Austria), bound by ties of clientship to
Rome. It was here that the north Germans first thrust themselves upon Roman attention. In 113, a numerous mass of
people bearing the name Cimbri broke into Noricum.[1] A consular army under Gnaeus Papirius Carbo engaged them in battle
and was soundly defeated. The invaders might have pushed
southward into Italy without resistance, but instead moved
westward to the upper Rhine and into Gaul. What lay behind
this sudden apparition of northern peoples in the Alpine regions
was much debated in Antiquity and is still mysterious. There
are several reports of requests by the intruders for land on
which they might settle; the protracted wanderings do support
the idea of a migration of land-hungry or dispossessed population, not the invasion of an army bent on plunder or conquest.

[1] G. Alfödy, *Noricum* (London 1974), 35–8.

The Cimbri appeared in southern Gaul in 109, now accompanied by the Teutones, who may have joined the migrants from north of the Alps after the victory in Noricum. After a number of indecisive battles, a major Roman army under the consul Marcus Junius Silanus confronted the Germans in a set battle and was defeated. The barbarians again asked for land but the Roman Senate would have none of it. The northerners retired into the interior of Gaul, where they are unlikely to have been welcome. In 105 the German host again appeared on the Rhone seeking land and food-supplies. Again their request was rejected and now they pushed south down the valley to Arausio (Orange), where they met and overthrew two consular armies in one of the greatest defeats ever suffered by Roman arms. With southern Gaul at their mercy, the Germans might have lodged themselves on the lower Rhone. But, presented with a wide range of choice, they seem to have been unable to define any clear objective. The native population of Gaul did not make common cause with them against Rome and this failure may have helped to impel them westwards toward Spain. There too native support was not forthcoming and the Germans now turned eastward, to threaten Italy. The Romans entrusted command against what they saw as a major invasion to Gaius Marius, who was to lead a reorganized army with the aid of competent officers. The German host was tracked from the Isère valley eastward until it reached the plain near Aquae Sextiae (Aix-en-Provence). There Marius' legions defeated it and dispersed the survivors. The first confrontation between German tribes and Rome was at an end. The episode is of more than passing interest.

Had the Cimbri and Teutones succeeded in finding a permanent home on the Roman borderlands, other northern peoples might have been emboldened to try their fortunes further south. But the barrier erected by Rome was an effective deterrent and it was forty years before another barbarian host crossed the upper Rhine and tried to establish itself in Gaul. This was a German force led by the warrior chieftain Ariovistus. They had been invited into eastern Gaul by the tribe of the Sequani to provide military aid against the Aedui, their rivals to the west. Ariovistus and his Suebic warriors, 15,000 of them in the original army, did their work well. But so attractive was the rich land of Gaul to the mercenary troops that they turned on the Sequani and began to take over their land. More Germans were invited in until, Caesar tells us, 120,000 had crossed the Rhine. All this was of pressing interest not only to the tribes of Gaul, but to Rome, whose province of Transalpine Gaul was threatened by a German presence on its northern border. The invasion of the Cimbri and Teutones half a century earlier still cast a shadow. The Aedui were allies of Rome and their call for Roman aid was greatly reinforced by the need to protect Rome's own interest in southern Gaul. Add to that Julius Caesar's search for a theatre of war in which a brilliant victory might be won, and the stage was set for the Roman conquest of the whole of Gaul. Had Rome not advanced into Gaul, there seems little doubt that further encroachment on eastern Gaul by the peoples from across the Rhine would have taken place. Before the arrival of Ariovistus and his Suebi, there had been a westward movement across the Rhine. *Germani cisrhenani* (Germans on this side of the Rhine) had established themselves in eastern Belgium. In that same region, the Tungri prided themselves on their German ancestry. Further south, the Treveri, whose very name may mean 'river crossers', had at least intermittent contacts with the tribes east of the Rhine.[2] The Belgic peoples as a whole retained a tradition of origins across the river and a migration to their territory in northern Gaul which probably went back to events otherwise unrecorded in the second or early first century BC. This westward drive towards the fertile lands of Gaul continued until Caesar carried Roman arms to the Rhine and could on occasion be exploited by Roman administrators. The Ubii had long wanted to settle west of the Rhine and their pro-Roman sympathies eventually earned them a territory about the site of Cologne, either in Caesar's day or early in the reign of Augustus. The Roman occupation of the Rhine valley thus again interposed a barrier to population movement which had a long history.

It is unlikely that any Roman commander before Julius Caesar had given serious thought to the extension of Roman power into central and northern Europe and even Caesar cannot have

---

[2] E. M. Wightman, *Gallia Belgica* (London 1985), 10–14.

long dwelt on the matter. The stabilization of the Empire under Augustus and in particular the consolidation of Roman authority in Gaul meant that attention could be turned to the peoples beyond the Rhine and the Alps, virtually for the first time. From 25 BC onward, when the peoples of the western Alps were conquered and a colonia founded at Aosta where the routes over the Great and Little St Bernard passes converged, the conquest of the Alpine regions was under way.[3] By about 16 BC forts were established at the nodal points of Basel, Zürich and Oberwinterthur, while further east the passes of Brenner and Reschenscheideck were brought within Roman grasp. In 16, two Roman armies, under Augustus' stepsons Tiberius and Drusus, swept through the Alpine valleys and in a fierce campaign conquered the tribes of the Alpenvorland plateau north of the mountain barrier. There can be no reasonable doubt about the purpose of these operations. The peoples of the Alps posed no serious threat to the security of northern Italy. The next phase could unfold quickly.

Campaign-bases already existed on the Rhine at Xanten, Neuss, Asberg, Bonn and perhaps Nijmegen by 16 BC, in which year an invasion by the Sugambri delivered an immense and unexpected shock to Rome. An entire legion under the Rhine command of Marcus Lollius was wiped out. The situation was serious enough to bring Augustus to Gaul, where he was to spend the next three years in a major reorganization of the province and its defences. The disastrous incursion of the Sugambri had revived fears about the military menace presented by the peoples east of the Rhine and prompted a reappraisal of how best it might be combated. By 13, it had been resolved to invade the territory of the Germans, probably without at that stage any very clearly defined long-term objectives.[4] In 12, the invasion began under the command of Drusus and for the next five seasons Roman forces were engaged in operations over a huge area between the Rhine and the Elbe, the latter river being reach by 9 BC. The magnitude of the task was

---

[3] C. M. Wells, *The German Policy of Augustus* (Oxford 1972), 35–58. The dating of some military sites is a few years too early.

[4] The Augustan master-plan for the conquest of Germania discerned by some modern scholars did not exist.

matched by the Roman war-effort. A major supply-base was established east of the Rhine, at Rödgen in the plain of the Wetterau, and the movement of men and supplies facilitated by the digging of a canal, the *fossa Drusiana*, linking the Old Rhine with the Ijsselmeer, and thus shortening the lines of communication with northern Germania.

Drusus died when returning from the Elbe in 9 BC. The scale of his success in the previous five years is difficult to assess. The difficult terrain had been overrun rather than fully occupied, but a measure of control had been achieved on which his successor could build. Several major routes were established across Germania, those running along the Lippe valley and north-east from the Wetterau being marked by the building of legionary bases. But such stations have not been detected on the Elbe or near it, or even on the Weser, so that operations so far to the east may have been mounted as rapid strikes from bases well to the rear. Tiberius immediately took up the task left by his brother and was perhaps able to organize what had so far been overrun as an embryonic province. But opposition was still strong. For some of the Sugambri and Suebi deportation seemed the only solution. By 8 BC some regrouping of Roman forces was necessary, perhaps indicating a belief that the first and most difficult phase of conquest was over. The events that followed Tiberius' retirement from the German command and from public life in 6 BC are obscure. It is clear, however, that there was Roman penetration from the south after 6 from the upper Danube valley. In AD 1, Lucius Domitius Ahenobarbus pushed northwards from the Danube, crossed the Elbe, established treaty relations with the peoples of that region and settled homeless members of the Hermunduri on land in the upper Main basin, where they were to remain as allies of Rome for a century or more. Elsewhere, active campaigning was still going on and the rise of a formidable Germanic power in Bohemia under Maroboduus meant that Tiberius' return to military command in AD 4 was more than timely. Bohemia was to be attacked from two directions, by Tiberius from the north and by Sentius Saturninus from the west. Just as the jaws of the pincers were to close, Roman troops had to be recalled to deal with a major revolt in Illyricum, leaving Maroboduus in control on the upper Elbe.

In the meantime, Publius Quinctilius Varus had been appointed governor of Germania, presumably to complete the organization of the province and to institute the customary impositions. But conditions in the interior still required the governor to take the field. Here Varus was out of his depth against a Germanic leader who had learnt his craft in the Roman army: Arminius.[5] By skilful exploitation of his knowledge of the terrain and the qualities of Roman troops, Arminius enticed the army of Varus into the densely forested land of the upper Weser, and there in the battle which has become known as the battle of the Teutoberg Wald three Roman legions were virtually annihilated. Roman ambitions to conquer the territory east of the Rhine were effectively ended by this shattering defeat and the reasons are not far to seek. The province of which Drusus and Tiberius had marked out included some of the most difficult terrain in western Europe and it was inhabited by the most intractable of tribesmen. The revenue which Germania could offer the Roman treasury was not great. There were no deposits of precious metals, no great expanses of cornfields. Its major resources were in manpower and these, for the greater part, were ranged against Rome. After AD 9, although Germanicus took an army along the Lippe valley in 15 and gave the dead on the battlefield decent burial, the emperor Tiberius' realistic appraisal, based on personal experience, of what Rome could hope to achieve in Germania would prevail. With Varus' troops were buried Rome's ambitions of setting her northern frontier east of the Rhine.[6]

After the recall of Germanicus in AD 16, the tale is one of consolidation until the reign of Claudius thirty years later. The eight legions on the Rhine and behind the upper Danube were held in strategic reserve, no doubt with a measure of control being exercised on the territory beyond the rivers. Diplomacy came into its own during these decades as an instrument of Imperial policy beyond the great rivers (below, p. 84f.). The fertile plain of the Wetterau had been under Roman surveillance

---

[5] D. Timpe, *Arminius-Studien* (Heidelberg 1970).
[6] It is debatable whether Augustus ever intended to establish a frontier on the Elbe. It is equally uncertain whether any such frontier would have had advantages over a frontier on the Rhine.

since the reign of Augustus, principally because of its potential for military supplies. But there were no serious attempts at extending the bounds of Roman authority.

Military operations were found to be necessary against the Bructeri in the Lippe valley in 78 and again in 94, but there was no thought of holding on to territory east of the lower Rhine. The Danube frontier, not that on the Rhine, now presented the major problem of provincial security. After wars against the Chatti in 83–5 and a revolt by his own commander of the upper German army in 88–9, the emperor Domitian reduced the strength of the Roman forces on the upper Rhine and began the process of frontier construction between the Rhine and Danube which was to result in the creation of the longest artificial frontier system in the Empire.[7]

Roman frontiers

The frontier which emerged from the last years of the first century was an *ad hoc* creation, not notably endowed with cohesive planning. At the northern end, it ran from the Rhine to enclose the fertile Neuwieder Becken and then crossed the Taunus hills before turning south to the Main valley and on to the broad plain of the Neckar. In its first form, the frontier was no more than a cleared strip of ground and a track, with timber observation towers at intervals of about 500 metres along its line. The whole was reminiscent of several sectors of the frontier which existed until 1989 between East and West Germany. A few small fortlets lay on the frontier, but the main garrison posts lay to the rear in support positions. Clearly, no major German incursion was expected from the thinly peopled lands immediately to the east. Later, as the functions of policing a static frontier developed, a few forts were added to the line, mainly at points where routes crossed it. Further south, a series of forts was erected across the Schwäbischer Alb to cover the

---

[7] D. Baatz, *Der römische Limes* (Berlin 1974); D. Baatz and F. -R. Herrmann, *Die Römer in Hessen* (Stuttgart 1983); H. Schönberger, 'Die römischen Truppenlager der frühen und mitteleren Kaiserzeit zwischen Nordsee und Inn', *BRGK.* 66 (1985), 321–497.

province of Raetia: this system was replaced by AD 100 by a broad military zone crossing Baden-Württemberg. At about the same date, a close-set line of small forts was built in the Odenwald, thus linking the Main and Neckar valleys. The geographical framework of the upper German and Raetian frontier was now virtually complete. The early second century saw consolidation on the existing line. More forts were added and in the region of Hadrian, probably after that emperor visited Germany in 121–2, a continuous palisade about 3 metres high was constructed. This was not a formidable military barrier: its purpose was to mark off the limits of Caesar's land from *Barbaricum*.

The artificial frontier against the Germans now ran from the Rhine opposite the Vinxtbach (the name retains an echo of the termination *ad Fines*) to the Danube near Eining. The final phase of frontier building came under Antoninus Pius, probably about AD 152–4, when the upper German sector was moved forward about 30 kilometres, most probably to take in a productive agricultural belt. Later still, perhaps at the end of the second century, an earthwork was added behind the palisade (the *Pfahlgraben*). Like the timber work it reinforced, this was not designed to serve as a military barrier. Now or early in the third century, the Raetian frontier was provided with a stone wall (the *Teufelsmauer*).

The river frontier on the lower Rhine had been stabilized since the reign of Claudius in the mid-first century. The Frisii of northern Holland had briefly regained their independence in 28 and, after the campaign of Corbulo on their territory in AD 47 and its abrupt conclusion, there was no further Roman attempt to hold the territory across the Rhine. Some form of control was, however, still maintained on the use of territory beyond the river, as the Frisii and Ampsivarii found in 58 when they were denied permission to settle on land reserved for Roman military purposes. The legion based at Bonn had grazing lands on the 'barbarian' side of the Rhine and it is likely that military interest in other resources on the east bank was not confined to this.

These frontier systems developed during a period when Roman military power could not be seriously challenged by the Germans and there was therefore no need for them to be designed to withstand constant pressure. When barbarian strength began to build after the middle of the second century, it was to be directed not at the frontier between the Rhine and the Danube, but at Noricum and Pannonia on the middle Danube. There, in the reign of Marcus Aurelius, a war erupted which gave warning of what would follow in the next century.

In 166, while the Roman world was struggling to recover from a major outbreak of plague, the peoples north of the Danube attacked the Roman frontier in strength, thus breaking sixty years of stability.[8] The wars which followed involved many peoples across a wide swathe of central Europe; about twenty-five tribes are mentioned as taking part in the wars that ensued – and it is clear from the nature of the fighting that the barbarian attacks were of a different order from anything the Roman frontier armies had experienced for a century and a half. Large masses of population were on the move, peoples rather than armies. Some tribes specifically sought land on which to settle, either in the Roman provinces or close to their borders; women appear in the fighting line; battles take place in winter. Behind it all is an ill-concealed hunger for land, probably induced by growth in numbers of population. What are usually called the Marcomannic Wars are more accurately to be described as a series of folk migrations, or attempted migrations, ultimately frustrated by the Roman determination to maintain the Danube frontier line. The main threat to that frontier came not from the peoples close to it, several of which had been clients of Rome for several decades or more; the greater pressure was exerted by tribes pushing south and west from afar. Early in the conflict, for example, we hear of Lombards from the Elbe valley now crowding on the Danube in upper Pannonia and soon other peoples from the east were swarming round the exposed bulk of Dacia. The danger of a major invasion of the Empire was real enough. One force of Marcomanni and Quadi broke through into northern Italy, destroyed the town of Opitergium (Oderzo) and laid siege to the city of Aquileia at the head of the Adriatic. This inroad sent shock waves through Italy and revealed how precarious

[8] A. R. Birley, *Marcus Aurelius* (2nd edn; London 1987), 217.

the security of the peninsula was once the Danube frontier had been pierced. The two emperors Marcus Aurelius and Lucius Verus themselves entered the field; the former was to spend much of the remainder of his reign in wearisome and costly wars against the northerners. Eventually, by 180, Rome was able to restore order along her northern frontier by exploiting the lack of any unified purpose among the barbarians, by defeating some of them in battle, by settling some on Roman soil in the Danube provinces (and even in Italy, an experiment which did not work well), and by forging alliances with others. But the struggle had been hard and the emperor had to take note of the increasing demands for land put forward by some of the invaders. In several ways, these wars foreshadow the barbarian assaults of two centuries later.

The period of the Marcomannic Wars and their aftermath saw a major realignment of Germanic peoples, especially in the eastern territories. It also witnessed a change in political geography which was to have far-reaching effects on later European history. In the decades that followed these wars we hear of new groupings of peoples, some of them confederacies built round a single large tribe, others probably amalgamations of numerous smaller groupings. The Alamanni appear in south-western Germania, apparently emerging from a confederacy of Suebi and neighbouring peoples west of the upper Elbe.[9] They are first mentioned in the surviving sources in 213, when Caracalla beat them back from the upper German *limes*, but twenty years later they were on the offensive again and this time they broke through that frontier and created havoc behind it. On the lower Danube, more and more was heard of the Goths and their allies from the early third century onward and by 250 this enlarged grouping had emerged as the single most potent threat to the northern frontier of Rome.[10] On the upper Danube, the Langobardi (Lombards) now established themselves as a major power, resistant to the blandishments of diplomacy. In the north there were moves towards larger federations during the first half of the third century. A confederacy

---

[9] R. Christlein, *Die Alamannen* (Stuttgart 1978).
[10] H. Wolfram, *History of the Goths* (Berkeley, Calif. 1988), 36–74.

under the name 'Franks' formed itself out of the many small groups settled between the Rhine and the Weser and soon began to threaten the lower Rhine frontier and later the Channel coast.[11] In the northern coastlands, the rise of another aggressive grouping is signalled by the increasing use of the name 'Saxones' to denote sea-borne raiders of the north-western provinces of the Empire. It would be false to assume that strong centralized powers lay behind these names. Their appearance, nevertheless, does mark a new phase in the relations between the northern peoples and the world of Rome. Barbarian ambitions were on the rise and the period AD 200–75 saw the first unmistakable signs that Roman power in central Europe was not unchallengable.

The first pressure-point, inevitably, was the exposed Roman frontier between the Rhine and the Danube. In 213, the emperor Caracalla conducted major operations against the Alamanni and the Chatti, apparently with success, for no further trouble is reported on this front for the following twenty years. But the growing barbarian threat was plainly not to be ignored by the civilian communities immediately behind the Roman frontier. Their urban centres were now given defensive walls for the first time and these provided invaluable protection against the next invasion. In 233 the Alamanni broke through the Danube frontier into the provinces of Raetia and Noricum, causing widespread damage there. The upper German frontier was also pierced and some at least of the communities behind it suffered severely at this time. Following this disaster, some of the extramural settlements around fort-sites were abandoned, while others were rebuilt on a much more modest scale. Many of the civilian population will have wondered how much longer the frontier would be held against the ever more dangerous Alamanni. Equally threatening to the security of the frontiers was the internal anarchy which the chaotic succession of military usurpers thrust upon the Empire from the elevation of Maximinus to the purple in 235 to the establishment of stable government by Diocletian and his colleagues nearly half a century later. The upper German *limes* was restored by Maxim-

---

[11] E. James, *The Franks* (Oxford 1988), 34–51.

inus and maintained by his successors, but its days were numbered. In 254, the Alamannic raids were resumed, if they had ever ceased. By 259–60 the old frontier line had been overrun, along with most of the civilian centres to the rear. The Raetian sector ceased to exist as an ordered frontier at the same time, as numerous coin-hoards demonstrate clearly. The defences of the Roman provinces were pulled back to the rivers Rhine and Danube, and there they would stay until the end of Roman authority in western Europe. The lands between upper Rhine and upper Danube given up by Rome, however, seem not to have been settled immediately by large numbers of Alamanni and other Germans. It may be that, once the prizes offered by relatively rich Roman provincial lands were removed, the edge was taken off barbarian interest in those areas. Not until the end of the third century or a little later are there clear signs of Germanic settlement on what had once been Roman land.

The eastern Germanic peoples were in tumult during the late second and early third centuries for reasons that had nothing to do with the aftermath of the Marcomannic Wars. Migrant groups moved south from the Vistula basin into the western Ukraine and spread towards the lower Danube during the later second century, combining there with more settled peoples. By the 230s at the latest, this federation began to assault the provinces on the lower Danube and Dacia, earning themselves subsidies thereby. The name 'Goths' was generally applied to this aggressive grouping of warrior bands, but almost certainly it included elements from numerous tribes. The southward spread of the Goths is less likely to have been a sudden migration *en masse* than a steady movement into the rich lands of the south Russian steppe. When we first hear of them they were threatening Moesia and Dacia in the 230s and 240s. It was not long before the cities of the Black Sea coasts and of Asia Minor experienced their sweeping raids. Little is heard of kings or centralized power at this time. The most formidable of the Gothic commanders, Kniva, is called a king by our sources, but may have owed his authority solely to his military prowess. In the middle of the third century, the Goths and their associates were the most resourceful and threatening of the enemies of Rome. They could strike deep into the rich provinces of Asia Minor and range widely on naval expeditions. They could attack the peaceful lands of Greece as well as an exposed province like Dacia. But as yet they made no concerted efforts to settle on Roman soil. The Black Sea hinterland offered them enough land for settlement and raiding provided them with ample profit, for the time being (below, p. 152).

Germans in the service of Rome

Increasingly from the later third century onward, the Roman army relied heavily on barbarian troops.[12] The origin of the practice lies far back in Rome's relations with native peoples, but pronounced new features emerged during the period of military anarchy in the third century and there were further developments in Constantine's day. Several of the third-century usurpers employed barbarian forces in their armies, in some cases because no other supplies of manpower were available to them. Others turned to the German and nomadic peoples because of their fighting qualities. By the late third century, recruitment among barbarians was well established and may have been viewed by barbarian warriors as a highly desirable entrée to fame and fortune. A decisive further impetus was given by Constantine's creation of a mobile army to support his Imperial ambitions, and specifically to attack Italy and unseat Maxentius. Constantine and his father Constantius had already employed German troops in Britain, and Constantine's elevation to the purple had been assured by the strong support of an Alamannic chieftain in Roman service. Constantine's new strike force was probably largely barbarian, drawn from captives, prisoners settled within the Roman provinces and volunteers from peoples outside the Empire. The latter group may have supplied many of the officers of the new units. Among the elite units there were several which consisted largely of Germans. These included the *scholae*, guard units which took on many of the functions discharged in the earlier Empire by the praetorians. Alamannic officers are prominent in the record in the first half of the fourth century, but this may be

---

[12] M. Waas, *Germanen im römischen Dienst* (Bonn 1969).

due to our reliance upon Ammianus Marcellinus, who knew a good deal about this German people. Franks appear in dominating roles as the fourth century progressed, along with representatives of other peoples.

Already before the middle of the fourth century, Germans were exercising senior commands within the Roman army.[13] Other commanders, possibly of barbarian origin, may be hidden behind Latin names. Several Germans achieved the highest military rank of all, that of *magister militum*. One such was Silvanus, *magister militum* in Gaul in the 350s, the son of a Frank who had attained high office under Constantine. Ammianus reports that Silvanus was a man 'dedicated to the Empire', but compelled to proclaim himself emperor to protect himself against plotters who had trumped up evidence that he did indeed harbour Imperial aspirations. He was later murdered by some of his own troops who had been bribed by another commander, Ursicinus. In the later fourth century it becomes difficult to identify holders of the most senior military posts who were certainly *not* Germans. This is particularly true in the West, from the reign of Constantius down to that of Honorius. The power of these men was by no means confined to the conduct of military affairs. When the emperor Julian was killed on campaign against the Persians and a new emperor was to be elected, both the western and eastern Roman armies had as their spokesmen barbarian officers. The two western representatives, Dagalaifus and Nevitta, were both certainly Germans. Western *magistri militum* of German origin exercised immense political authority under Valentinian I and II. Merobaudes twice attained the consulship, an exceptional honour for someone not of the Imperial house, and it was he who was largely responsible for the proclamation of Valentinian II as emperor. When he abandoned the cause of the emperor Gratian, the power of that emperor was significantly impaired and the way was opened up for the usurpation of Magnus Maximus. Even greater power was wielded by another Frank, Arbogast, the leading commander of Valentinian II and possibly the son of yet another leading barbarian general, Bauto. After the defeat

---

[13] J. H. W. G. Liebeschuetz, *Barbarians and Bishops* (Oxford 1990), 7–25.

of Magnus Maximus in 388, Arbogast was assigned the role of supreme military commander in the West under Valentinian II, but he also held sway over other matters of state. His supremacy was such that after a quarrel with his emperor, he felt secure enough to murder Valentinian or to drive him to suicide, and replace him with the nonentity Eugenius. Arbogast had gone beyond what even a powerful German could get away with. The eastern emperor Theodosius moved against Arbogast and his puppet, overthrew them and killed them both. Supreme power in the West now passed to the German, or half-German, Stilicho, who acted as regent to Honorius, the feeble son and successor of Theodosius. From 395 until his execution in 408, Stilicho was effectively the ruler of the Roman West, the last and greatest of barbarian commanders who fulfilled the military role which was properly that of an emperor.

We hear of few German commanders in Roman service who later returned to their own peoples and this is significant. The most notable exception was Mallobaudes, a Frankish commander under the emperor Gratian. He later returned to the Franks beyond the Rhine as a king and conducted a successful war against the Alamanni in 378. How he was able to pursue this course is not certain, but it is highly likely that Roman support was made available to him in the hope that he would reduce Alamannic pressure on the frontier. Otherwise, high-ranking German generals and probably many of their warriors adjusted easily to life within the Empire and showed no marked eagerness to return to their earlier lives.

4

The Living and the Dead

The forms of settlement

The history of settled agricultural communities in northern
Europe is very long and archaeological study of them has
made enormous advances since the 1950s. Exploitation of the
resources of the land began at least 4,000 years before the
Germanic peoples make their first appearance in European
history and from an early date in that long period community
settlements of some size and sophistication existed. The settlements of the peoples of early historic northern Europe must
thus be seen within this long continuum, and not as a process
which began when the Classical world became aware of the
inhabitants of these regions. We are now very much better
placed to construct an account of settlement in the Germanic
world, within its appropriate social and economic context, than
any writer of Classical Antiquity. The point has to be clearly
stated, for efforts are still made to fit the archaeology of
settlement within a framework based ultimately on the accounts
of Caesar and Tacitus. It is increasingly obvious that this
approach is, at best, inadequate and liable to lead to error.
Vastly more data are now available to us from a far wider
geographical and chronological span than were at the disposal
of any ancient observer. There are constraints on how we can
use it and limitations on what it reveals, but the growing
coherence and consistency of the archaeological record are
guarantees of its fundamental reliability.

The coastlands of northern Holland and Germany offer a

landscape in which many ancient and medieval settlements are still clearly visible; in which indeed there is a marked degree of continuity from prehistoric time to the present. In the clay-lands near the coasts of Friesland many early settlements are revealed in the form of mounds, often rising to a height of some metres above the surrounding flat land.[1] In many cases modern villages and hamlets occupy the mounds, their church and churchyard lying at their centres. Many are far less promi-nent, now appearing as barely distinguishable platforms in pasture fields. In Holland, these mounds are referred to as *Terpen*; in Germany the dialect words *Wurt, Warft* or *Wierde* are used to describe them, these elements often figuring in the place-names of the region. The mounds are most probably the *tumuli alti* (high mounds) and *tribunalia manibus exstructa* (platforms raised by hand) which the Elder Pliny saw or heard about on his northern visit in the mid-first century AD. Many of the larger *Terpen* have been severely damaged by later activities. The farmers of later times found that the organic material sealed within the mounds made excellent fertilizer, with the result that many sites were quarried away almost to extinction. Smaller mounds have been vulnerable to ploughing and drainage schemes, so that many short-lived sites have also disappeared. But large-scale excavation of a number of *Terpen* has brought rich rewards in information on settlement-plans and history. The fact that many *Terpen* have been waterlogged or very wet over long periods of time means that structures and artifacts often survive in exceptional state, providing a clarity of detail which is rare on dry sites.

The earliest known *Terpen* belong to the sixth or seventh century BC. Their erection may have begun as part of a coloniz-ation movement on to the claylands from the drier areas of Drenthe to the south. But much more significant is the spread of *Terpen*-building towards the end of the first millennium BC and further development thereafter. In certain areas of the coastland, for example in parts of Schleswig-Holstein, local conditions may have severely restricted settlement until the first century AD. Of sites so far excavated, the great majority began

[1] H. Halbertsma, *Terpen tussen Vlie en Ems* (Groningen 1963).

as flat settlements, their subsequent increase into mounds being due partly to the natural accumulation of debris and occupation material on a restricted space, and partly to the deliberate dumping of clay to form platforms for structures. Numerous sites did not progress beyond the phase of flat settlement or the first stages of mound-building. At Paddepoel, near Groningen, five or six substantial dwellings coexisted in the same area, but apparently independently of each other, during the first century AD.[2] All were abandoned before the mound progressed beyond its primary stage of building. But many *Terpen* are the result of a long and continuous occupation of the same site. One such is Ezinge in Groningen province, which originated as a flat settlement in the mid-first millennium BC, went through several stages of small *Terp*-building, before developing into a sizeable settlement of 12 to 15 long-houses, laid out on a radial plan, by the late pre-Roman Iron Age. By this time the mound was nearly 3 metres high and 150 metres across. This settlement continued, with frequent renewals of its buildings, down to the late Roman period, when it was transformed into a numerous series of *Grubenhäuser* (sunken-floored dwellings). Although other *Terpen* followed this kind of development over a similar period, not all attained the size of the Ezinge settlement. Many were probably single farmsteads or small hamlets, occupied over a relatively short timespan and vulnerable to change in personal fortunes and the natural environment. Numerous sites in the coastlands will have been affected by the advance of the sea which is widely attested in northern Europe from the later third century onward. This major natural change may have stimulated the growth of larger and higher mound-settlements during the later Roman period.

The most extensive and in all ways most important excavation of a coastal mound-settlement to date has been the work at Feddersen Wierde, near Bremerhaven, overlooking the Weser estuary, from 1955 to 1963.[3] A large irregular mound, over 100 metres across, has been more completely examined than any other settlement of the type, with outstandingly important

---

[2] W. A. van Es, 'Paddepoel', *Palaeohistoria*, 14 (1968), 187–352.
[3] W. Haarnagel, *Die Grabung Feddersen Wierde, vol. 2: Methode, Hausbau, Siedlungs- und Wirtschaftsformen, sowie Sozialstruktur* (Wiesbaden 1979).

results for the social and economic ordering of the place during the Roman period. As the site was occupied for some five centuries, the mass of data recovered is immense and not all has yet been published. But the outline history of Feddersen Wierde is clear. Occupation began in the later first century BC, at a time when the immediate area was still vulnerable to flooding. By the early first century AD, at least, substantial long-houses existed, along with attendant store-buildings. Each of these dwellings occupied its own low building-mound: amalgamation into a single mound came later. The settlement grew steadily in size during the early Roman period, developing a radial plan also seen in some of the Dutch *Terpen*. Shortly after AD 100, there was an important development at the south-eastern margin of the settlement. A large house, set within its own palisaded enclosure, from now on dominated the settlement. Around this dwelling and its ancillary structures lay a number of buildings which were used by craftsmen working in a wide range of materials, including wood, leather, bone and iron. This craftsmen's quarter was plainly under the control of the occupants of the adjacent house and some close relationship involving obligations of service would seem to be in evidence here. This further indication of social differentiation from the early Roman period is important confirmation of the evidence seen in the case of settlements in Holland (below, p. 68). What is so interesting about the arrangement at Feddersen Wierde is that it was to endure for some two hundred years. Such a degree of stability may have been fostered, in part at least, by the conditions which obtained in the coastal marshland. How common such dominance of individual families was in northern Germania is not clear. But it must be noted that in Jutland, for example, there are signs of a different social structure in the late Roman period.

There are other glimpses of an elevated social group in settlements of a very different type. At Peelo, near Assen, and at Fochteloo, both in Drenthe,[4] substantial long-houses lie in their own purlieus, with a few ancillary buildings, but with no

---

[4] P. B. Kooi, G. Delger and K. Klaassens, 'A chieftain's residence at Peelo', *Palaeohistoria*, 29 (1987), 133–44; A. E. van Giffen, 'Prähistorische Hausformen auf Sandboden in den Niederlanden', *Germania*, 26 (1958), 35.

concentration of other dwellings nearby. In both cases, the long-house is a large structure, 19 metres long at Fochteloo, 27 metres at Peelo. Both sites date from the earlier Roman Iron Age, that at Fochteloo from the first century AD. If they were indeed chieftainly residences, as seems most likely, then it follows that significant social distinctions were present within society in this part of Germania at a relatively early date. The Frisii had, of course, long been in contact with Rome, so that a stimulus to such differentiation had been applied early. We hear of the first-century Frisian leader Cruptorix, who had served in the Roman army, in possession of his own villa in his tribal territory. That it took some such form as the sites at Fochteloo and Peelo would not be surprising.

Community settlements of the pre-Roman Iron Age have long been known in Jutland and the Danish islands, most notably at Grøntoft, where successive palisaded villages of aisled long-houses existed from the middle of the first millenium BC. Later settlements, though larger in scale, seem to have been very similar in their general character. At Hodde in south-west Jutland, for instance, orderly settlements are recorded over some five centuries, beginning in the late first century BC.[5] These settlements shifted their position within the main area of occupation on several occasions, without abandoning it entirely. The same shifts in settlements are evident at Vorbasse in southern Jutland.[6] In the late Roman period, this was a grouping of perhaps twenty long-houses, each with ancillary buildings, and each set within its own fenced enclosure. Craft-working as well as agriculture was a marked feature of the local economy at this period, suggesting a community which diversified its activities to exploit to the maximum the natural resources at its disposal. In contrast to the dominance of an individual or a single family at Feddersen Wierde, the impression conveyed by Vorbasse is of a much more egalitarian community consisting of a number of families of equal status.

[5] S. Hvass, Hodde. Et vestjysk landsbysamfund fra aeldre jernalder (Copenhagen 1985).
[6] J. Jensen, The Prehistory of Denmark (London 1982), 214–20. S. Hvass, Die völkerwanderungszeitliche Siedlung Vorbasse, Mitteljütland, Acta Arch. 49 (1978), 61–111.

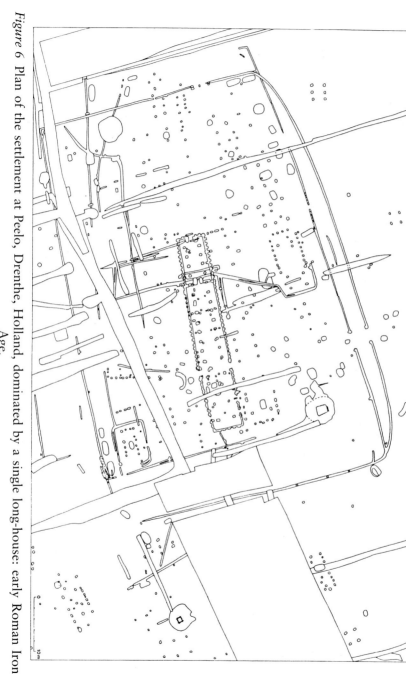

Figure 6 Plan of the settlement at Peelo, Drenthe, Holland, dominated by a single long-house: early Roman Iron Age.

It is, of course, possible that the settlement was subject to a chieftain who chose to site his residence elsewhere. The existence of large settlements like these, and others at Ginderup, Mariesminde and Nørre Fjand, plainly demonstrates a marked increase in population during the Roman Iron Age, with a peak attained in the fourth century. The significance of this increase, and the concomitant rivalry over land and other resources, will clearly have been great. Its role in promoting both internal and outward migration may have become steadily more important.

The emergence of large communities is attested by the evidence of settlements in northern and central Holland during the Roman Iron Age. The most compelling single picture is provided by the settlement at Wijster, also on the sandy lands of Drenthe.[7] This grew from a single farmstead or hamlet in the first century BC through a steadily evolving settlement-plan, into a regularly planned settlement of perhaps fifty or sixty families in the later Roman period. The degree of planning evident in the layout of streets bounded by palisade-fences and a shared alignment of the principal long-houses indicates a central authority invested with considerable power, though it is not clear whether the focus was a single figure or family, or a more widely based group. The territory supervised by the Wijster community must have been large and what it produced is likely to have been more than sufficient for the community itself. A ready market for its surplus production, of course, lay some 100 kilometres to the south, in the garrisons and settlements of the Roman province on the lower Rhine. Smaller communities than Wijster also maintained themselves over long periods. At Bennekom in Gelderland, only 40 kilometres from the Roman frontier, a settlement steadily grew from the second to the fourth century, at its greatest extent consisting of four substantial farmsteads and their ancillary buildings.[8] As at Wijster, the most prosperous phase at Bennekom was the third and fourth centuries. With the collapse of Roman power on the Rhine, the principal prop to the economic order in this part

---

[7] W. A. van Es, 'Wijster: A native village beyond the Imperial frontier, *Palaeohistoria*, 11 (1965), 29.

[8] W. A. van Es, M. Miedema and S. L. Wynia, 'Eine Siedlung der römischen Kaiserzeit in Bennekom, Prov. Gelderland', *BROB* 35 (1985), 533–652.

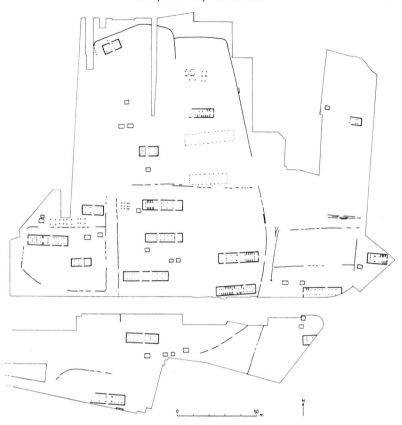

Figure 7 Plan of the settlement at Wijster, Drenthe, Holland: a planned layout of the fourth century AD.

of Germania was removed. Both Wijster and Bennekom faded out early in the fifth century.

The regions immediately east of the Rhine are much less well documented than Holland and the coastland. Present indications are that a variety of settlement types existed here, but excavations on a large scale have been few. An extensively excavated site is that at Haldern, near Wesel, close to the Rhine.[9] The central part of this settlement was dominated by

[9] R. von Uslar, 'Die germanische Siedlung in Haldern bei Wesel am Niederrhein', *Bonner Jahrb*, 149 (1949), 105–45.

two or three rectangular structures which were not the familiar
aisled long-houses. One of these was a large hall in a manner
suggestive of cruck construction. Another building was unusually wide, measuring 9 metres by 6 metres, and may have
had a social or religious function rather than a purely domestic
purpose. Around these structures lay *Grubenhäuser*, providing
work-places and housing for dependants. The known period
of occupation at Haldern was the first and second centuries
AD, but it may be suspected that settlement later shifted to a
nearby site.

Settlements in the eastern regions of Germania have not yet
been studied so extensively as those in the north-west. There
are, however, clear signs that community settlements existed
from an early date. At the Bärhorst, near Nauen, 50 kilometres
west of Berlin, a compactly planned settlement lay within a
timber palisade on a roughly square layout.[10] About thirty
long-houses may have existed at one time and these were
carefully planned on the same east–west alignment, leaving an
open space at the centre of the enclosure. Very few *Grubenhäuser* or other subsidiary buildings were present for a settlement of this size, though the long-houses themselves varied in
type and may have formed a hierarchy now difficult to discern.
The dating evidence for the Bärhorst was not published, but
the place may have reached its peak of development in the
third century. Other sites are known in the Berlin region,
and their layout shows considerable diversity. At Kablow, 30
kilometres south-east of the city, settlement began as two rows
of houses but had developed into a sprawling community of
more than sixty buildings, including aisled long-houses and
large oval *Grubenhäuser*, by the third century. At the northern
end of this large settlement was situated a substantial dwelling,
with a row of store-buildings adjacent to it. This was quite
possibly the headquarters of the local chief or headman. After
this long period of stable settlement on one site, the place was
progressively abandoned during the third century and replaced
by another extensive village nearby.

---

[10] O. Doppelfeld and G. Behm, Das germanische Dorf auf dem Bärhorst bei
Nauen', *Prähist. Zeitschrift.* 28–9 (1938), 284.

Hill-forts and other fortified places seem at present to have played little part in the settlement history of the early Germans.[11] This may, however, be misleading for relatively few hilltop sites have been examined in the heartland of the Germanic peoples. There is suggestive evidence from a number of sites for occupation in the Roman Iron Age and migration period, but at very few has such evidence been followed up with appropriate excavation. In south-western Germany and in Czechoslovakia in particular, where the tradition of hill-fort building long preceded the arrival of German settlers, it may be expected that hilltop strongholds were either reused or built anew, especially in the disturbed conditions of the later Roman Iron Age. That this did occur in the regions between the upper Rhine and upper Danube is certain. On the Glauberg, some 5 kilometres east of the Roman *limes*, a prominent flat ridge had been settled by a succession of prehistoric communities, before a great hill-fort was erected in the early first millennium BC. This was abandoned before the building of the Roman frontier in the Wetterau and lay empty until that frontier was given up about AD 260. Not long afterwards, the hilltop was again fortified, this time by a stone wall. The builders and occupants were Alamanni, perhaps the dependants of a local chieftain or *regulus*, now beginning to move into areas hitherto denied them by the Roman military presence. The Glauberg was occupied from the early fourth century until the end of the fifth, for the earlier part of that period maintaining close links with the Roman world, through either trade or the terms of a local treaty. The internal arrangement of the settlement is poorly known, the records of the excavations of the 1930s having been destroyed in 1945. But the foundations of stone dwellings were identified, along with workshops. Further south, in Mittelfranken, the hill-fort of the Gelbe Burg near Dittenheim was also occupied in the fourth and fifth centuries. The defences of the late Roman phase were exceptionally powerful, consisting of a massive stone rampart, over 13 metres wide, of two dry-stone walls revetting a mass of stone and earth. A timber breastwork may well have lain on top of this huge wall. Within

---

[11] G. Mildenberger, *Germanische Burgen* (Münster 1978).

there was abundant evidence for occupation from the fourth
century onward, chiefly in the form of brooches and other
ornaments, belt-parts and weapons, as well as both Roman
and Germanic pottery. The strongly military character of the
finds suggests that this use of the hill-fort was by a warrior
group, quite possibly in Roman service.

Although strongly fortified sites do not at present figure
prominently among the settlements of the Germanic peoples,
there are evident signs that local strongholds did exist. These
are not the impressively defended hill-forts of Celtic Europe,
though use of some hilltop sites is known. Most of the known
Germanic *places-fortes* are relatively small enclosures, sited on
low ground and surrounded by timber palisades rather than
massive earthwork defences. One such is the Heidenschanze,
near Bremerhaven, an enclosure of 10 hectares (24 acres) protected by a strong palisade set in a foundation trench and
backed by an earthen rampart revetted at the rear by a wall of
planks. This site originated in the first century BC and continued in use, with several renewals of its defences, into the
earlier Roman period. Within the defences, occupation does
not seem to have been intensive and the significance of the
Heidenschanze may have had more to do with commerce than
settlement. It was carefully positioned to overlook land and
river routes which converged on the Weser estuary, itself a
major approach from the sea, and was thus well placed to serve
as a distribution point for goods leaving the coastal zone and
as a reception area for imports.

A striking series of fortified sites has been excavated on
the sandy lands of Drenthe in northern Holland, all of them
occupying ground which gave no tactical advantage.[12] These
are mainly rectilinear palisaded enclosures, four of which have
been extensively excavated, at Zeijen, Vries and Rhee, all of
them dating from the period 200 BC to the first century AD.
There is no doubt that the defensive aspect of these sites was
very important. Zeijen I, of the later pre-Roman Iron Age, was
protected by a rampart nearly 4 metres wide, fronted and

---

[12] H. T. Waterbolk, 'Walled enclosures of the Iron Age in the north of the
Netherlands', *Palaeohistoria*, 19 (1977), 97–172.

backed by stout timber palisades, while Vries in its latest form was girt not only by a strong rampart, but by three additional palisades outside it. These sites show considerable variation in their internal arrangements. Zeijen I had a carefully planned interior, six large long-houses being placed close to the defences, and the central area containing only four- and six-post structures of a type usually interpreted as stores for grain and other products. The later site of Zeijen II contained mainly storage buildings set close to the ramparts. The enclosure at Vries contained few buildings in any of its phases, recognizable dwellings being particularly scarce. The tightly planned Rhee, by contrast, was essentially a dwelling enclosure, with long-houses

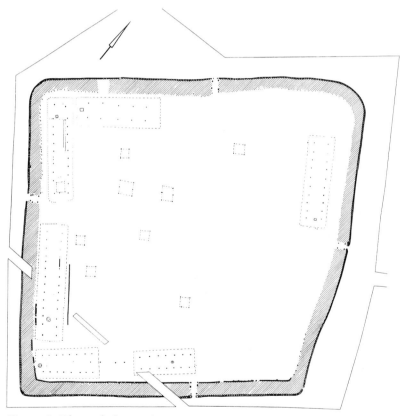

Figure 8 Plan of the settlement at Zeijen I, Drenthe, Holland: an enclosed settlement of the early Roman Iron Age.

occupying much of the interior throughout its history. Both Rhee and Zeijen I may be seen as the seats of powerful local families, intent on dominance of the resources and the landscape of the area. The enclosures containing mainly storage-buildings may have served as repositories of their wealth, thus requiring defences as powerful as those around the residences. The picture of localized power, and of the rivalry that went with it, is as clear as archaeological evidence can present. That such *Herrensitze* (chieftains' residences) probably existed in other parts of the Germanic world at this early date is surely to be expected.

Not all structures can be easily fitted into such categories as habitations, store-buildings and defensive works. In a large-scale study of the North Frisian island of Sylt, a number of Iron Age settlements have been located. Among them lies the Archsumburg on a small eminence. This has been shown to be a roughly circular structure, surrounded by a turf wall 5 metres thick originally and defining a space over 100 metres in diameter. Within the enclosure lay timber buildings with wattle walls and centrally placed supporting posts. A number of other earthworks of this kind are known on the Frisian islands. They are not convincing as works of defence and their true significance is not yet clear. A function connected with cult might be reasonably considered, as might places of assembly for the island community. That such earthworks might have existed on the mainland is also possible, for their remains are not substantial and are vulnerable to later agriculture.

A wide range of simple structures existed on Germanic settlements in Holland, many of them leaving behind very slight remains. In recent works in the Assendelft polders, small houses up to 10 metres in length have been identified, defined largely by gullies running alongside exterior walls which were probably of turf. Even the larger buildings in these settlements were framed on small timber uprights, scarcely more than stakes. These discoveries indicate that the record of early German buildings is still far from complete.

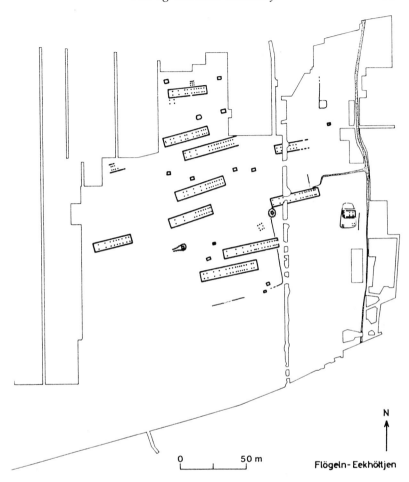

Figure 9 Plan of the settlement at Flögeln, Kr. Cuxhaven, Germany: fourth to fifth centuries AD.

The agricultural economy

Animal husbandry played a very significant part in the agricultural economy of the early Germans.[13] For many, their wealth

[13] Much of what follows is summarized in G. Kossack, K. -E. Behre and P. Schmid (eds), *Archäologische und naturwissenschaftliche Untersuchungen an ländlichen und frühstädtischen Siedlungen im deutschen Küstengebiet vom*

Figure 10 A reconstruction of a Roman Iron Age settlement at Lejre, Denmark.

lay in their flocks and herds, as Tacitus asserted, and the point is fully supported by the domestic settlements of Germania and by the animal remains found in them. Studies of animal bones from a considerable number of northern settlements reveal that cattle were everywhere of the greatest importance, as producers of meat and milk and as beasts of burden, followed by pigs, sheep and, further behind, horses. Other domesticated animals such as goats and chickens are poorly represented on most

5. Jahrhundert v. Chr. bis zum 11. Jahrhundert n. Chr., vol. 1 (Bonn 1984) – and in M. Todd, *The Northern Barbarians* (2nd edn; Oxford 1987), 100–14.

been remarkably little influenced by cross-breeding from other parts of Europe. Non-selective breeding over centuries inevitably led to a reduction in the size of the animals, so that certain species would appear to us almost as miniature animals.

The cattle from the northern coastal settlements were small, no higher than 1.1 metres at the shoulder, slender and with short horns. Horses, too, were generally short and solidly built, many measuring only 1.4 metres at the shoulder. Pigs were proportionately small, even though they seem to have been derived from a large, wild ancestral breed. Sheep and goats, by contrast, were not much smaller than those of the contemporary Roman world or the Middle Ages. On almost all sites, cattle were the dominant domesticated animal. At Feddersen Wierde, they account for well over half the total of animals kept. At Wulfshof, the proportion is nearly 70 per cent. In the coastal marshlands, where there was abundant pastureland, sheep came next. In areas where there was a greater tree-cover, swine husbandry followed that of cattle. Horses were nowhere very prominent and were probably mainly kept as draught animals. But marks of butchery on some horse bones indicate that they were eaten on occasion. Dogs were present in small numbers at most settlements and were presumably employed in herding and as watchdogs. At Feddersen Wierde, dogs were frequently buried under the thresholds of houses as symbolic guardians of the home. Domestic chickens appear in the record very occasionally. The range of meat available to the household was thus considerable and the fact that a relatively high proportion of animals was slaughtered at an early age is a clear proof that succulent meat played a major part in the diet. About a third of sheep in several settlements were killed in their first eighteen months. Young pigs were also slaughtered in some numbers, calves somewhat less so. Cattle were clearly kept for their milk and the products derived from it. The skins of mature animals were in due course turned into leather for a variety of uses.

Surprisingly, the hunting of wild animals played an extremely minor role in the supply of food. On the most fully studied sites, the remains of wild mammals amount to less than 1 per cent of the total. And yet there was an abundance of wild meat on the hoof in Germania, notably the aurochs, wild boar, roe and red deer. The furs of the fox, beaver and otter were also

available, though there is scarcely a sign that these animals
were hunted on any scale. The red deer was probably the main
target of the hunter, partly for its meat, partly for its antlers,
which were used to make a number of implements. Sea mammals make a limited showing among the bones found on settlements. Dolphin- and whalebone presumably were gathered
from stranded animals. Seals were abundant and were easily
hunted on the sandbanks of the Baltic and North Sea. Their
bones were fairly common finds at Feddersen Wierde, and
these creatures could have provided meat, oil and skins in
fair quantity to coastal communities. Fishing made a more
significant contribution to diet than the hunting of mammals.
Sturgeon and salmon were both taken, probably in nets as they
moved into estuaries from the open sea. But cod were also
caught and that implies offshore fishing from boats. Plaice and
flounders could be more easily fished for in coastal waters.
Shellfish, too, were collected, especially mussels, but not in
great quantity. Some coastal communities may have depended
heavily upon fishing for their livelihood, for example Nørre
Fjand in Jutland, where large quantities of fish bones were
found.

The crops grown by the farmers of northern Germania are
well established in a variety of sources, chiefly pollen spectra
and finds of seeds and other plant remains in dated deposits.
Barley had been grown in quantity from the second millennium
BC and it was to continue as the most prevalent form of
grain crop until the early medieval period, especially the hulled
varieties. Oats were also widely grown, having been originally
collected as a weed among cultivated grain. Various forms of
wheat, including emmer and Einkorn, were widely cultivated,
as they had been since the Neolithic. Rye and millet appear in
varying quantities, as do other seed-bearing plants such as gold-
of-pleasure. The main vegetable crops seem to have been beans
and peas. Flax was grown mainly for its oil-bearing seeds but
also for its fibres which could be made into linen. Various wild
vegetables were available and could have been gathered. These
include celery, spinach, the brassicas and dandelion, radishes
and lettuce.

There is little sign that wild fruits and berries were collected,
and certainly no evidence of organized fruit-growing. Elder-

berries, strawberries and blackberries are attested on settlements but only in small quantities. These could have been used to make fomented drinks as well as consumed in their fresh state. Apples and pears were apparently not known, but the plum, wild cherry and sloe all appear, as does the hazelnut. In sum, this adds up to a very modest supplement to the northern Iron Age diet. A plant which was grown or gathered for another purpose was woad, recorded at Feddersen Wierde and in Denmark. This was used as a dyestuff for textiles.

The early German thirst was legendary and the adjuncts to drinking, the horns, glass vessels, bronze containers and silver goblets, are familiar components of Germanic grave furniture throughout the period. What was actually consumed is not as well established as it might be. The drinking of Roman wine is often assumed but is not supported by the archaeological evidence. Although silver and bronze drinking sets were imported from the Roman world, there is little indication that wine crossed the Roman frontiers in any quantity. Roman wine amphorae are very scarce in Germania, in contrast to their import into the earlier Celtic Europe, and other indications of wine consumption are slight. The principal drink of northern Europe was that based on fomented grain. A beer-like drink has been identified by chemical analysis of residues in drinking-horns found in Denmark. The abundance of barley among the cultivated grains of the north may be partly explained by its use in the making of beer. There were other forms of drink, based on fruit juices, also identified in drinking-horns. A horn found at Skydstrup in Denmark contained traces of a drink based on honey, the mead later popular in several parts of Germanic Europe. But it was beer, above all, that flowed at German feasts, and the size of some of the vessels that held it tells its own story. Some hold several gallons; even one drinking-horn might contain 2 or 3 gallons.

Burial of the dead

The study of the Germanic peoples relies heavily upon information derived from cemeteries and observances for the dead. Cremation was well established in the second millennium BC and it remained the dominant rite of burial throughout the next thousand years and into the historic period. The first inhumation graves began to appear in the first century BC, but these were confined to fairly limited areas, in Denmark, southern Sweden and the lower Vistula region. In northern Germania generally, a series of richly furnished inhumations, the so-called Lübsow group, has been often assigned to an elevated level in society, since the graves are usually set apart from the common cremations and their furnishings indicate access to luxury goods from the Roman world. Inhumation seems to have been more widely practised in southern Scandinavia than elsewhere, these graves being often placed beneath a barrow or cairn of stones. The great majority of burials in all the Germanic territories before migrations were cremations, often in extensive flat cemeteries, the largest of which might contain thousands of graves. Most graves were simply furnished with one or two pottery vessels, a brooch or other ornament, a knife or a spindle-whorl. Offerings of food and drink were provided in many cases, as finds of animal bones testify. A relatively small proportion of graves in most regions contain weapons or tools. In certain parts of northern Germania, distinction between male and female cemeteries was observed, as is clear from the grave-goods. The majority of cemeteries, however, are those of entire communities and they reveal little in the way of distinction in social status or wealth. The graves of children and babies are rare in cremation cemeteries and it is likely that the bodies of the young were less formally disposed of. At the Tisice cemetery in Bohemia, for example, only nine graves were those of children out of a total of 104 and none of these was an infant. Occasionally, however, a child burial was accompanied by rich grave-goods suggestive of high rank, as in the case of a boy at Bornitz, buried with a belt, two knives, two spurs, silver dress-ornaments and a drinking-horn.

Cremation might take one of several forms. The commonest is the urn-grave in which the cremated remains have been collected together and placed in a pot or occasionally a metal vessel, or a wooden or cloth container, the whole being then buried in a small pit. Another widely distributed grave-form contains the remains of the funeral pyre and grave-goods as well as the ashes of the dead (*Brandgrubengrab*), while in a third type the cremated remains were kept separate from the urn and other grave furniture (*Brandschüttungsgrab*). The last-named mainly occurs in the north but is encountered elsewhere. Empty pits are also found in cemeteries, perhaps cenotaphs or sacrificial *putei* (ritual pits). In the eastern territories, notably in Poland, cemeteries occur in which individual graves do not exist. The remains of the dead and the offerings to them were scattered in a layer on the ground and then covered with earth.

Richly furnished burials are rare before the late first century BC, at which date imports of Roman luxury goods began to enter the northernmost parts of Europe, chiefly vessels of silver, bronze, glass and pottery. Once imported, items of high quality might circulate for long before being consigned to the earth. Some graves in Denmark of the first century BC contain Etruscan and Campanian bronzes which were at least three hundred years old when buried. The outstanding quality of the finest imports is well exemplified by the two splendid Augustan silver cups and the bronze utensils, amounting to a full banqueting service in a grave at Hoby on the Danish island of Lalland. The silver cups are among the finest products of the Graeco-Roman metalsmith's craft and they are by no means the only representatives in the North (below, p. 92f.).

Inhumation had long been a more favoured rite among the eastern peoples and in Scandinavia. In the later Roman Iron Age it spread widely through northern and central Europe, perhaps under the influence of changing practice in the Roman frontier provinces. Those Germans who settled in the provinces from the fourth century onward quickly adopted inhumation, the most notable exceptions being the Anglo-Saxon invaders of Britain, a majority of whom adhered to the rite of cremation long after they migrated. The Goths inhumed their dead from before their entry into the Empire and continued to do so when they settled in Gaul, Italy and Spain. The grave-goods deposited with the dead were usually modest in character, consisting generally of personal ornaments. Weapons and war-equipment were rarely included in Gothic graves, thus often making such burials difficult to distinguish from those of other Germans or Roman provincials. Other peoples, such as the Burgundians, seem to have adopted the burial practices of the provincial population among whom they settled and thus are almost invisible in the record. The same may be true of the Franks as they expanded southward.

Elaborate tomb monuments which stood above ground were not part of the Germanic observance of the dead. Theoderic's mausoleum at Ravenna is essentially a Roman structure. Even simple mounds or other constructions over graves seem to have been relatively rare in most regions, though barrows were erected by the eastern peoples and stone cairns were built over graves in Scandinavia. Stone settings in the form of a ship are also found in Scandinavia and, of course, burials of actual ships and boats for the more illustrious dead, especially in migration period Sweden.

The most widespread form of cemetery among the Germans of the migration period was that of *Reihengräber*, in which the inhumation graves were set out in long distinct rows, the interments often extending out from the earliest burials at the centre. Such cemeteries were frequently in use over very long periods of time. They are found from the early fifth century on both sides of the Rhine, become widespread among the Franks, Alamanni and their neighbours, and eventually spread over much of western and central Europe. The origins of row-grave cemeteries are still in dispute. A link with the spread of Christianity is possible, but not wholly convincing.

There is a general conservatism about Germanic burial rites, an adherence to practices and locations over long periods, as is seen in the huge urnfields of the North, in the *Reihengräber*, and in the continuance of cremation by some of the Anglo-Saxons. Changes rarely came with dramatic suddenness. Nobles and kings could still be buried with their earthly treasures long after the triumph of Christianity among their peoples and long after it was fitting for the great to be laid to rest in churches.

One feature of cemeteries, particularly of the migration period, which is perhaps unexpected given the care devoted to the deposition of the dead and their grave-goods, is the phenomenon of grave-robbing. This is very widely attested, in graves differing greatly in the richness of their contents. It is now certain that intrusion into graves and the removal of their contents often took place not long after burial. Some very richly furnished graves were all but emptied in this way. Several obvious explanations are to hand for the disturbance and robbing of graves, including theft and the need to recover a body for reburial. It has been argued that the authorized recovery of grave-goods may also have to be allowed for, after an interval which may not have been prolonged. The grave may have been viewed as a temporary resting-place of the dead. Once the soul was lodged elsewhere, there was no longer any need for the grave-goods to remain in the ground. This is an ingenious interpretation, but it does not account for the survival of so many splendidly furnished burials, undisturbed and with their contents intact. Probably, then, most grave-robbing had less to do with views of the afterlife than with normal human greed.

5

Trade and Diplomacy

Roman diplomacy and the early Germans

Advanced cultures and powers, when faced with primitive peoples beyond their borders, are usually active in developing systems of control, sometimes directly through military supervision, more often by means of diplomacy and political manipulation. 'Divide and rule' was a commonplace of Roman statecraft and the principle was widely applied among the northern peoples of Europe, and with conspicuous success. Although the main aims were political, some of the results of Roman policy had an impact on other aspects of Germanic society, so that some grasp of the process and its consequences is needed.

Roman efforts at controlling Germanic tribes from within their own societies had made considerable progress before the climactic year of AD 9.[1] In no case were they more energetically pursued than among the Cherusci, the core of the group of tribes which inflicted the crushing defeat on the army of Quinctilius Varus. The Cherusci had elected Arminius as their military leader in AD 6, probably not long after he had seen service in the Roman forces as a commander of German troops. We may well guess that the election of Arminius was at the time not unwelcome to Roman commanders. Arminius was not the only Cheruscan with experience of service with Rome and of the rewards it might bestow. His father-in-law, Segestes, had

[1] E. A. Thompson, *The Early Germans* (Oxford 1965), 72–108.

proved to be an outstandingly loyal servant of Rome during the time when Roman forces occupied the lands east of the Rhine after 12 BC; he had been rewarded with Roman citizenship by Augustus. How the loyalty of Segestes had been bought is unknown, but, as he later declared that he believed that Rome's interests were the same as those of the Germans, it must have been in a most attractive currency. Segestes was firmly opposed to the idea of a revolt against the Roman occupation and did what he could to relay Arminius' plans to Varus. When matters came to a head in AD 9, he and his following did take part in the campaign against the Roman forces and received some of the spoils after the final battle. But he remained with the people, at odds with Arminius and still cherishing the dream of a Roman return east of the Rhine. Finally forced out in AD 15 during the campaigns of Germanicus, he was rescued from the forces of Arminius and given a home within the Roman provinces of Gaul. He managed to bring with him his daughter and her (and Arminius') unborn son, who was to grow up at Ravenna.

The career of Segestes is instructive, and not merely for the details of the case. We hear about Segestes because he was the father-in-law of the great liberator of Germany and because his story is intertwined with greater events. How many chieftains were there like Segestes, unnamed and unknown, but staunch supporters of Roman power all the same? How many saw that there could be still greater benefits for Germans than service with the Roman army? Virtually at the beginning of German relations with Rome, a theme is introduced which would resonate while Roman power continued in western Europe.

An even closer relative of Arminius, his brother Flavus, also followed a strongly pro-Roman career. He had served as a cavalryman in Tiberius' army after AD 4 and was still in service under Germanicus in AD 15. His support for Rome remained steadfast throughout a time when the prospects for an ultimate Roman victory in Germany faded away entirely. When reconstructing a debate between Flavus and Arminius on the merits of their respective causes, Tacitus makes Flavus put forward his monetary rewards, military honours, the wealth of the emperor, the greatness of Rome and the terrible punishment which awaited her enemies as his reasons for adherence to the

Empire. These made up a sound Roman view, but they also fairly summarize what most impressed a German leader. The same motives may be ascribed to Boiocalus, a chieftain of the Ampsivarii. During the great revolt, Arminius had to confine him in chains. That did not deter Boiocalus from serving Rome. He remained loyal to a succession of emperors for fifty years, a record which earned no special treatment for his people when they sought more land on which to settle.

What is most clearly reflected in the careers of these men is the power of Roman money, as expressed in a variety of forms, and the relative ease with which it might be used to exploit and deepen the divisions between the leading men and the main body of the tribe. These divisions opened up remarkably quickly when Roman arms were extended beyond the Rhine and Danube. It is easy to understand why. Access to wealth barely dreamed of before the advent of Roman power enabled Germanic leaders to enrich and enlarge their retinues, and thus bid for power within a society which thus far had seen relatively little in the way of social differentiation. The opportunities opened up by the acquisition of Roman money were not to be missed, even if this meant dividing the loyalty of a tribe. A formidably anti-Roman people such as the Cherusci could be weakened in this way, and finally torn apart by internal struggles fomented by Roman wealth. Roman successes in this area of diplomacy were considerable, not only in the reigns of Augustus and Tiberius, but later also, especially in the lands north of the middle Danube.

When the Cherusci again appear in the historical record, in the 40s AD, these diplomatic processes had worked to devastating effect. In only thirty years almost all of the leading men of the tribe had been removed from the scene. One notable survivor remained, Italicus the son of Flavus and nephew of Arminius, born at Rome and still resident there. In AD 47, the emperor Claudius restored him to rule among the Cherusci, not as their native king but as a Roman citizen holding power over an external people. Such a position was bound to lead to strains within tribal society and a struggle ensued between the rank-and-file Cherusci, who supported their leader, and a group of warriors who found his coercive power too strong for their liking. Italicus won that round, but later offended the mass of his people by his exercise of total power and was driven out. Eventually he was reinstated with the aid of Lombard warriors.

Diplomacy played a large part in Roman efforts to maintain the peace on the middle Danube. Drusus Caesar established the Quadan Vannius as ruler of a large tract north of the river in AD 19. Vannius greatly enlarged this kingdom by annexations in Bohemia and Moravia before he was expelled by his own people in 50. His place was taken by his nephews Sido and Vangio, who also found Rome ready to assist them with monetary subsidies and even military support over the next twenty years. Vannius and the rest of his family were not abandoned by Rome, but were provided for in case their time to serve Roman interests might come around again. Much later, in the third and fourth centuries, the lands north of the middle Danube were to enjoy a special relationship with the Roman Empire, to the extent that life there may not have been far removed from that of the frontier provinces themselves (below, p. 148).

After the first century, little further is explicitly recorded of diplomatic exchanges between Rome and German leaders, though there is every reason to believe that they continued to figure as an essential part of the controls which Rome placed on the peoples settled close to her frontiers. The assignment of a king to the Quadi in the reign of Antoninus Pius, at the request of the tribe, was viewed as sufficient of a success to merit record on Roman coinage (*Rex Quadis datus*). Subsidies paid in Roman coin, resorted to by some first-century emperors, were certainly provided by second-century rulers, as an increasingly usual means of ensuring loyalty or quiescence. Other support, such as military aid or supplies of food, could be offered when appropriate. Rich gifts also crossed the frontiers to barbarian leaders and elites, there to leave their mark on the archaeology of the Germans in a variety of ways. The processes of gift-exchange and trade are difficult, if not impossible, for us to disentangle, not least as they were closely intertwined in their operation.

Trade with the Roman Empire

Roman commercial activity among the Germanic peoples is astonishing in its range and geographical scope.[2] From northern Holland, across the north German plain, into Norway and Sweden, over the Vistula basin, into western Russia and the eastern Baltic lands, across the plains of the Ukraine and up the valleys of the Dnieper and the Don, the products of workshops in the Roman provinces are encountered in quantities that are often surprising, not least when it is recalled that what has been recorded is a tiny fraction of what originally reached barbarian hands. The high levels of survival of certain kinds of goods in graves and votive deposits mean that some features of the pattern of trade are more fully known than others. Vessels of bronze and silver, glassware and pottery have understandably received more attention than less striking objects such as brooches. Other imports from the Roman Empire such as textiles and foodstuffs, may be largely invisible in the archaeological record, but may have played an important part in the traffic. Some imports pose particular problems for the interpreter. What is to be made of the considerable quantities of Roman weaponry found in the north in the later Roman period? Is this booty resulting from successful warfare or could some have reached the north through trade processes? The presence of Roman coinage, most commonly silver *denarii*, in hoards and single finds, also poses problems. Who used this coinage and to what purpose? Was it a true currency, however limited in function, or was the attraction of the coins merely that of their bullion value? The silver plate, too, can be variously interpreted. Some of the pieces are of such outstanding quality that they are convincingly explained as high-level gifts from Roman officials, even from emperors in some cases. Such magnificent objects were not normal trade commodities.

---

[2] There have been several important recent contributions to the subject, especially J. Kunow, *Der römischer Import in der Germania libera bis zu den Marcomannenkriegen* (Neumünster 1983); and U. Lund Hansen, *Römischer Import im Norden* (Copenhagen 1987). H. -J. Eggers, *Der römischer Import im freien Germanien* (Hamburg 1951) is still of significance.

The organization and regulation of trade across the Roman frontiers is poorly documented. Roman *negotiatores* have left little trace behind them of their activities, apart from their goods, and when they are mentioned there may sometimes be suspicions that their interests were not confined to trade. In Nero's reign, a Roman knight travelled to the Baltic lands where he visited *commercia* (trading-posts), returning with large quantities of amber for the adornment of the Imperial games in Rome. He would also have had opportunity to make other contacts and perhaps gather information which had nothing to do with trade. We are on firmer ground with Quintus Atilius Primus, who operated north of the Danube among the Quadi, probably in the second or early third century.[3] He had been an interpreter and centurion in the Roman forces and had either later turned to commerce among the German settlers north of the frontier, no doubt exploiting contacts made during his military career, or had superintended trade relations. He died in the territory of the Quadi and it is a fair guess that he had organized his commercial operations from a base there. Other such agencies must have existed but have not been identified. Men like Atilius were in a good position to engage in activities other than commerce. Intelligence-gathering, whether occasional or systematic, has often been a secondary occupation of traders and businessmen who cross frontiers and maintain contacts on the other side. The Austro-Hungarian Empire relied on Jewish traders to keep its commanders informed about military deployment in Russia. An ex-soldier like Atilius would know what to look out for and any information supplied by him would be regarded as more soundly based than that gathered from non-Roman agents.

The Germans were not simply the passive recipients of trade-goods supplied by Roman traders. The Hermunduri, north of the upper Danube, engaged in trade with the provinces not only under controlled conditions on the frontier but in the principal city of Raetia, Augsburg. It is certain that they were

---

[3] T. Kolnik, 'Q. Atilius Primus – Interprex, Centurio und Negotiator', *Acta Arch. Hung*, 30 (1978), 61.

not alone in such an enterprise. During the late second century, Marcus Aurelius regularized the places and days for trading between the Marcomanni and the frontier provinces, after a period of unregulated commerce.[4] Probably most of the commercial exchange between German and Roman was conducted at recognized trading-posts in Germania or at major bases. The western Baltic attracted so much in the way of imports from the Empire that we must take seriously the idea that here, probably on one of the Danish islands, there was at least one centre of redistribution, from which goods were redirected to other parts of southern Scandinavia. Such nodes of commerce are demanded by the geography of the region. That there were counterparts in the Roman Empire to the later emporia at Hedeby and Birka does not seem fanciful.

The archaeological record is eloquent about some of the goods which passed from the Empire into German hands. Large quantities of bronze vessels (more than 1,600 are recorded) are known from burials and other finds of the first and second centuries. The first-century objects are overwhelmingly of Campanian manufacture, the principal types being elegant wine buckets, *trullei*, or pans with flat handles, jugs and flat platters. Although produced in bulk, these are objects of some quality; some may have been gifts to leading Germans rather than traded goods. Many of the imported bronzes were drinking-sets: the bucket for temporary storage, the ladle and strainer for serving, the cup, either of silver or glass, for drinking. As time went on, products from Gaulish factories began to enter Germania, eventually to dominate the barbarian market by the later second century. The most distinctive item from the north-western provinces was the so-called Hemmoor bucket, a small handled pail, often with a figured frieze below its rim, issued by workshops near Aachen in Lower Germany. Other bronze vessels came from the middle Danube lands, others again from the northern Balkans.

Fine glassware is another prominent feature of the early Roman imports. Many pieces are probably Italian in origin but precise identification of the location of workshops is hazardous;

[4] Dio Cassius, lxxii. 15.

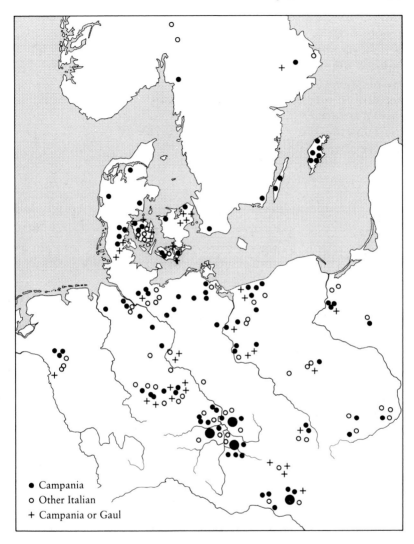

Figure 11 Imports of early Roman bronze vessels into Germania. (after J. Kunow)

many production centres seem to have existed at the same time. It is clear that glass vessels of high quality were prized by leading Germans. The western Baltic finds, which come mainly from graves, are particularly striking, but fine drinking cups and bowls are also found in Sweden, Poland and widely across central Europe. A few vessels are very rare, or even unique, and were probably carefully chosen gifts or presentation objects. One such is the blue glass bowl with a silver overlay and a rim-band bearing the legend EVTVTWC ('good luck') from a third-century grave at Varpelev on Zealand. Other, later products probably had a particular appeal to Germanic taste, for example the glass drinking horns made in the Cologne factories in the third century. The bulk of the known glass finds date from the third and fourth centuries. Not all the vessels need be products of the northern Roman provinces. The cities of the Black Sea shore could well have exported goods into south Russia and northward to the Vistula basin and the eastern Baltic. But certainly western are the well-known cylindrical cups painted with human and animal figures, of which more than twenty examples are recorded, mostly around the Baltic coast and the islands. Such a distribution seems to underline the sea-borne nature of this traffic. Among types with a likely Black Sea origin are tumblers of rather thick, olive-green glass. Interestingly, these found their way not only to the eastern Baltic, but also to southern Norway, where as many as fifteen have been found so far. The taste for glassware of good quality was not lost when the Roman production centres ceased manufacture. Frankish glass continued to reach the northern regions in the fifth and sixth centuries, there to furnish aristocratic feasts.

The most conspicuous of exports were silver vessels, originally intended for the table and often of outstanding quality. Individual finds are normally in graves, especially in the richly furnished graves of the Lübsow group, dating from the first and earlier second centuries AD. The finest vessels have thus far appeared in the north German plain, Denmark and the Danish islands; later on, they figure north of the Danube and in the Black Sea hinterland. It is easier to see these fine pieces as diplomatic or other high-level gifts than goods of trade or booty. That is certainly true of the two cups from the grave at Hoby, which formed part of a lavish table service of silver and bronze vessels dating from the middle of the reign of Augustus. Both bear the name of the maker Cheirisophos, the graffito of an earlier owner Silius, (plausibly the upper German legate

Caius Silius) and the all-important weight of the pieces. To find close analogies for the Hoby cups, we have to turn to the treasure of Boscoreale, near Pompeii. Silver plate, understandably, does not occur as the occasional find or normally in hoards. But there is one magnificant exception.

The most spectacular silver find of the early Empire is that recovered by Prussian infantryman near Hildesheim in 1868.[5] This consisted of over seventy silver vessels, mostly in good condition, though many had seen use and repair over decades before their final concealment. Some of the pieces are of excellent quality and would not be out of place on the most distinguished dining tables of the Empire. These include a dish with an emblem of Athena in its base and another with the infant Hercules in high relief. A series of table sets seems to

Figure 12 Silver dish with emblema of Athena, from the Hildesheim hoard.

[5] E. Pernice, *Der Hildesheimer Silberfund* (Berlin 1901); R. Nierhaus, *Die Kunde*, 20 (1969), 52 for the date.

form the core of the hoard, but there are also trays and the folding tripod for a table, all in silver. The date of the Hildesheim hoard has been much debated. The earlier emphasis upon the first century BC, burial in the Augustan period and connection with Quintilius Varus has now been abandoned. It is difficult to imagine Varus clanking through the Weser forests with this in his baggage and in any case some of the vessels are too late for him. A Neronian to early Flavian date is more satisfactory for the burial, the individual vessels ranging in date over the previous century. What brought them to Germania? They do not comfortably sit with other traded goods. Their quality is high; no other hoard like this is known in Free Germany: most of the other silver imports occur in graves. It is better to see it as made up of a sequence of imports, perhaps from the Augustan period to the middle first century AD, intended as gifts to leading Germans, even to a single dynasty or tribal group, in the region between the Weser and the Elbe, with which lingering contacts were maintained after AD 9.

We now have to confront a major body of evidence, significantly enlarged in the 1980s. Since the nineteenth century, finds of Classical and Byzantine silver and bronzes have been intermittently reported from sites in south and western Russia. Greek pottery and metalwork had been penetrating inland from the colonies on the Black Sea from the sixth century BC onward and more attention was paid to this material than to the less impressive Roman imports. Work since 1979 has largely transformed our view of what was finding its way into south Russia.[6] Not merely occasional silver vessels, but a wide range of goods are now recorded, and not only in the Black Sea hinterland, but far into the centre of European Russia. This new information is only just beginning to be made acccessible to Western scholars and any account of it must be provisional. It must also be emphasized that what we know of it at present is a tiny and not necessarily representative sample. What is already evident is that the dwellers on the Russian steppes were receiving not only goods from the Black Sea and Aegean cities,

---

[6] V. V. Kropotkin, *Rimskie importnye izdelija v Vostocnoj Evrope* (Moscow 1970).

but also from Italy, the middle Danube provinces and perhaps even Gaul. The bulk of the known imports seems to date from the period from the first century BC to the second AD. In large measure they represent the same classes of object that passed into Free Germany.

A series of large barrows in the lower valley of the river Don have been known from the nineteenth century to contain very rich grave-goods and furnishings.[7] Several of these burials have been excavated since 1970, with astonishing results. Roman bronzes of the first and second centuries abound, many of them the same types found beyond the Rhine and Danube. Fine silver vessels occur, from Mediterranean workshops ultimately but probably passing through the trading cities on the Black Sea shore to the lower Don steppe. This is a region with a complex and disturbed history. It would be rash to assume that this material reached the local chieftains through only one agency. Loot from the vulnerable and rich cities around the Black Sea may account for as much as trade. The lower Don was also a frontier region, between the steppe ranged over by nomads and the more varied landscape inhabited by more settled agricultural peoples. The situation was one which called out for diplomatic control, and some of the fine imports might find their place here.

Roman imports are far more widely spread in western Russia than is usually realized. It is unlikely that anything like a corpus could yet be assembled that would hold any meaning. But it seems increasingly clear that Roman commercial and other contacts reached well to the east of the Germanic peoples, perhaps as far as the rivers that drain into the Caspian Sea. It is not therefore entirely surprising to encounter a chieftain's grave on the middle Don at Tretyaki, which contained alongside Roman imports metalwork from Han China.

Roman weapons and other military equipment also found their way far beyond the frontiers, to the Elbe basin, Jutland and the Baltic islands, and northward to Sweden and Norway. The most spectacular examples are in the great votive deposits

---

[7] B. A. Raev, *Roman Imports in the Lower Don Basin*. British Arch. Reports, International Series 278 (1986).

in the peat-bogs of Thorsbjerg, Nydam, Vimose, examined in
the mid-nineteenth century, and of Ejsbøl and Illerup, excavated
in recent years. But they occur with some regularity in burials
across the north German plain and in southern Scandinavia,
from the early second century onward, becoming much more
frequent from the mid-third. The later weapons, especially the
swords, included some items of high quality. Pattern-welded
blades with steel edges are remarkably common in the votive
finds of Jutland, while a series of swords with inlaid figured
designs is represented from the Ukraine in the east to Norway
in the west. Among other equipment, there is the occasional
helmet, many spears and javelins, shield-parts and horse-
harness. How this weaponry got to the northern peoples still
provokes debate. It is obvious that a variety of explanations
will have been involved, including goods brought by Germans
returning from service with Roman units, booty from raids or
longer campaigns, gifts to highly placed barbarians and the like.
But we should not discount trade, both illicit and recognized.[8] It
is true that from the early third century, if not before, exports
of weapons, armour, iron, horses, money, grain, salt and anything else that might benefit an enemy were forbidden by law.
But how effective could such a ban be in the conditions of the
Roman Empire? And can we be sure that Roman commanders
observed the interdict at all times and against all temptations?
It is easy to think of modern European states that break sanc-
tions or ignore bans on arms sales that they have themselves
imposed. The sheer numbers of Roman weapons in the north,
especially swords, when compared with the scarcity of native
equivalents must make some traffic in armaments a proposition
to be taken seriously. Whether this was no more than unofficial
private enterprise or something connected with selective support for external powers the available evidence cannot determine.

All who have studied Roman trade with the Germans have
noted how poorly informed we are about what passed from
Germania to the Roman world. There were no precious metals,
few other minerals, except possibly iron, and not much else to

---

[8] The point is well made by J. Ilkjaer and J. Lønstrup apropos the votive
deposit at Illerup: *Germania* 61 (1983), 95.

attract record by ancient writers. Women's hair for the cords of *ballistae*, geese and lard can only have been minor elements in trade across the frontiers. The staples will have been slaves, animal products such as hides and meat, and perhaps other products of agriculture. At best, these will be rare visitors to the archaeological record.

The most noted of the exports from Germania was perhaps one of the least significant in economic terms: amber from the Baltic coast. Trade in amber had a long prehistoric past before Roman merchants began to follow the routes from the Danube to the eastern Baltic and the Samland peninsula in particular.

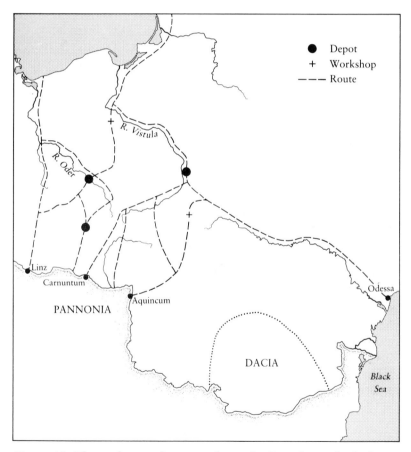

Figure 13 The amber trade-routes from the Danube and Black Sea to the Baltic.

That they were doing so by the reign of Nero is certain; probably they were following the northward routes well before that. The archaeological evidence for the trade in amber has been significantly enlarged in recent years. Large depots of raw amber have been identified around Wroclaw at the crossing of the Oder. But these are dated to the early first century BC and their intended destination may not have been Italy. The clearest indication of Roman exploitation of amber, apart from the objects of worked amber in the Roman world itself, is the dense distribution of Roman coins, especially *sestertii*, close to the Samland. The warfare of the later second century seems to have interfered with the traffic from the Danube lands to the Baltic, and the later focus seems to be Cologne on the lower Rhine. But amber was still reaching the lower Danube in the fourth century, perhaps through Sarmatian intermediaries. It is hard to believe that this was a major trade. We would expect more evidence than we seem to have of the great economic resource of the Baltic in later centuries; skins and furs.There is just a hint of this resource in the *Germania* of Tacitus, but no other certain reference to a fur-trade seems to be extant.

A major centre of trade has long been suspected to exist on the Danish island of Fyn, most particularly in the area of Gudme in the east of the island, only 5 kilometres from the sea.[9] Over a century ago, a pioneering regional study of this area by Frederik Sehested revealed, among much else, a major concentration of rich finds of the late Roman and migration periods around Gudme. In the recent past, this material has been augmented by many new finds – coins, brooches and other ornaments, silver plate fragments, bracteates and the like – from a relatively restricted area. Settlements and burial sites of the period are also emerging and connections with sites on the coast are being traced, the whole recreating a picture of a power-centre with wide overseas connections from the later Roman Iron Age onward.

The mass of gold and silver finds from several sites at Gudme

[9] H. Thrane, 'Das Gudme-problem und die Gudme Untersuchung', *Frühmittelalterliche Studien*, 21 (1987), 1–48; K. Randsborg, 'Beyond the Roman Empire: archaeological discoveries in Fudme on Funen, Denmark', *Oxford Journ. Arch.* 9 (1990), 355.

is astonishing and so far without parallel in Germania. The Roman silver and gold coins are especially remarkable, since they are for the most part single finds, not the contents of hoards. Most of them probably were lost in the fifth and sixth centuries, but some were deposited in the third and fourth centuries. Other gold and silver objects are equally striking, and it is clear that some were brought here to be reworked by craftsmen. This was the fate of pieces of Roman silver plate, broken up into pieces for resmelting. Gold bracteates and brooches are also present in quantity and like the other objects are found over an immense area. The size of the area inhabited or used in the late Roman and migration periods may be as large as 200 hectares.

The link with sea-borne commerce is also emerging from detailed survey of the area. This was first hinted at in 1833, when a large hoard of gold, weighing over 4 kilograms, was found at Lundeborg, a harbour site on the coast near Gudme. This is still the second largest migration period gold hoard from Denmark. Work on the coast immediately north of the harbour has now revealed a large site dating from the late Roman period onward, like the Gudme sites very rich in arti-facts, including precious metal pieces and Roman imports. Craftworking was being carried out at Lundeborg, but its primary significance may have been as a harbour or *emporium*, a forerunner of the well-known Viking period *emporia* at Hed-eby and Birka. Other harbours clearly must have existed in the western Baltic, but only recently have they begun to reveal themselves. One seems to have lain at Nyborg about 17 kilo-metres north of Lundeborg in the migration period. A clearer example is the rich site at Dankirke, near Ribe in south-western Jutland, where fifth-century imports, notably of glass, are to the fore. Another likely site is Sorte Muld, near Svaneke on the island of Bornholm. Here, a major complex of settlements lies only 2 kilometres from the sea. Roman imports are prevalent, especially silver coins, and a wide range of crafts was pursued, including the making of fine jewellery. Later, imports were being received from the Rhineland. The precise commercial mechanisms at work in places like Lundeborg and Sorte Muld are not yet absolutely clear. What is certain, however, is that local leaders in the western Baltic were engaged in contacts, perhaps direct contacts, with the Roman world from the later Roman period and were able to acquire substantial quantities of gold, silver, the other metals, and probably other commodities which do not appear in the record.

The most familiar feature of commercial relations between Rome and the northern peoples is coinage, and the large quantities of Roman coins, especially silver coins, found in Germania have been a frequent subject of discussion.[10] They occur both in hoards, often of substantial bulk, and as single pieces. More than 500 hoards are now known, but that is certainly a small fraction of what was once consigned to the ground and a still smaller fraction of what was current beyond the Roman frontiers. If about 1 per thousand coins has been recorded in modern times, then the total number once in circulation must have run into millions. The phenomenon was well known to Tacitus, writing at the end of the first century AD. The Germans nearest the frontiers used coinage in trade transactions, he remarks, whereas those in the interior engage in barter-exchange. They preferred the older types of coinage, those with the serrated edge and bearing the design of a two-horsed chariot. This might seem to make good sense, as Republican *denarii* of the types which Tacitus refers to contained a higher proportion of silver than later issues, but the observation is not borne out by first-century finds in Germania. Although Republican coins did cross the frontiers, they did not do so in immense numbers. It might have been expected that issues of emperors from Augustus to Nero might have found particular favour in Germania (that is, coinage struck before Nero reduced the silver content of *denarii*). But this, too, does not hold good. Coins of the later first and second centuries were used and hoarded in great quantity. Only with issues of Commodus in the 180s is there a marked diminution in the flow of silver, partly due to a marked reduction in bullion value, and partly perhaps as a result of changing relations following the long Marcomannic Wars. Coins still arrived in the early third century, but older issues made up the bulk of the coinage. It is

---

[10] S. Bolin, *Fynden av romerska mynt i det fria Germanien* (Lund 1926); L. Lind, *Roman denarii found in Sweden*, Vol.-1 (Berlin 1979); Vol.-2 (Stockholm 1981); U. Lund Hansen, *Römischer Import*, 229–32.

not uncommon to find coins of the first and second centuries in hoards buried in the fourth or even the fifth century.

Roman coinage went further east than is often appreciated. The volume of coinage that got to western Russia was substantial. Again, silver currency is to the fore, gold rare and bronze occasional. The main concentration is in and about the Dnieper basin, with other finds occurring eastward to the Volga. Hoards appear to be more prevalent than single coins, but this is probably no more than a reflection of the still scanty record. Most of the coins are of the later first and second centuries, with a peak between 160 and 180. From the reign of Commodus, the flow was checked, though here too old coins went on circulating and are still found in hoards a century or two later. What carried this coinage into the Ukraine? There had long been commercial connections between the Black Sea cities and the fertile plains in the interior. The attraction was grain and other products of the land, welcome imports to the Roman provinces. If the Republican *denarii* found in such quantity in Romania arrived in exchange for slaves, the coinage in the Ukraine may also have been drawn to the same objective and the restless warfare of nomads and semi-nomads on the steppe would have provided a steady flow of supply.

The amount of gold coinage which entered Germania appears to have been relatively small. A scatter of gold finds of Augustan date in the upper Weser region may represent loot from the ill-fated army of Quintilius Varus. Otherwise, *aurei* of the first and second centuries are found only sporadically ouside a small number of hoards. Not until the later third century was this picture significantly changed. A currency of such high intrinsic value was presumably less attractive than silver, a fact that may say something about how coinage was employed. Tacitus does not mention bronze coinage, but it, too, crossed the frontiers, and this also may be significant. It is not found in great quantity, but the fact that it is there at all is worth noting. First-century bronze is widely spread and not merely clustered near the frontiers. Around Lodz in southern Poland, for instance, over 200 miles from the Danube, a scatter of first- and second-century *aes* of all denominations has been recorded. Around the Baltic shores, too, bronze coins appear, thinly but consistently. In what is now Latvia and Lithuania, a surprisingly large number of *sestertii* appear in graves and on settlements, possibly one local reflection of the trade in amber. Bronze coins of the late Empire are not common, but they occur more frequently than is generally realized. All in all, *aes* coinage appears on a scale and over a geographical spread to indicate that it did not drift across the frontiers merely as curios or ornaments.

To return to the silver hoards, it is abundantly clear that their composition matches that of hoards amassed within the Roman provinces. The pattern of issues represented within them is broadly similar to that seen in the hoards buried in the Empire. No obvious processes of selection seem to have been deployed, as has often been alleged. The implication of this for the function of coinage in *Barbaricum* should be clear. The coinage on both sides of the frontier responded to the same economic forces, and was subject to the same principles of selection when it was withdrawn from currency.

What then did coinage *do* beyond the frontiers? It is increasingly difficult to resist the idea that Roman silver coinage acted as a form of primitive currency, not only close to the frontiers as Tacitus states, but much further afield. The very wide distribution, from the Rhine to the Volga, the presence of single finds as well as hoards, the composition of those hoards, and the presence of small quantities of bronze: all this in combination takes us far from imported coin merely as bullion. We must stress a *primitive* form of currency, one used to discharge obligations and pay for services, and to act as a medium for gifts, rather than a facilitator of everyday transactions: closer in fact to the Celtic coinages of pre-Roman Europe than to Roman currency. In this setting we also have to accommodate Roman subsidies of coined money, mentioned from time to time by our sources, but probably a more frequent instrument of control beyond frontiers than is evident from literary sources alone. The mere fact that subsidies could be paid in coin must indicate that coinage had functions that went beyond ornament or bullion. Most of the earlier commentators on Roman exports to the northern peoples, and several of the more recent, limited their explanatory model to a system in which goods were exchanged for goods or for money. Purely commercial exchange, however, will not adequately explain all the material we encounter beyond the frontiers, nor will it satisfy economic anthropologists who study the relations between advanced states and primitive societies. Most exchanges between such disparate polities, we are told, do not involve trade based on markets and middlemen. Most transactions are connected not with commerce, but with social relations, diplomacy, political status and recognition. This does not mean that commerce of a kind we would recognize did not flourish in Free Germany, nor that *negotiatores* were not active beyond the frontiers: we know this did go on. But we are invited to take a wider view of the exchanges which took place in *Barbaricum* and to acknowledge that we are dealing with a very complex subject, and one we do not yet fully understand.

One approach towards understanding at least the more luxurious exports from the Roman world is to relate them to the aspirations and needs of barbarian elites. Germanic society was dominated by warlike elites rather than rulers endowed with permanent power. Roman goods were deployed beyond the frontiers, not on the principle of an open market, but within a loose system of directed trade, observing relationships that were not merely or primarily economic. The targets of this trade were the barbarian *principes*, the leading men who formed the retinues of kings and other leaders, the men whose loyalty it was worth acquiring, by their own rulers and by Rome, and who were likely to be masters of whatever commodities the northern lands could offer the Empire: fighting men, slaves, animal products; nothing very dramatic. These arrangements will explain most of the Roman imports of the first and second centuries. Later, matters changed, and trading functions were widened. More humdrum objects crossed the frontiers and reached a wider market. This is not difficult to explain. The advantages of being able to control exchange will have become obvious to barbarian leaders: more profit, more prestige. Such contact with the Empire was thus not insignificant for the barbarians who engaged in it. On the contrary, it might have provided major support in their extension of political influence among their own peoples.

6

Cult, Art and Technology

Deities and their sanctuaries

The written sources for early German deities are very limited before the Viking period.[1] The reports of Roman writers are naturally cast in a form which a Mediterranean audience could respond to and that meant linking Germanic cults, where possible, with those of Roman deities. Thus, the leading Germanic deity in the early Roman period, Tiwaz, was identified by Tacitus with Mars because Tiwaz was pre-eminently a god of war. Tiwaz was a powerful god among the early Germans, honoured as much for his wisdom as for his dominance in war. His name is derived ultimately from the Indo-European word *dieus*, which simply meant 'god'. The Greek Zeus and Roman *Dyaus*, an early name for Jupiter, come from the same source. Tiwaz was thus probably the supreme god of the sky for the early Germans. But his rule over the battlefield was unchallenged. One form of his name, Tyr, appears in early runes on weapons, and possibly on the inscription on the Negau helmet as early as the second century BC (above, p. 12). Later, in Scandinavia, he was to be superseded by the grim god Odin, the lord of the battlefield. His power as a ruling god is probably referred to in Roman inscriptions set up to Mars Thingsus,

---

[1] J. de Vries, *Altgermanische Religionsgeschichte* (Berlin 1969); H. R. Ellis Davison, *Gods and Myths of Northern Europe* (Harmondsworth 1964).

Mars of the Thing or assembly of the people, the guardian of law and order in the community. A god of battle who was also an arbiter in the affairs of men involves no contradiction. In a society so geared for warfare as that of the Germans it is predictable that the god who presided over war should also be concerned with the proper conduct of society. Little is known of any specific rites in honour of Tiwaz. The supreme god of the Semnones, worshipped in a sacred grove with human sacrifice, may have been Tiwaz. Those who entered the grove were bound, to symbolize the power of the god to bind his devotees, as Tyr or Tiwaz bound the wolf in myth.

The German god Donar was easily identified by Roman writers with Hercules. Like the Graeco-Roman deity, Donar was physically powerful and involved himself in great journeys and struggles against monstrous forces. Even the favoured attribute of Donar, his hammer, could be likened to the club of Hercules. Donar, in later form Thor, was a god of Thunder and possibly of the sky. Thunder-gods were frequently worshipped in forests by early European peoples, including the Celts, Balts and Slavs, and this was so with Donar. A forest in the Weser basin was particularly sacred to him. In the account of the gifted Icelandic scholar Snorri Sturluson, compiled in the thirteenth century, Thor or Donar was the eldest son of Odin and Earth. His great strength was provided by his belt, one of three great treasures in his possession, the others being his hammer Mjöllnir and gloves with which to hold it. Two other gods appear to have been worshipped from an early date, Njord and his son Freyr. Njord was master of the sea and the winds and thus supervised seafaring, while Freyr controlled the sun and the rain, thus providing the blessings of fertility. Freyr's twin sister Freyja, the most famed of female deities, also seems to have been honoured from an early date. She was concerned with love and marriage but also held sway over the dead. There was a multitude of other gods in Snorri's book, but most probably represent later appearances in the north German pantheon. The world-picture presented in the Scandinavian tradition may possibly contain early elements, such as the world-tree, Yggdrasil. This was a great ash-tree at the centre of the universe, whose branches spread over heaven and earth. There were three roots, one passing into the world of the gods, another to the world of the giants, and a third to the world of the dead.

Certain west German deities were worshipped in the Roman provinces. At Domburg on the island of Walcheren, near the mouth of the Old Rhine, a temple of the goddess Nehalennia stood during the second and third centuries, and was much frequented by traders making the crossing from lower Germany to Britain.[2] Over a hundred pieces of sculpture and altars, many of them inscribed, have been recovered from the tidal channel into which the temple eventually collapsed, so that the iconography and concerns of Nehalennia are unusually well documented. The goddess is often shown seated on a throne, with grain or fruit in her lap. A ship frequently appears beside the throne, as does a dog, the only animal associated with her. Her concern with fertility is obvious, and as with many fertility deities her power extended to the underworld. The dog represents this side of her interests, as possibly does the ship. The protective power of Nehalennia was extended to sailors on the Rhine and the open sea, and the reverence in which she was held is evident in the fine quality of the sculpture and inscribed altars at Domburg itself and in dedications to her from as far up the Rhine as Cologne.

In the Roman province of lower Germany, many dedications are encountered to the Matres and Matronae with strong localized associations. These are indicated by soubriquets such as Aufaniae and Austriahenae. These goddesses were also plainly concerned with fertility, but in several cases links with the afterlife are patent. It must be stressed that we see these deities in their Roman provincial guise only. There is no reliable evidence for the pre-Roman character of their cults or even for their existence. Nor is it certain that triads of mother-goddesses were worshipped east of the Rhine. Nevertheless, these local goddesses stand for the myriad localized cults which existed all over Germanic Europe and which have left little or no trace of their former dominance over the affairs of men.

[2] A Hondius-Crone, *The Temple of Nehalennia at Domburg* (Amsterdam 1955); *Deae Nehalenniae* (Middelburg/Leiden 1971).

Figures of deities and other supernatural beings are relatively rare in any medium. There are bronze statuettes which may portray gods, but no convincing identifications can be offered. A series of small bronze figures of cattle from central Europe can plausibly be linked with fertility cults, but there is little else to say about them. The most imposing representations of divine or supernatural figures are a number of wooden idols found at sanctuaries in peat-bogs. These are usually male, occasionally female, in some cases occurring in pairs. A striking pair of male and female figures has been recorded at Braak in Holstein, the male figure being 3 metres high and the female somewhat shorter. The sexual features of both came in for careful delineation. The vigorously carved male figure from Broddenbjerg in Jutland was shown with an aggressively erect sexual organ. This idol had stood on a stone cairn in a peat-bog and around it offerings of food in pottery vessels had been placed. Another idol probably linked with fertility cult is the male figure from Rude Eskilstrup on Zealand, which wears a massive torc or collar round its neck and holds a loaf or some such object in its lap. In some peat-bogs, tall posts without any embellishment were erected and offerings, which might include both animal and human sacrifices, were laid at their feet. Such foci of observances are mentioned at a late date in pagan Germany. A tall wooden pillar called the Irminsul was worshipped by the Saxons until the late eighth century when it was destroyed by Charlemagne, along with the richly furnished sanctuary in which it stood.

Springs, wells, streams, and rivers received votive deposits, as in other parts of Europe. The most fully recorded is the series of offerings made at the Brodelbrunnen, a mineral spring at Bad Pyrmont in lower Saxony. These began in the late pre-Roman period and continued until the third century. Over 200 Roman brooches were dropped into the spring, a similarly large number of Germanic brooches and other metal pieces, three *denarii* and a large enamelled Roman *patera* (pan). The Brodelbrunnen was resorted to in the Middle Ages, and later, for its healing properties and these may have been appreciated in much earlier times. Specially dug cult-shafts and pits are also recorded in Germanic Europe, though not in great numbers. The most striking is a shaft up to 3.5 metres deep, cut into chalk bedrock at Greussen in Thuringia, in which six cult vessels had been placed. One of these assumed the shape of a boar, another had boar-masks applied to its sides, and a third was in the form of a bird of prey. The boar was frequently used as a symbol of fertility, but may also have had chthonic powers, as a guardian of the dead. A pottery vessel in the shape of a boar occurs in the cemetery at Liebenau in lower Saxony as a container of grave ashes, and a boar figurine stands on the lid of another vessel in the cemetery at Issendorf.

The best-known of Germanic cult-places are the great votive deposits in pools and peat-bogs, mainly in Denmark and northern Germany. Several were examined between 1858 and 1865 by Conrad Engelhardt, notably those at Nydam, Thorsbjerg and Vimose, and his findings still form a significant basis for knowledge of this form of cult-observance.[3] A number of bog-deposits have been studied more recently, with important results, the largest being those at Ejsbøl, Illerup and Skedemosse on the island of Öland. These large deposits date from the later Roman and migration periods, but the deposition of objects, animals and even humans in pools and peat-bogs has a very long history, now known to extend back to the Neolithic in northern Europe. The larger deposits, in some cases made repeatedly in or near the same place, seem to begin in the later first millennium BC and involve the dedication of considerable quantities of war-gear. The earliest major deposit of this kind is that at Hjortspring on the Danish island of Als. The great bulk of this material was probably placed in the bog at one time, though this is not entirely certain. The most unusual item in the deposit was a ship, 19 metres long, clinker-built and constructed from five large timbers held together without iron nails. This was not a vessel for the open sea, but in the bays and inlets of the western Baltic it could have conveyed up to twenty-four men fairly easily. Around the ship lay weapons and other war-equipment, including 150 shields, 20 mail garments, over 130 spearheads and 6 swords in their scabbards. There were less warlike objects also, such as wooden vessels,

---

[3] C. Engelhardt, *Thorsbjerg Mosefund* (Copenhagen 1863); *Nydam Mose-fund* (Copenhagen 1865); *Kragehul Mosefund* (Copenhagen 1867); *Vimose Fundet* (Copenhagen 1869).

boxes and a bucket. This deposit, if it is indeed homogeneous, perhaps results from a military engagement in this area around 100 BC or somewhat later. Smaller deposits of weapons were made during the next three centuries, but not until the late second century are large votive offerings of war-equipment again recorded. These become more and more prominent during the third century at Nydam, Illerup and Ejsbøl. This increasing emphasis on the equipment of war in votive deposits is obviously related to increasing Germanic success against Roman opponents, and also to the growth in significance of localized powers in northern Europe and the competitive rivalry between them. Success in battle was commemorated by the dedication of the spoils, or some of them, to the gods who had made it possible. That successive deposits were made at some of the votive sites underlines the importance that these places might have over a lengthy period. At Thorsbjerg, for instance, deposits of various kinds were made in the same bog over more than three centuries. It may be supposed that ceremonies preceded the depositions. Many of the weapons and other pieces were damaged or destroyed before being thrown or laid in the peat, perhaps symbolizing the defeat of an enemy and the ending of his power, a practice also widely attested in the earlier Celtic world.

One of the largest and best-studied of the large deposits is that made in the bog at Thorsbjerg, about 20 kilometres north of Schleswig. This was not only a rich and varied deposit, but also one that had accumulated over a lengthy period. The brooches found here ranged from the second century BC to the fourth century AD, while the pottery vessels also spanned several centuries. Small deposits of personal ornaments, pottery and animals were made during the early Roman period, perhaps mainly to fertility deities in return for fruitful crops. Late in the second century, the character of deposition changed. War-equipment became the dominant element in deposits and remained so during much of the third century. The material includes numerous Roman items, notably the face-mask of a silver parade helmet, part of another in bronze, shield-bosses, swords, javelins, parts of mail coats and brooches. There were also two bronze discs covered with silver-gilt foil (below, p. 126). The Germanic weaponry is equally varied, including spears with ash shafts, shields, longbows, arrows, horse-harness and reins. There were also fine woollen garments, two cloaks, two pairs of trousers and a magnificent long-sleeved tunic. A terminal date for the deposition of the war-equipment is probably to be set in the later third century, but there was at least one later deposit, a small number of sword and scabbard parts.

Large deposits of military gear continued throughout the fourth century at a number of cult-sites in the north. Some 32 kilometres north of Thorsbjerg is the peat-bog of Nydam, where votive finds were made over an area of 1,000 square metres. The bulk of the objects are of the third and fourth centuries, and a large proportion probably were deposited on two or three occasions within that period. There were over a hundred swords, most of them pattern-welded blades of Roman manufacture, over 500 spears and javelins, more than 40 bows and 170 arrowheads, along with belts, brooches, pottery vessels, agricultural implements and Roman coins. Three ships lay in this peat-bog, of which one was successfully excavated and is now preserved in the Schleswig museum, another was removed from the bog only to fall victim to the Danish–German war of 1864, while the third still remains in the peat. Probably all the ships had been laden with equipment before being deliberately sunk. The surviving vessel is about 20 metres long and nearly 3 metres wide amidships. It was composed of eleven long oak planks, five of them to each side above a massive keel. There were fifteen rowlocks to each side fixed to the gunwales, the thirty rowers being accommodated on narrow benches attached to the ribs. There was no housing for a mast, so that the ship was propelled entirely by its oars. it was fairly clearly a warship, well suited to the tideless waters of the Baltic. The Nydam vessel, along with many of the weapons recovered from it, dates to the later fourth century and presumably was sunk in the peat-bog following some military encounter on or near the strait which divides the island of Als from the mainland.

Thorsbjerg and Nydam were excavated in the mid-nineteenth century and, although well studied and published by the standards of the day, still pose major problems of interpretation. The modern examination of votive deposits at Ejsbøl, Illerup and Skedemosse add significantly to the record. At Ejsbøl, two distinct complexes within a peat-bog have been identified, one near the centre, the other near to the edge of the moss.[4] The larger group of objects lay near the centre, about 500 items in all, dating from one time in the late fourth century. The smaller deposit near the shore, also laid down at one time, was made early in the fifth century. The central group of finds is remarkably homogeneous, suggesting that the equipment of up to 200 warriors was consigned to the bog at one time. There were over 200 javelins, 190 spears, at least 160 shields, along with 60 swords, 60 belts and 62 knives. In the force of about 250 fighting men, there would appear to have been 60 warriors equipped with swords. The main deposit at Illerup, near Aarhus, was earlier, about AD 200, and included a huge number of objects, at least 10,000 of which have been recovered.[5] This mass of equipment had been deposited in a lake covering an area 400 by 325 metres, apparently at one time. More than 100 swords were thrown into the water, over half of them bearing stamps which indicate Roman manufacture.

Not all the votive deposits of the later Roman Iron Age were dominated by weaponry. At Skedemosse on Öland, the deposits began in the third century and extended to the sixth, most falling in the fourth and fifth centuries.[6] Gold snake-headed rings and finger-rings were sacrificed, along with other personal ornaments. Weapons were present, but not in overwhelming quantity. More striking are the remains of animal sacrifice, especially of the horse, and the sacrifice of humans. More than 100 horses are represented in the skeletal remains and horse-trappings are prominent among the metal objects in the bog. Probably a horse-god was honoured by these offerings. The human remains included about fifty individuals, both male and female, and of all ages. The theme of human sacrifice requires closer examination.

---

[4] M. Ørsnes, 'The weapon find in Ejsbøl Moss at Haderslev', *Acta Arch*, 34 (1963), 232.

[5] J. Ilkjaer and J. Lønstrup, 'Der Moorfund im Tal der Illerup-Å bei Skanderborg in Ostjütland', *Germania* 61 (1983), 95.

[6] U. E. Hagberg, *The Archaeology of Skedemosse* (2 vols; Stockholm 1967).

Human sacrifice

One of the earliest descriptions of the cult-practices of a Germanic people, that by Strabo on the Cimbri, dwells on their practice of human sacrifice. White-clad priestesses supervised the sacrifice of selected prisoners of war by suspending them over great bronze cauldrons and cutting their throats, so that their life-blood flowed down into vessels below. Orosius had also heard of the sacrifice of prisoners by the Cimbri, along with the spoils taken from defeated foes:

Following a strange and unusual vow, they began to destroy all that they had taken. Clothing was cut to pieces and thrown away. Gold and silver was thrown into the river, the breastplates of men were cut to pieces, horsegear smashed and the animals drowned in whirlpools. The men were hanged from trees with nooses round their necks.

The dedication of defeated enemies and their equipment to the god or gods of war recurs frequently in the sources for the Roman Iron Age and for later pagan Scandinavia. The Chatti and Hermunduri went to war over possession of a river which ran between their territories, each side vowing to sacrifice their foes and the spoils of battle to their respective war-gods. The victorious Hermunduri fulfilled their vow. But the sacrifice of humans was by no means confined to ceremonial honour to the gods of war. Fertility deities might also be propitiated by the offering of a human victim. The tribes of Jutland and Schleswig-Holstein honoured a female deity of fertility called Nerthus, who visited the human domain on occasion, probably annually, being drawn in a wagon which only her priest might touch or look inside. The sanctuary of the goddess was a sacred grove on an island in a lake and on returning there after each progress, her image and her wagon were ritually washed in the lake by slaves, who were then drowned.

Specific instances of sacrifice, or of ritualized killing, of human beings, both men and women, are attested in the archaeology of the early Germans, on occasion in dramatic form. The original significance of these acts is now all but impossible to establish. Particular distinction between religious sacrifice and judicial penalty is difficult to make. But in at least a few cases, the circumstances seem to point clearly to significant ritual acts which involved human victims. The evidence is provided by human remains found in peat-bogs and dated to the pre-Roman and Roman Iron Age by associated objects or technical study of the deposits in which they lay.[7] The remains range from complete, and often remarkably well preserved, corpses to parts of bodies or groups of disarticulated bones. The most celebrated finds are the complete bodies recovered at Tollund, Grauballe and Windeby, all in Denmark, but corpses in peat-bogs are found widely over northern Europe, including northern Germany, Poland, the Netherlands and the British Isles. The practices which led to these depositions in marshes or pools were by no means confined to the early Germans. The Celtic peoples of

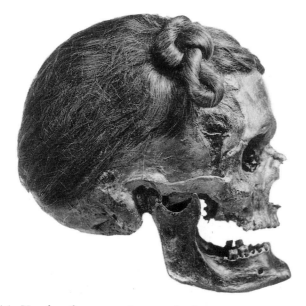

Figure 14 Head of a warrior with hair tied into a Suebic knot, indicating high status: from a peat-bog at Osterby, Schleswig-Holstein.

[7] A. Dieck; *Die europäischen Moorleichenfunde* (Neumünster 1965).

Britain followed similar practices, as the find of a bog-body at Lindow Moss in 1980 reveals.

The well-known corpse of a man found at Tollund, now dated to about AD 200, bears all the marks of a special sacrifice, prepared for by a distinctive meal of seeds and grains, and carried out with due deliberation in accordance with an established rite. The same seems to be true of the corpse found at Grauballe in Jutland, that of a man of about thirty years of age, naked and with his throat cut. Like the Tollund man, his stomach contained the remains of a meal consisting of a gruel of many different kinds of seeds. Other corpses occur in peat-bogs in somewhat different circumstances. At Windeby in Schleswig, a bog contained at least two bodies, one a young girl of about fifteen and, five metres away, a man. The girl's body, naked but for an ox-hide collar around her neck and a blindfold over her eyes, bore no indications of how she had died; probably she had been drowned, for the corpse was covered in branches and a large stone. The man had a branch of hazel around his neck, with which he had apparently been throttled. He, too, had been held down in the water and mud by branches.

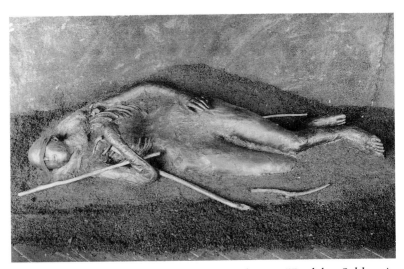

Figure 15 Body of a girl found in a peat-bog at Windeby, Schleswig, blindfolded and with hair shorn; wooden stakes had been placed over the body.

In some cases, there are signs of post-mortem acts. The corpse of a thirty-year old man found at Dätgen in Schleswig showed that he had been killed by stabbing through the heart. He had later been decapitated and most of his skin removed. He, too, had branches thrust over him, a formality in his case. The Windeby and Dätgen corpses may fall into a category of those condemned to die by their communities for some crime or social misdemeanour. Tacitus knew of punishments meted out for adultery and vice which involved those found guilty being thrown into marshes and held down by hurdles. It is possible that the known victims in the northern peat-bogs met their ends for a wider range of reasons. Some may have been outcasts from their communities, objects of fear or loathing, such as the insane or the psychotic; some may have been traitors or others who had harmed the social group to which they belonged. The decapitation and flaying to which some corpses have been subjected might support this notion, for this is treatment which suggests an apotropaic element in the procedure. Although victims of sacrifice are singled out only with great difficulty from the majority of bog-corpses, there are certain recurring features which fit easily within the framework of ritualized killing with a religious purpose. First, it is clear that a number of the best-preserved bodies are those of people who have not engaged in manual labour and who presumably came from the higher social ranks. This is true of the man from Tollund and of a woman from Haraldskjaer, a rather plump fifty-year-old. Secondly, a considerable number met their deaths by hanging or throttling, a rope or thong being sometimes found still around the neck. Thirdly, when the contents of the stomach have been well enough preserved for analysis, it is frequently evident that the final meal consisted of a gruel of seeds, often very varied in composition. This is unlikely to represent the standard diet of later Iron Age man and most probably is a ritual meal, possibly related to the purpose of the sacrifice. These are circumstances more easily explained as attendant on sacrifice than in any other way. But to what purpose? Here, only speculation is possible. There is no obvious connection with the deities who presided over war.

Myth and ritual

Glimpses into the world of early Germanic myth and ritual are fleeting, but one such glimpse is long enough to reveal a richness of detail which underlines how much has been lost. The two famous golden horns found at Gallehus in southern Denmark, one in 1639, the other in 1734, now known only in engravings, are clearly connected with the supernatural world of northern Europe, even though motifs derived from elsewhere are present in the design.[8] The decorative details place the two horns in the first half of the fifth century. The maker has recorded his name on one in runes: 'I Hlewagast son of Holt made the horn.' The scenes on the two objects have been much debated from the seventeenth century. Without understanding the significance of all of them, it is likely that they record a cycle of ceremonies and cult festivals. The two horns show obvious links in their subject-matter; some individual figures are found on both. The scenes depict quite specific practices and rites, often in remarkable detail. It is possible that the scenes follow a sequence, related with the sequence of cult-practices. These in turn may have followed a seasonal cycle. It has been plausibly suggested that one horn depicts the rites of spring and summer, the other those of autumn and winter. This is not beyond all question, and it still leaves numerous scenes and symbols unexplained. But some cycle of myth and cult seem the likeliest basis for the overall design. It is clearly a challenge to attempt to identify known deities among the figures. On the topmost panel of the horn with the runic inscription are shown two figures, largely naked but wearing helmets with curved horns. One holds a sickle and a rod, the other a spear, rod and ring. The legs of both are bent, as though they are leaping or dancing. To either side of these is a warrior, wearing a torc and holding a sword and shield. These, too, appear to be dancing. The helmeted figures have been identified by some as Tiwaz and Freyr or Tiwaz and Wodan. There seems no firm basis for this. They could equally well be priests or devotees of those or of

---

[8] E. Oxenstierna, *Die Goldhörner von Gallehus* (Lindigö 1956).

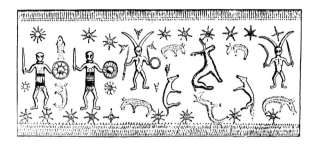

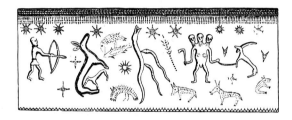

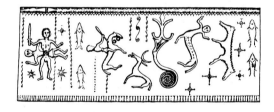

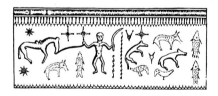

*Figure 16 Motifs and inscription from one of the gold horns found
at Gallehus, Denmark.*

other gods. Another possibility is that they represent the twin gods reported by several sources in northern Germania: Tacitus named them the Alcis and wrote that they were worshipped by the Naharvali; other writers locate them on the North Sea coasts. Of individual cults, those of fertility may appear in the form of animals and snakes suckling their young. The cult of the horse, perhaps in connection with a sky-god, is prominent on the horns. A horse is twice shown being shot at by an archer, once being ridden and once being led by a man holding a sickle or a curved knife. There seem to be references to horse sacrifice here, recalling the horses and their trappings in the bog at Skedemosse on Öland (above, p. 111). The horns bear other scenes and symbols which may be connected with sacrifices and other rites. An archer is shown aiming at a stretched-out animal skin surmounted by a human head, the target perhaps symbolizing fertility as it did in later Scandinavia. A three-headed monster holding an axe and leading a goat also has counterparts in later European myth which were linked with fertility, appearing at midwinter feasts and weddings. The Gallehus horns remain mysterious, but they leave us in no doubt about the richness of the supernatural world of the northern Germans in the early migration period. They also make it clear that contacts with a much wider world had contributed to that wealth of imagery and symbolism. They therefore comprise a document of priceless worth in revealing cultural and religious links across immense distances. The inhabitants of the northernmost Germanic lands were by no means remote from the rest of Europe at this time of profound change.

Another range of symbols appears on a series of engraved and originally painted stones on the island of Gotland.[9] These begin in the fifth century and continue down to the eleventh. The loss of the painted details means that interpretation is hazardous, but there is general agreement that the stones as a class commemorate the dead, presumably the more distinguished members of the island community. Some occur in small groups, others within low stone cairns, while a few are

[9] S. Lindqvist, *Gotlands Bildsteine* (2 vols; Stockholm 1941–2).

known to stand over the sites of graves. Among the recurrent symbols, a circular design is prominent, often occupying much of the upper part of the stone. Smaller circles may be drawn within the main design, often shown in whirling motion. These are plausibly identified as the sun-disc, a symbol found much earlier in Scandinavia, and thus linked with the worship of a sky-god. Dragon-like monsters, occasionally shown pursuing men, are frequently present, probably representing death and the fate that waits for all men. The ship motif may also be connected with the voyage into the afterlife, though it has also been linked with the journey of the sun across the sky. One stone, found at Sanda, shows a tree along with a monster and a ship. The tree may be the world-tree, Yggdrasil, the symbol for the universe. A number of smaller stones, thought to be of the fifth century, contain other symbols. The flight of geese or ducks may represent the journey of the soul. The horse recurs, recalling the horses on the Gallehus horns and perhaps related to the cult of a sky-deity. The tradition of erecting these striking memorials continued into the Christian period, some of the later stones depicting in some detail myths and episodes treated in the sagas.

Divination played an important part in the religious practices of the early Germans and those who foretold the future and conveyed messages from the gods to men occupied an honoured place in society. The most famous practitioners of divination were women. Veleda, who gave her pronouncements from a tower, was an honoured seeress of the lower Rhine Germans at the time of the revolt of the Batavi and their allies in AD 69, and had considerable influence with the rebel leader Julius Civilis. A little later, the seeress Ganna was to divine the future before the emperor Domitian. Observation of the flight and song of birds was a favoured means of divination in northern Europe, and certain birds, including the raven, were held to have the power to foretell the future by much later peoples. Horses, also, might provide guidance for the future, their snorts and neighs being interpreted by a priest or king. Perhaps more widespread was divination from marks cut into twigs from fruit trees or other pieces of wood. Such a method recurs among many primitive peoples and within the Germanic world naturally brings to mind the use of runes.

The Germanic peoples remained largely illiterate until well into the migration period. Not until the fourth century is there any clear record of an attempt to commit a Germanic language to written form and the attempt when made seems almost superhuman. In the mid-fourth century, Ulfila, bishop of the Goths north of the lower Danube, translated the Bible into Gothic, having invented an alphabet for that specific purpose. Earlier, however, a system of communication using signs had been developed, although its employment was specialized and limited. The origin of these signs, known as runes since the seventeenth century (the ancient name is unknown), is wrapped in uncertainty.[10] The earliest runes that can be dated belong to the later second century AD, though it may be that their beginnings lie further back in the preceding century. Most of the early signs represent a single word and occur on weapons and personal ornaments. The largest concentration has been found in the lands around the western Baltic, where the majority of the later runic inscriptions are also found. There are no obvious models for the runes. The Greek and Latin alphabets have had their proponents, but neither seems plausible on grounds of typology or historical likelihood. Four signs may be linked with Latin letters, but the other twenty characters in the early runic futhark have no obvious relation with Latin. More substantial is the claim that nine of the runes are close to letters in several north Italic scripts. These were current in the Alpine regions down to the first century AD, so that some overlap with the ancestors of runes is possible. But several major problems are left unsolved by this hypothesis. Not all the signs are likely to have originated in Italic letter-forms. At least twelve signs in the futhark seem unrelated to any letter yet known. And there is an enormous geographical gap between the north Italic inscriptions and the earliest known runes in Germania. That runes on perishable material such as wood may have filled this gap is possible but has not yet been demonstrated. The matter remains undecided, but the links between certain signs and letter forms in the Italic and Latin scripts do seem to be real and the likeliest region in which

---

[10] R. I. Page, *Runes* (London 1987).

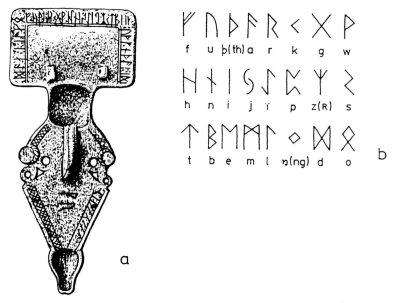

ᚠ ᚢ ᚦ ᚨ ᚱ ᚲ ᚷ ᚹ
f u þ(th)a r k g w

ᚺ ᚾ ᛁ ᛃ ᛇ ᛈ ᛉ ᛊ
h n i j ï p z(R) s

ᛏ ᛒ ᛖ ᛗ ᛚ ᛜ ᛞ ᛟ
t b e m l ŋ(ng) d o   b

Figure 17 (a) Brooch with inscription in runes from Charnay (Dép. Saône-et-Loire), France: later sixth century; (b) the runic futhark.

such links could have been forged is the Alps and the lands immediately to the north.

Christianity

There are very few indications that Roman religious cults had any impact on the German peoples outside the Empire before the fourth century. Germans who served in the Roman army brought their own cults with them, as is known in the case of some of the units on Hadrian's Wall in the third century. It is possible that some who entered the Roman provinces became devotees of one or more Roman gods and took that devotion back to their homeland, like the Alaman who became a worshipper of Serapis and later named his son after the god. But there is no reason to think that such transmission of cults was common. With one major exception, the impact of Christianity on the Germans before they entered the Empire was scarcely greater. There were no organized attempts at converting the barbarian peoples to Christianity before the sixth century, though the Rugi on the middle Danube, or some of them, did become Christians before moving into Noricum. Conversion of individuals beyond the Roman frontiers was occasionally recorded.

Shortly before 397, a Christian travelled from Italy to the land of the Marcomanni beyond the middle Danube. There he met the queen Fritigil and talked to her of the great Ambrose, the formidable bishop of Milan. Fritigil was so impressed by what she heard that she accepted the teaching of Christ and asked Ambrose through her visitor for instruction in the faith. The bishop responded by sending her a letter which served as a catechism. The case is interesting, but it stands almost alone. No comparable contact between a Christian leader and a barbarian ruling house seems to have been recorded before the main period of migration. It must in any case be noted that Ambrose did not initiate the correspondence, but merely exploited the opportunity when it was offered. What issued from his letter to the Marcomannian queen is unknown, but probably nothing of moment. If other such contacts across frontiers did occur, they are unlikely to have been numerous.

One Germanic people did receive Christianity before entry to the Empire.[11] The spread of the Christian faith among the Goths is inextricably bound up with the life and work of Ulfilas, or Ulfila, born a Goth and later to be bishop to his people and a tribal leader. He was born about 311, the grandchild of a Cappadocian captive, taken in one of the great raids before 270. Christianity had more than merely survived in Gothic communities beyond the Imperial frontiers. Many captured Romans had been taken north of the Danube and the Black Sea after 250 and those who were Christians had attracted some of their Gothic masters to the faith. How large the Christian community in Gothia was is impossible to estimate, but it was clearly significant enough to warrant the attentions of Roman and Greek missionaries. Many of the displaced Roman Christians may have been centred in the kingdom of the Bosporus, which recognized Christianity as the

---

[11] E. A. Thompson, *The Visigoths in the Time of Ulfila* (Oxford 1966).

official faith about AD 300. Which strata of Gothic society were most influenced by the imported religion we have no way of knowing, but Ulfila himself evidently enjoyed a high social position, as he accompanied a Gothic delegation to Constantinople while in his twenties. He was also acquainted with Latin and Greek, and had the means and leisure to travel. At the age of thirty, in 341, he was consecrated bishop of the Christians in the land of the Goths, a mission which he was to pursue for forty years. For the first seven of these, he ministered to the Goths north of the Danube. Driven out from there, he moved to the province of Moesia and led the Goths there until his death. In Moesia he engaged in preaching and also in a greater work, the translation of the Bible into Gothic. In order to do so, he had first to create a Gothic alphabet, using Greek letters as a basis and adding to them characters from Latin and runes.

Although most of the Germanic peoples were pagan when they entered the Roman world, nearly all were converted to the faith within a generation or two of their arrival. The reason is not far to seek. Christianity was largely identified with the polity and society of the Roman Empire. Those who lay outside the Roman civilisation therefore also lay, normally, beyond the reach of Christ. Once inside the frontiers, the Germanic peoples followed their leaders in accepting the official religion of the provinces in which they settled, the Christian faith. Very many of them, however, became not Catholics, but converts to that form of the faith associated with Arius, an Alexandrian priest who had set the eastern Church in uproar early in the fourth century by asserting that Christ was closer to the creation than to the Creator, that the Son of God was not of one substance with God himself. Arius received support from powerful bishops, and what had begun as a localized dispute became a bitter schism. The fact that several major German peoples accepted the Arian faith meant that divisions were more sharply drawn than they otherwise might have been. Within the Germanic kingdoms, however, there was a general tolerance of Catholic Christianity, the exception being the regime of the Vandals in Africa. The Arianism of the Germanic settlers, and particularly the Goths, continued to provoke both theological and political problems until the sixth century, often being used in support of action against an opposing faction or power.

Figure 18 A page from the Gothic Bible of Ulfila.

With the conversion of the Visigoths to Catholicism in the
580s, echoes of the ancient controversy slowly faded away.

Crafts and craftsmanship

Since there were no natural deposits of gold in the lands occupied by the Germanic peoples, working in the metal could make no progress until external contacts made the raw material available. The flow of gold was modest in the first and second centuries, most of it provided by the Roman world, but with a contribution coming from the Black Sea region. The flow perceptibly increased during the third century and went on increasing later, especially from the later fourth century. In Scandinavia, the fifth and sixth centuries witnessed a flood of gold, in the form of imported coinage, from the eastern Roman world (below, p. 229). The earliest gold objects produced by Germanic craftsmen are small ornaments, mainly pendants and rings, dating from the later first century AD. Few sizeable objects in gold are yet known from the early Roman Iron Age, the most striking exception being a superb torc or neck-ring, found at Havor on the island of Gotland, within a small fortified site, perhaps a chieftainly stronghold.[12] The torc had been buried in a hoard which also contained six Roman bronze vessels of the first century AD; the hoard had been concealed about or shortly after AD 100. The ring of the torc, measuring 24 cm in diameter, was composed of gold wires, rectangular in section, twisted together. The terminals are hollow bulbs, plain except for a single cable of filigree. The plain surfaces of the bulbs are in satisfying contrast with the cone-shaped supports of the terminals, which were ornately treated with filigree cables defining crescents into which a steer's head was set. The design of the Havor torc is so mature and confident, and the technical standard so high, that the piece is clearly recognizable as the work of a master goldsmith. Where did he operate? One torc with similar characteristics is known in Scandinavia, at Dronninglund in Denmark. At least three torcs of the same broad type are recorded in south Russia, one at Olbia on the Black Sea, the other two in a hoard found near Kiev. Other

---

[12] E. Nylen, 'Die älteste Goldschmiedekunst der nordischen Eisenzeit und ihr Ursprung' *JRGZM* 15 (1968), 75.

goldwork in the Black Sea hinterland shows a general similarity of design to these torcs, and to the pieces from Havor and Dronninglund. It seems fairly clear that the origins of the design and the technical expertise lay in the area north of the Black Sea. But designs and expertise in metalworking can be transmitted by one agency or another. Craftsmen can move and it is not impossible (though perhaps not very likely) that a skilled metalworker made his way to southern Scandinavia from the Black Sea lands in the late first century AD. Apart from the Havor and Dronninglund torcs, a number of small gold objects have appeared in the western Baltic in early Roman Iron Age contexts, revealing the same effective use of filigree. The possibility of a workshop on one of the Baltic islands is thus not to be dismissed out of hand.

From the late second century onward, there were evident advances in the design of gold jewellery, especially in the introduction of semi-precious and other coloured stones. Richly furnished graves increasingly contain brooches and other ornaments with inset garnets and other stones. A grave at Hassleben in central Germany, of the end of the third century, contains a splendid gold brooch with two garnets *en cabochon*, as well as rich filigree ornament. Another chieftainly grave, at Aarslev on the island of Fyn, included a brooch with a large garnet over the bow, a garnet inset on the foot and six other stones on other surfaces. The development towards a polychrome style in fine jewellery is one of the most distinctive features of the late Roman Iron Age and one which opened up the most brilliant chapter in Germanic metalwork. The artistic influences at play were many and various. It is no longer satisfactory to ascribe the advances in technique and design to the cultural influence of Gothic craftsmanship from the later fourth century onward. The impact of Roman jewellers, themselves exploring the possibilities of polychrome insets in gold and silver from the third century, must be allowed for. Nor should the inventiveness of northern German craftsmen be underrated; for that there is increasingly abundant evidence in a variety of fields.

The use of gold and silver-gilt foils on jewellery, belt-mounts and even weapons is another marked feature of Germanic metalwork in the late Roman Iron Age. The inspiration for this technique is to be sought in Roman metalwork, which found its way into Germania in some quantity, most particularly the Hemmoor bucket type, which bore friezes of animals and other motifs below the rim, and ornamental discs, of which the most distinguished examples are the two *phalerae* (ornamental discs) found in the votive deposit at Thorsbjerg.[13] These were bronze discs, covered with gilded silver foil. One is fragmentary, but it clearly bore a frieze of running animals in its outer zone. The more complete disc has an inner zone containing nine full-face male masks, and in the outer four large roundels interspersed with four seated figures of Mars. This is probably provincial work of the late second or early third century. At

Figure 19 One of the two Thorsbjerg phalerae, a Roman military ornament with additions by a Germanic craftsman.

[13] J. Werner, *Die beiden Zierscheiben des Thorsberger Moorfundes* (Berlin 1941).

some time in the third century, a German craftsman had added a number of animal figures in solid gold, in a thoroughly Germanic style. These little figures are among the earliest figured depictions in Germanic art. Broadly contemporary are a number of small disc-brooches bearing animal figures.

Ornaments exclusively of gold were produced in some quantity in the later Roman period, prominent among them being torcs decorated with snake-headed terminals, well known in the western Baltic lands. In the fourth century, a workshop near the lower Rhine was producing torcs ornamented with close-set punched and stamped designs. Still more elaborate torcs and collars were made in southern Scandinavia from the early fifth century. These were based upon tubes of gold covered by rich filigree and granulation. Filigree work, in which tiny globes of gold were soldered or heat-sealed to wires or flat surfaces reached a peak in the collars from Ålleberg, Möne and Färjestaden, all dating from the later fifth or sixth centuries. Already by this date, *cloisonné* work was dominating fine jewellery in all parts of Germanic Europe and the greatest of

Figure 20 Gold collar from Ålleberg, Sweden: fifth century AD.

all Germanic artistic achievements in metalwork were about to be realized.

The widespread connections of the Germanic peoples, extending from the south Russian steppes to Scandinavia and from Byzantium to Gaul, had enormous repercussions on the finest metalwork of the fifth and sixth centuries. The supply of gold to the Germanic and nomad world greatly increased in the fifth century, as is evident in the finds of *solidi* and medallions far beyond the Roman frontiers. Gold plate and bars of gold bullion were presented to barbarian leaders in staggering quantity. Germanic leaders had never been hesitant about putting their wealth on show. Now they had even more to display and the craftsmen who were in their service were no doubt encouraged to develop styles of ornament which would express the flamboyance of the age. The advances which were made in fine metalworking from the late fourth century were once attributed to the cultural influences released by the breakup of the Gothic powers on the northern shore of the Black Sea after the Hun invasion of the 370s. It has steadily become clear that this explanation is not satisfactory. Finds of rich graves and hoards in the lower Danube region and in the Carpathians have added significantly to the record. It is now clear that innovative craftsmen in gold and precious stones were working as a group in a limited area north of the lower Danube from the first half of the fifth century. The magnificently furnished graves at Apahida, near Cluj, found in the nineteenth century, are now known not to have been the only princely burials at this site.[14] Another has been located close by, all the burials dating from about the middle of the fifth century. Not far distant, at Cluj-Someseni, a hoard of gold objects including a pectoral and the fittings of a superb belt is to be related to the same princely milieu. These treasures and those from Apahida were probably made by the same craftsmen. From the same region has come the richest and most astonishing hoard of the fifth century yet to be unearthed, the great treasure of Pietroasa,

[14] K. Horedt and D. Protase, 'Das zweite Fürstengrab von Apahida', *Germania, 50 (1972), 174–220.*

found in 1837.[15] This is a collection of gold and silver pieces
of such exceptional range and quality (and of weight; the hoard
contained 18 kg of gold) that it was for long linked with one
of the main events of early Gothic history, the destruction of
the Gothic kingdoms by the Huns after 370. The burial of the
hoard is, however, too late for that connection to be made.
The objects in it are products of the late fourth and early fifth
centuries, and the whole collection was consigned to the ground
about 450. This was not a grave-treasure. It may have been
the treasury of a leader or, possibly, a religious treasure, buried
for safe-keeping in some disturbed time.

There are a number of unique and idiosyncratic pieces in the
Pietroasa hoard. The most imposing is a solid gold dish, its
interior decorated by a frieze of deities and other figures in
high relief. In the centre sits a throned figurine of a female on
a circular throne, holding a goblet in cupped hands. The encirc-
ling frieze represents a group of divinities, some in Classical
guise, others with attributes more easily assignable to the Germanic pantheon. A powerful male god holding a club and
cornucopia, and seated on a throne in the form of a horse's
head, is probably closer to Donar than to Hercules. A heroic
warrior in full armour and wearing three hair-knots is plainly
a barbarian kingly god, while a trio of goddesses presumably
represents the German *matres*. The seated goddess who presides
over the entire ensemble is also not easily placed in the Classical
order. She is better viewed as a barbarian mother of the gods.
There are products of late Roman workshops among the Pietroasa pieces; these include a plain gold platter and jug, the
platter weighing 7 kg. But four immense gold brooches in the
form of birds of prey, designed to perch on the shoulder of the
wearer, obviously belong to a barbarian world. Two polygonal
gold cage-cups, once encrusted with precious stones and with
handles in the form of springing panthers, carry the marks of
Pontic or even Persian style in their design. More familiar pieces
are four torcs, one of which bears the runic inscription *Gutani*

Figure 21 Brooch in the form of an eagle, from the Pietroasa treasure, Romania.

*Figure 22 Cage-cup with handles in the form of panthers, from the
Pietroasa treasure, Romania.*

o wi hailag, which may be interpreted as a dedication to the
'god who protects the Goths, most holy and inviolate'.

From the Danube lands, the taste for exuberant work in gold
and precious stones was transmitted to Italy, Gaul and northern
Germania by high-level gifts. By the late fifth century, a Frankish king could be buried in northern Gaul surrounded by fine
objects which would not have been out of place in a Germanic
court in any part of Europe.

Silver was reaching the Germanic peoples in some quantity
as early as the first century AD and work in the metal was
making steady progress from that date onward. A tiny silver
cup in the rich grave at Hoby may be the earliest known silver
vessel produced by a Germanic smith. It was followed by two
cups from one of the graves at Lübsow, no fewer than five from
Leg Piekarski in Poland, and two from Dollerup in Jutland. The
fairly rapid response to the import of Roman silver vessels is
interesting, though the standard of execution of these early
pieces was not high. Silver was widely used as a decorative
element on other metals. Inlay was a particularly favoured
decorative technique, on both bronze and iron, though filigree
was also widely used. Inlay requires only the use of an engraving
tool and a hammer. A groove is cut in the surface to be
decorated, its edges inclining slightly inwards at the top. The
silver wire to be inlaid was then hammered into place and was
held there by the overhang. Silver inlay was applied to many
items of personal ornament, buckles, belt-plates and weaponry.
Some of the finest pieces are spurs, in which the basal surfaces
are covered in filigree, while the thorns are criss-crossed by a

mesh of inlay. These began to be made in the later second century. Bracelets and rings of solid silver are frequently encountered in richer graves from the same period, a favoured type being the bracelet or armlet with snake-headed terminals. Brooches of silver also occur, as do pieces covered with silver foil, occasionally gilded. More ambitious products were a series of small silver cups, five of which have been found on the island of Zealand, their probable place of origin. Two come from rich graves at Himlinghøje, two from Vallöby and another from Nordrup. They were evidently inspired by Roman vessels, for all five bear friezes in gold foil below their rims, recalling the friezes on Hemmoor buckets. The cups from Himlinghøje show galloping animals and men holding daggers, engaged perhaps in some act of ritual. The others have simpler animal designs. All of these pieces belong to the later third century and may be seen as work of a locally based group of craftsmen for a limited chieftainly clientele.

Ancient writers, most notably Tacitus, had a false impression of the scarceness of iron in Germania and the lack of expertise shown by the Germans in working the metal. The fact was that there were numerous, extensive and accessible deposits of ironstone in northern and eastern Germania, the most important of those exploited in Antiquity being those in the Ruhr valley, the Harz mountains, Schleswig-Holstein and Jutland (mainly deposits of bog-iron), Bohemia, Slovakia, Silesia and the Lysa Gora mountains of Poland. The last-named area contained the richest deposits of all, particularly near the modern towns of Opatow and Ostrowice. Large quantities of slag and the debris of furnaces here point to the existence of sizeable workshops in production over a long period from the first to the fourth centuries AD. Most of the ironstone was won by opencast working, but mine-shafts also might be dug. At Rudki, for example, a shaft was dug to a depth of 18 metres and from its base a number of galleries were opened up along the lines of mineral veins. From the Rudki mine there were recovered shovels, wedges and other mining tools, as well as pottery of the Roman Iron Age. The Lysa Gora hills have produced large numbers of furnace-sites, over fifty having been recorded, some of them with large numbers of furnaces. One workshop, at Stara Slupia, has so far produced over 150 furnaces. The degree of centralized production implied by these sites is surprising and it is reasonable to ask where the metal produced by these sites was marketed. Not only neighbouring areas may be in question, but also perhaps the Danube provinces of Rome. Substantial workshops have also been identified in Bohemia. Installations of this scale were obviously operated by specialists working within an ordered community which was at least partly industrialized. This is an unexpected picture of a highly centralized craft.

The smelting of iron was carried out in a variety of furnaces. Probably the most widespread, and certainly the most effective, was the clay shaft-furnace, a type of installation well established in the Roman provinces. The shaft-furnace had been introduced to Germania by the first century AD, from an unknown source. It was in essence a short clay chimney, normally between 50 cm and a metre high, set over a firing chamber dug into the ground. The chimney was pierced near its base to allow entry of a draught of air. The lower part of the shaft was packed with ore and a fire was lit in the firing chamber below. Once it was alight, the draught of air would in normal conditions be enough to sustain the process of smelting the ore. Bellows could be used to provide additional assistance if needed. Furnaces of this type are now recorded in the Elbe basin, in the Rhine–Weser region, in Schleswig-Holstein and in the coastal lowlands. Although they were simple to construct and relatively straightforward to operate, they were capable of producing iron of fairly high quality. Iron ore begins to reduce at about 700°C and the shaft-furnace was capable of producing temperatures of up to 1200 degrees. At about 1,050°C iron becomes liquid and runs down to the bottom of the shaft. The slag could then be tapped off and the raw iron recovered after cooling. The metal could be made into ingots or directly fashioned into implements and weapons. The quality of the iron produced by Germanic smiths could be high, perhaps as high as much of that produced in the Roman Empire. A particularly hard form of iron was manufactured by smiths in the later Roman Iron Age and used in sword and knife blades. The proficiency of German smiths is not in doubt, their skills being surrounded with an exceptional mystique in later legend. The fact that smiths might be accompanied by the tools of their trade in their graves suggests that they possessed a recognized and significant status in early Germanic society, long before this was defined in the early medieval laws.

The pottery of the early Germans has often been unfavourably compared with the fine products of the La Tène cultures of central and western Europe. The prevailing uniformity of hand-made vessels found in the large urn-fields of the north has tended to obscure the fact that pottery of excellent quality, often with handsome rouletted or stamped ornament, was produced in many regions of Germania. Nor was it by any means all hand-made. The potter's wheel was certainly in operation in several areas, including Silesia, Brandenburg, the Harz, and the region between the Oder and Weser, in the third century. Some of the vessels produced on the wheel at this time seem to be versions of Roman wares and the possibility that Roman craftsmen, perhaps prisoners from the frontier provinces in some cases, were active in Germania cannot be dismissed. Although much of the common pottery used in Germanic settlements was fired in hearths or possibly clamps, well constructed pottery kilns have now been recorded in many areas, from Jutland to southern Poland. The kilns are of the updraught type widely represented in the Roman provinces. In these, the firing chamber is usually a pit dug into the subsoil, over which the kiln is built. The vessels for firing were placed in the dome-shaped kiln made largely from clay. The heat generated in the firing chamber had to reach 750° to 850°C to fire the pots effectively, the natural draught carrying the heat up to the kiln. The temperature level in the kiln could be controlled by releasing the hot gases through one or more holes provided in the outer wall. In some areas, it is clear that the finer pottery was produced by specialists in the craft, not merely by the housewife or domestic servant. The fine, polished wares in dark grey and black fabrics of the middle and lower Elbe, for example, with their geometric zones of rouletted ornament, were presumably produced by centralized workshops. Likewise, the concentrations of pottery kilns on some sites in southern Poland indicates reasonably orderly production by centralized workshops. That this occurred elsewhere, especially in the later Roman Iron Age, is at least highly likely.

The craft of weaving woollen textiles had a long prehistory

in northern Europe, garments of excellent quality being known from the early Bronze Age in Scandinavia.[16] By the later first millennium BC, a wide range of weaves was in use. The commonest and simplest type of weave, the plain weave or tabby, in which the threads pass over and under one another, seems to have been in use over most of the Germanic territories. Twills, in which the weft thread passes over and under a number of warp threads, are increasingly found from the later Iron Age; these offered opportunity for considerable variation in the treatment, including herringbone, chevron and dog-tooth twills. The quality of woollen textiles shows a marked improvement during the Roman period. At its best, Germanic weaving was capable of producing textiles as fine as anything made in the Roman world. Professional craftsmen must have been responsible for garments of outstanding quality, like the Thorsbjerg mantle and the Vehnemoor cloak, though no doubt a great deal of textile-weaving was carried out in purely domestic circumstances. Within certain settlements, for instance at Wijster (above, p. 68), numbers of loom-weights and spindle-whorls seem to indicate large-scale weaving in one or more major workshops. Sheep are known to have been kept to a mature age in numerous northern settlements, so that they could have provided wool as well as milk and meat. Linen was also available from the flax plant. Tacitus mentions undergarments made of linen, though these have not yet been found in the north. Three centuries later, when the Goths began to settle in the Empire, their linen garments were much admired by the Roman provincials.

We are in the fortunate position of having a relatively large number of surviving garments from the northern peat-bogs, as well as depictions of Germans on Roman sculpture and coins, so that knowledge of dress is unusually full. Women are most commonly shown on Roman reliefs wearing a full-length dress, gathered below the breast or occasionally at the waist, frequently with no sleeves. A blouse or short skirt might be worn below the dress and a neckerchief about the throat. One garment from Huldremose in Denmark was a full-length dress

---

[16] M. Hald, *Olddanske Tekstiler* (Copenhagen 1950).

with wide sleeves, gathered at the waist and with a large fold at the neck which might serve as a hood. This was a versatile garment, well suited to northern cold and rain. The other outfit from Huldremose was more varied. Above a woollen skirt was worn a skin cape and a shawl fastened with a bone pin. Men's dress included a thick tunic or shirt worn over trousers, and a cloak which might be long or short. Trousers were usually full-length, even sometimes with covering for the feet attached, but knee-length breeches are also known. Almost complete examples of full-length trousers have come from the Thorsbjerg peat-bog. The tunic was often belted at the waist and might reach to the hips or thighs. Shoes of leather bound with leather straps were worn, but probably not by everyone. Germans of both sexes are usually shown bare-headed on Roman reliefs, though occasionally head-coverings are found in peat-bogs, as in the case of the leather cap worn by the man from Tollund. The essentials of male dress survived little changed into the migration period. As late as the seventh century, representations of Frankish or Lombard warriors show them wearing tunics and trousers like those found at Thorsbjerg.

Skilled working in wood is evident in a wide variety of objects, from houses and ships to small domestic containers. The raw material was present in superabundance and wood-working to high standards had developed from at least the Neolithic onwards. Only one carpenter's workshop has been identified, at Feddersen Wierde, where the waste from a lathe has been found, but it is likely that the craft was pursued at most settlements. The tools of the carpenter included many still in use today: the mallet, axe, adze, awl, chisel, plane, rasp, auger and knife. The high quality of craftmanship attained is well seen in the surviving wooden platters, goblets, bowls and buckets found in waterlogged deposits and wells. It is also evident in larger products, such as the aisled long-houses, ships and carts.

The origins of Germanic art

The roots and inspiration of Germanic art are various. The earliest surviving works which can be designated as distinctly

Germanic date from the later second and early third centuries, a formative period for many aspects of Germanic culture. What does survive is pre-eminently work in metal, a medium in which later Germanic craftsmen were to produce some of the finest works of art in early medieval Europe. This does not mean that fine craftsmanship was not pursued in other materials, merely that very little has survived in other media. From an early date, imported Roman objects had considerable impact on the motifs and designs chosen by Germanic artists. The human and animal forms on metal and glass vessels brought in from the Roman Empire inspired imitation, as is well seen on the silver cups from Zealand (above, p. 132). Representation of men and animals was very rare before the late second century. Thereafter, it is increasingly found on disc-brooches, *phalerae*, drinking-vessels, weaponry, and in the form of figurines. Celtic forms are also evident in Germanic metalwork, in some cases at a surprisingly late date. It has long been remarked that some of the motifs on the Gallehus horns of about AD 400 are drawn from a Celtic repertoire.

Perhaps the single most formative influence on Germanic art in the late fourth and earlier fifth centuries was chip-carved metalwork of Roman provincial origin.[17] Along the Rhine and Danube frontiers, workshops producing mainly bronze objects bearing this ornament were active in the later fourth century, among their most distinctive pieces being the buckles, belt-plates and strap-ends which decorated the broad military belt and other accoutrements of the warrior. Some of this equipment found its way into the hands of German soldiers in Roman service who carried it back to their homelands in northern Europe. There, it would be copied and transferred to a wider range of objects, which in turn were to supply models for craftsmen over the next three centuries. The designs of chip-carving (or *Kerbschnitt*) seem more appropriate to wood-carving than to metalwork and may have originated in that craft. They include geometrical and chequered patterns, as well as circular rosettes, plaits and spirals. In their metal form, these designs were cast in bronze, retouched with an engraving tool,

---

[17] On the origins of Germanic ornamental styles, G. Haseloff, *Die germanische Tierornamentik der Völkerwanderungszeit* (3 vols; Berlin 1981).

often silvered or part-gilded and polished. When gold became more plentiful in the fifth century, the gilding of chip-carved designs became heavier and more lavish. In due course, the technique of chip-carving was to spread through the Germanic world and create one of the most familiar elements in early medieval ornamentation.

By the late fourth century, there had emerged a distinct ornamental style in the north, in which animal forms had been added to chip-carved decoration. This style is evident on brooches and other ornaments in the large votive deposits at Nydam and Ejsbøl, and in richer graves. The bodies of animals and birds were used with great skill within the designs, often in sinuous curves, the heads of the creatures being turned over their backs. Animal heads were often confronted by a twin head, occasionally with a human head or other object clasped between them. We may suspect that some of these designs are symbolic, but if so, their meaning is lost to us.

About the same time there were major developments in fine metalwork far to the south-east. As early as the third century precious and semi-precious stones had been applied to jewellery and weapons, producing a polychrome style which could be crude and flashy, but in its best exemplars brilliant in effect. The origins of this style of ornament owed much to contacts between the eastern Germanic peoples and the nomads of southern Russia and northern Iran. Its westward spread was for long linked with the movements of the Goths and their associates in the later fourth century, but this explanation seems less and less satisfactory. A major centre of the manufacture of the finest objects in this style from shortly after 400 now seems to have been situated in the area north of the lower Danube in the shadow of the Carpathian mountains (above, p. 129). But the style was quickly disseminated across Europe, to Gaul, Italy and Scandinavia. The most distinctive of the decorative stones used in this jewellery was the garnet, which was acquired in part from Bohemia, in part possibly from India via nomad intermediaries, and perhaps also from Asia Minor.[18] It was to become the most favoured decorative stone of Ger-

---

[18] B. Arrhenius, *Merovingian Garnet jewellery* (Stockholm 1985) is an important recent study.

manic jewellers from the fifth to the seventh centuries, its glowing hues combining to such brilliant effect with gold.

From the fifth century, northern craftsmen in metal developed a distinctive style of ornament in which a four-footed animal is shown in profile. The lines of the creature are sinuously drawn and the main emphasis is upon the head and legs. Often, a pair of such beasts is shown confronting each other, with a human mask or figure between them. The ultimate origin of the motif lay in late Roman metalwork designs, but the rather bland model has been transformed into a mysterious image conveying both savagery and dread. The style was first studied in detail by the Swedish scholar Bernhard Salin and called by him Style I.[19] Its motifs, in a wide range of manifestations, were to be used by metalworkers over much of western Europe in the fifth century. Towards the end of the century, ornament based on interlace spread northward from the Mediterranean world and after 500 was increasingly combined with the animal forms of Style I. A major impetus to the spread of these new designs was given by contacts between the Franks and the Ostrogoths in Italy and their Byzantine successors. In the course of the sixth century, the fantastic interlaced animals of Salin's Style II were an abiding presence on fine metalwork, becoming ever more elaborate and entwined, and eventually reaching their artistic summit on Scandinavian and Anglo-Saxon jewellery in the seventh century.

Some of the influences at work on the northern craftsmen were more direct. Imperial gifts to German leaders in the form of gold medallions are found beyond the frontiers, most strikingly in the case of the hoard at Szilagy-Somlyo in Hungary. This contained twenty-four medallions of the emperors Maximian, Constantius II, Valens, Valentinian I and Gratian. The latest piece in the treasure dates to AD 367. This is in essence a collection of costly gifts, amassed by a local dynasty over several generations in return for their loyalty to Rome. Some of the individual pieces have been given their own gold settings by Germanic craftsmen, one being further embellished

[19] Salin's book *Die altgermanische Thierornamentik* (Stockholm 1935) is still worth attention.

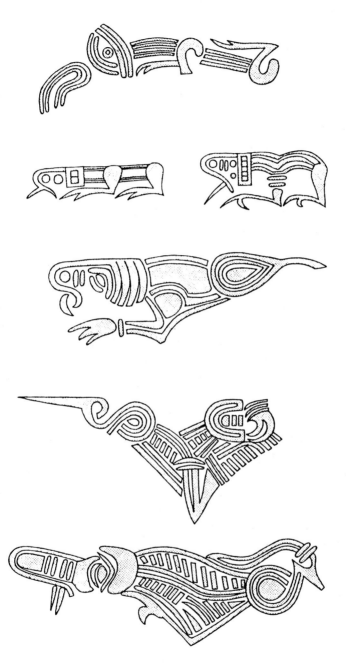

Figure 23 Details of Style I ornament (after G. Haseloff).

by a frame of garnets. Other gold medallions found their way to Scandinavia in the later fourth century, there to provide models for imitation. Most probably arrived there after 360, a time of considerable turbulence on the Rhine frontier. These and later imports of gold medallions were the prototypes for the bracteates, one of the most distinctive of northern ornaments in the migration period.[20] The main distribution area of bracteates is southern Scandinavia, especially Denmark, where more than 260 of a total of over 600 have been found. Like their models, they were probably gifts to warriors by their leaders. They may have been worn not only as marks of distinction but also as protective amulets. The early designs are clearly based on the profile portraits of Roman emperors on coins and medallions. As time went by, the heads became more and more grotesquely

Figure 24 Bracteate from Åsum, Sweden.

[20] M. B. Mackeprang, *De nordiska Guldbrakteater* (Aarhus 1952) is still useful, though there have been major new finds and discussion on manufacture.

Figure 25 Detail of bracteate from Gerete, Gotland.

treated until they vanish and are replaced by curvilinear ornament in Style I. Before that stage was reached, there were evident links with the sphere of gods and heroes, beings who could offer protection to the wearers of these objects. The manufacture of bracteates has provoked a great deal of discussion, particularly on the point of whether they were produced by dies of metal or clay, or by matrices of some organic material such as wood, padded with cloth or leather. There seems to be supporting evidence for the use of matrices rather than dies, for the series of identical or near-identical bracteates are relatively short. No dies have been recorded, while the pressing of a thin gold blank on to a matrix does fit well with some of the minor details seen in the finished designs. Although the greatest number of bracteates occurs in Scandinavia, they are also found in Germany and elsewhere in central Europe, in Frankish Gaul and in southern England.

Part II
Germanic Europe

Frontier Societies

Frontiers maintained for centuries between tribal societies and an advanced centralized state were bound to have impact on both sides in a variety of ways. These aspects of Roman frontiers have begun to engage attention in several parts of the Empire, just as the formative effects of medieval frontier systems have been explored by historians. What is observable on and beyond the northern Roman frontiers, from the third century onward, is the emergence of frontier societies, neither purely Roman provincial nor entirely barbarian. Typically, such societies on long-established frontiers develop a material culture which draws on elements from both sides while remaining part of the dominant political order. When that order weakened or collapsed, a frontier society often remained in being and filled the political vacuum. Along the Rhine and Danube frontiers it is possible to discern a number of such societies from at least the later third century.

On the lower Rhine, economic connections across the frontier seem to have strengthened from the second century onward, partly at least in response to the need to supply Roman garrisons with food and other commodities. The economic koine thus created is discernible at settlements like Wijster and Bennekom (above, p. 68). It is not only the regular planning of sites like these that suggests the working of a system which owed much to the Roman provincial order; the concentration of economic activities at individual sites suggests that external forces were active, either within the framework of private commerce or directly driven by official Roman needs. In the fourth century, the links reveal a changing relationship. Warrior graves containing both Roman and Germanic equipment are found on both sides of the old frontier, along with hoards of Roman gold coins. By 400, German settlements were established in the Meuse valley and perhaps elsewhere within the provinces. The old frontier virtually ceased to function as a military obstacle; it was no cultural boundary either. It had given rise to an increasingly independent frontier society.

On the upper Rhine, matters are less well defined, but there are pointers to a closer relationship between the Alamannic cantons and the frontier land than is often accepted. After the fall of the *limes* about 260, there was a slow but perceptible shift of barbarian interest towards what the provinces had to offer. Alamannic groups were taken into the Roman army; some villa estates were settled by barbarians; in the Rhine valley itself, Germanic material found its way to some of the frontier forts and watch-towers.

More striking is the situation north of the middle Danube. There had been a long history of close diplomatic relations with German leaders in this region, beginning in the reign of Tiberius, if not before. When the historical sources fall silent, the archaeological record continues to reveal close connections between the provinces and the peoples settled in Moravia and Slovakia. Buildings of Roman style went up in barbarian territory on sites which were probably the seats of favoured chieftains. Roman imports abounded, not merely of luxuries, but of the widest range of common objects. The material culture of this region was not far removed from that of the adjacent Roman provinces. What was once referred to as the 'moral barrier' on the Rhine and Danube frontiers had been radically modified by the fourth century and in some places removed entirely.

The implications of these developments for the origins of migration are probably considerable. Many barbarians were to enter the Empire, not from some remote part of Europe, but from regions relatively close to the frontiers, on which Roman goods and standards of life had already left their mark. In some of those regions, interaction between barbarians and provincials had been close for a century or two before the main migrations began. When the Germanic peoples did pass into the Roman world, it was for many of them by no means into the unknown.

7

The Gothic Kingdoms

Gothic origins

The rise to prominence of the Goths in the third century is no better documented than the emergence of the Franks and Alamanni. The Goths' own traditions derived them from Gothiscandza, a vaguely designated southern Scandinavia, and told of long struggles with their neighbours the Vandili and Lugii.[1] They moved from their long-established homeland between the Oder and Vistula because of overpopulation, the legend ran, and moved in a body to the south-east, settling north of the Black Sea. A large-scale migration is not given any support by the archaeological evidence and is almost certainly merely the founding myth of the Goths. What is revealed is a slow shift of the cultural assemblage of the Oder–Vistula region into the Ukraine from the late second century AD onward, a process which continued for up to a century. That a movement of population was involved is probable, but it need not have been the migration of a tribe *en masse*. It is easier to see the movement as one of warrior bands drawn to the south-east by the rich lands of the Ukraine and the wealth of the cities of the Black Sea coasts. On the way, these bands may have been joined by others with similar aims, notably from the peoples on the western steppes. The Goths entered a region which had seen much intrusion from the east in the preceding centuries

[1] R. Hachmann, *Die Goten und Skandinavien* (Berlin 1970).

and which thus contained a very mixed population indeed. Probably from the beginning, the people whom the Romans called Goths were a very heterogeneous gathering and it would be impossible to define what was distinctively 'Gothic' about them. What is certain is that by the middle of the third century these Goths were the most formidable military power beyond the lower Danube frontier.[2]

The first certain indication of the presence of a rising barbarian power north of the Danube came in 238, when an army of Goths broke across the Danube close to its mouth and pillaged the province of lower Moesia. They extracted payment from the Roman government before they withdrew and returned prisoners, though it is possible that they had been receiving monetary subsidies before this. Soon afterwards, Goths appear in the Roman armies led against the Persians by Gordian III, perhaps under the terms of a formal treaty struck in 238. The payment of subsidies was stopped in the afterglow of Roman successes on the Danube front in the 240s, which simply provoked a massive invasion by the Goths and others in 250. On this occasion the barbarian leader was the Gothic king Kniva, one of the most astute and able of Germanic leaders. He led a force drawn from the Carpi, Bastarnae, Taifali and Vandals as well as the Goths; he even acquired some Roman deserters. The campaign was unusually well organized, three main thrusts being delivered to separate targets. The Carpi attacked Dacia, a Gothic force drove into the Dobrudja plain, while Kniva himself led an army into lower Moesia. The attack on Dacia did not go well and the Carpi were pushed out. But Kniva skilfully deployed the other two armies, attacking Nicopolis and laying siege to Philippopolis. He then turned on the Roman army at Stara Zagora and drove it off. Philippopolis fell to the invaders, an unusual case of a well-defended city falling to a barbarian force, though it came as a result of a power-play among the defenders that went astray. The Goths were emboldened to overwinter in the Roman province and then in the following spring of 251 began their return. They were confronted by a Roman army on marshy ground at

[2] H. Wolfram, *History of the Goths* (Berkeley, Calif. 1988), 42–55.

Abrittus, a terrain on which Kniva's tactical expertise could have full play. The Goths won a comprehensive victory, the Roman emperor lost his life, and the remains of his army were extricated with difficulty and only after payments had been made to the victors.

This Gothic success inaugurated a series of major invasions of the northern Balkans and Asia Minor. The fact that so much had been destroyed and pillaged in the areas close to the Danube frontier meant the invaders were compelled to go ever further afield in the search for booty. From 255, the Goths and others, especially their Sarmatian neighbours, added a new arm to their attacks, raiding from the sea. From harbours on the northern Black Sea shore, once the preserve of Greek and Roman traders, the barbarians took ship and quickly appeared before the walls of cities which had seen no serious warfare for centuries. In 256 the city of Pityus fell to them. Then, more stunning still, the wealthy city of Trebizond was taken, its garrison simply fleeing when the enemy approached. The following year saw an invasion by sea on a scale which few could have imagined possible. The Goths and their associates crossed the Black Sea, sailed through the Bosporus and encountered a Roman force at Chalcedon. Again, the garrison of the city decamped without offering resistance. The rich lands of Bithynia now lay wide open and the invaders quickly took Apamea, Nicomedia, Nicaea and Prusa. The plunder taken in this invasion must have been immense. Numerous prisoners were removed from Asia Minor to the Gothic homeland, where they, or those who came later, were to implant the Christian faith (above, p. 122).

A decade later came the greatest and most devastating of the Gothic invasions of the eastern provinces, the raid on Greece. A large fleet conveyed Goths from the Dniester and Heruli from the Sea of Azov to the Bosporus, there to attack Byzantium, without success. It passed on into the Aegean and at Athos divided into three flotillas which thereafter operated independently. Bands of Heruli attacked Thessalonica and other towns in Chalcidice. A mixed force turned to Asia Minor once more, attacking Crete and Cyprus on the way, and then pillaging Troy and the temple of Artemis at Ephesus. The army which landed in Greece seized the greatest of the prizes:

Olympia, Argos, Corinth, Sparta and Athens all fell to them. But the return from Greece and the Aegean was not to be easy. The huge fleet (we hear of 2,000 vessels) was vulnerable to the north Aegean winds and there were many losses. The Heruli around Thessalonica were confronted by the emperor Gallienus, who deployed heavy cavalry against them to great effect. The Goths in Greece headed into the mountains of Epirus, there to suffer a crushing defeat at the hands of the new emperor Claudius, thereafter Gothicus. The remaining warbands were rounded up, to be taken into service with the Roman army or settled on the land in the Danube provinces, which for most would have seemed more acceptable than a return to their homes.

These Gothic successes came to an abrupt end just as they seemed to threaten still greater invasions of the eastern Mediterranean. In 270, Aurelian defeated the Vandals in Pannonia and the Iuthungi in northern Italy. In the next years, a Gothic army either entering the Empire or leaving it after a raid was pursued by the emperor and destroyed on their home territory. Little is known of the battle, except that the Goths lost many warriors; 5,000 dead were reported, among them their king Cannabaudes. The Roman victory was decisive and it was followed by a major reordering of the barbarian peoples of the east. The Bastarnae, probably the greater part of that people, settled within the Empire. The Carpi, too, were brought into the northern Balkans and were there joined by other barbarian groups. At the end of the third century the Gepids appeared north of the Danube on land which divided two large blocs of Goths. The broad division of the Goths into Visigoths and Ostrogoths arose from this series of movements, the Tervingi occupying the land to the west of the Dniester, the Greutungi lying to the east behind the Sea of Azov. For the following half-century and more, the western Goths consolidated their hold between the Dniester and the Danube, largely at the expense of the Sarmatians. Relations with the Roman Empire were stabilized by a treaty in 332, which provided an annual payment in return for troops and allowed a resumption of trade with the Danube provinces. The Goths were probably federates of Rome before 332, but Constantine's treaty is the first sure record of the relationship. Until the tumult released by the invasion of the Huns, Gothic power north of the Danube was secure.

The Visigoths

In 376, larger and larger numbers of Germans began to gather on the lower Danube, thousands of them, desperately looking for shelter on the southern bank away from the rapacious Huns. Only two years later this army of landless refugees inflicted on Rome her greatest defeat for many decades and killed her emperor. Thirty years on, their sons would range over Italy and take possession of the Urbs itself. The way to these triumphs was arduous and when the prize was won the gain proved to be fleeting. The first of the great invasions of the Roman Empire was to bring as much suffering to the barbarians as to the Empire and it was to be two generations before the Visigoths found a secure home in the western provinces. Their struggle to find a permanent place in the changing world and the efforts of their chiefs to gain at least a share in the power of Rome struck the first mighty blow at the very heart of the Empire, one from which Rome was never fully to recover. In little more than thirty years, from the banks of the Danube to the palaces of Rome, Visigothic tribesmen began the transformation of western Europe from provinces of a Mediterranean Empire into barbarian kingdoms which, in their several ways, aspired to be like Rome.[3]

The battle of Adrianople might not have been fought. Fritigern, the Visigothic leader, entered into secret negotiations with the eastern emperor Valens, claiming that he would only ally himself with Rome, but could not control the savage temper of his Goths or win them over to an alliance unless Valens made a show of force before them. It is probable that this proposal was seriously meant. Fritigern had little to gain by playing a double game while all the time the armies of the western emperor were drawing nearer to the Balkans. And he was right in his assessment of the mood of the Goths. The

---

[3] Ibid., 117–50.

appalling treatment they had received from Rome over the previous two years did not dispose them in favour of any alliance with Rome, even if it did seem to hold out the prospect of land at long last. Nor was it unreasonable that Valens should take Fritigern's overtures seriously. The two leaders may have been in favour of an outcome by negotiation; others were not. Two Roman officers opened hostilities without reference to their superiors and within a single day a large part of their army was destroyed by the Gothic infantry or scattered by the horsemen, their emperor dead or mortally wounded.

Before the battle, Fritigern had distanced himself from the mass of his people by negotiating secretly with the Roman emperor. Two years earlier, in bitterness at their treatment by Roman commanders, the Visigoths had sworn solemn oaths to each other that they would harass the Romans by every means in their power and rest only when they were masters of the Roman Empire. Fritigern was now behaving like many another barbarian adherent of Rome and after Adrianople the new emperor Theodosius, unable to confront the Goths in battle, was soon sapping and mining the will of their leaders by diplomacy. Gifts and honours were pressed on to high-ranking Goths and it was not long before a sizeable Roman faction was building up among then, led by one Fravittas, who had married a Roman woman and taken the name Flavius. Theodosius succeeded fairly easily in seducing the Gothic nobles from their defiant oaths sworn so recently, but the rank and file of the Goths had no good reason to show devotion to the Roman cause. They had gained little or nothing from the victory at Adrianople. They were still confined to a small area of a far from rich province of the Empire and another Roman army was already being mustered against them, its ranks including disaffected Goths. Some of the leading Goths entered Roman service at this time, among them Modaharius (Modares), who was soon into action, wiping out a force of Gothic plunderers. Rome was quickly gaining the upper hand. In 380 the cavalry formations of Alans and Huns which had contributed to the success of Adrianople were settled as a federate group in Pannonia, and in 382 the main body of Goths accepted the terms of a *foedus* (treaty) and were established in Thrace and Moesia between the Danube and the Balkan mountains. The main outline of the agreed settlement is known.

The area ceded to the Goths was theirs to hold without being taxed, but it remained Roman territory. The barbarians were admitted to membership of the Roman state, but not to the right of *connubium* (legal marriage with Romans). In exchange they were required to provide military service to Rome but were to be commanded by their own leaders. The Goths were thus not confined to an enclave on the frontier, but were dispersed over a wide area and lived there alongside the Roman population 'under one roof'. The arrangement was to be arrived at in settling other federates in several of the western provinces.

From the Roman viewpoint the Gothic settlement was probably the best that could be hoped for and much practical sense lies behind the loose integration of barbarians into the structure of provincial society. The lower Danube frontier, too, gained in stability, at least for a time. There was still barbarian movement north of the river but no great invasion followed on these events, even when the Danube froze over in 384–5. There was still contact, however, between the Goths outside the Empire and those now within. The princess Gaatha travelled from Gothia north of the Danube to Cyzikos in Asia Minor accompanied by her daughter Dulcilla, carrying with her martyrs' relics; later she was able to return to her barbarian home. There may have been a diplomatic or political motive behind this journey: Gaatha's son Arimir led a group of Tervingi, a pagan people hostile to Rome, though their nobles were probably open to conversion. Gaatha's mission was not without risk: on the return journey her companion was stoned by pagan Goths. Whatever this lady was attempting, her travels reveal the complexities of a world in which Christian Goths could carry holy relics to an ancient Greek city and on their return could fall foul of their own pagan countrymen.

The rank and file of the Visigoths gained far less than they might have expected from the victory at Adrianople and the *foedus* that resulted from it. They were effectively contained within Thrace and Dacia, and their leaders were intent on expanding their own wealth and influence within the world of Rome, not on the overthrow of the Empire. In 400, two Gothic officers serving with the Roman forces, Gainas and Tribigild, rebelled against the government, but only in a bid for more personal power. Gainas was then himself given the task of quashing the revolt and was thus able to exercise power in Constantinople (the new name for Byzantium since Constantine had made it capital of the Roman Empire) and at the same time retain a hold on his Gothic warriors. When he was eventually defeated and forced out of the Empire, it was by another Goth, Fravittas, in command of a motley 'Roman' army. Nothing illustrates better the influence of Gothic leaders in the highest places at this time, and the loyalty of the Visigothic warriors to whatever cause their leaders might espouse. While Gainas' career was running its brief and futile course, the Goths had another ruler who was to forge that loyalty into a more powerful weapon and turn it against Rome.

By about 395, Alaric, one of the Goths settled in Moesia, had emerged as the recognized leader of the federates. He had first come to the fore in 391 as the leader of a barbarian force which had thrust south of the Balkan mountains, thus breaking the treaty of 382. Alaric's long career as a warrior-chieftain is so dominated in retrospect by the successes of 408–10 that it is possible to overlook the fact that he lost many minor battles and failed to win any major engagements until Roman military organization had virtually ceased to exist in Italy. Yet he maintained a hold over his people for fifteen years, perhaps because he stuck to the aim of finding a territory on which the Goths could finally settle. But he also fulfilled the terms of his various agreements with the Roman government, as his predecessors had done since crossing the Danube. Even here, however, no lasting success was achieved, and when Alaric died the Visigoths still had no homeland in the Empire.

The first phase of Alaric's operations centred on Greece and Illyricum. In 397, Epirus and its cities were given up to him and he was soon appointed *magister militum* in Illyricum. Consolidation in the Balkans might have given Alaric the chance of taking control of Constantinople, but in 401 he chose instead to leave that prize to Gainas and turned his attention to Italy, where his own ambitions and those of his people might be more fully satisfied. For the next decade the Visigoths occupied tracts of northern Italy and grew ever bolder in their

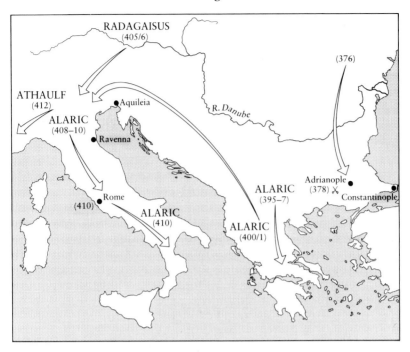

Figure 26 Movements of the Visigoths from the Danube to Gaul.

assaults on the great cities there. In 401–2 they marched on Milan, forcing the emperor Honorius to retire to Ravenna. Thereafter, Stilicho's formidable diplomatic skills had to be reinforced by armed strength, some of it drawn from the Rhine frontier and Britain. At Easter 402, the Roman army, strongly supported by Alan cavalry and under the command of the Alan Saul, attacked the Goths while at their devotions outside the city of Pollentia and dispersed them. Although claimed as a great Roman victory, this engagement did nothing to lessen the Gothic threat to the north. Alaric's force was attacked again, at Verona, and again defeated but not destroyed. It was time for him to withdraw out of Stilicho's reach, into Illyricum and Pannonia. One report has him conspiring with Stilicho at this time to attack Constantinople, a not entirely incredible story. In the brief lull that followed, Italy suffered another Gothic invasion, by a mixed and reportedly large army led by Radagaisus, a former associate of Alaric. The very size of this force may have been its undoing, for it could not support itself in the rough country of the Apennines and was soon starved into ignominious defeat.

The lesson of his own reverses at Pollentia and Verona, and of the fate of Radagaisus, will have convinced Alaric that his best chance of lasting success in Italy lay in taking possession of Rome. In 408 he again descended upon the peninsula and pushed on to the city, ignoring lesser targets, investing it in September. After extorting a huge amount of gold, silver and other riches, Alaric was prepared to raise the siege and withdraw, content with what he was now able to hand to his followers. His own position remained undefined, for he held no formal office and no part of Italy was assigned to him and his people. The time was ripe for a definitive solution to the main problem of Gothic settlement and the chance was missed. Next year the city was blockaded once more and again negotiations centred on Alaric's relations with Rome. The Goth's demands were modest, considering the virtual stranglehold he had on Italy. He now sought a settlement for his people in Noricum, offering to evacuate northern Italy, in return for military aid against any enemy of Rome. Those conducting the negotiations must have considered this more than they could have hoped for, but still the final sanction was withheld by Honorius. This confused situation was bizarrely resolved when the citizenry of Rome hailed as emperor the prefect of the city, Attalus, who promptly made peace with Alaric and appointed him commander-in-chief of the army (*magister utriusque militiae*) and his brother-in-law Athaulf commander of the household troops (*comes domesticorum*). Alaric's attention was now caught by Africa and her grain supplies to Rome, though he failed to persuade Attalus to send a Gothic army there to keep the ports open. Again he failed to seize control of affairs, leaving Rome and moving back to the north. The position of Attalus, never very secure, collapsed early in 410 and Alaric turned now to Honorius and offered his allegiance. Peace between Rome and the Goths was within easy reach, but again the hope was frustrated, this time by the intervention of a Goth, Sarus, a former adherent of Stilicho. What his motives were for standing in the way of a treaty between Honorius and the Goths cannot be guessed at. A private grievance against

Alaric and Athaulf or a blood-feud between the leading Gothic families are plausible explanations, but both are without proof.

Alaric moved southwards once more to Rome, this time without having to invest the city for long. On the night of 24 August the Goths broke through the city wall by the Salarian Gate on the northern side, close to the Pincian Hill and the Gardens of Sallust. This was not the most vulnerable sector of the defences and the suspicion must linger that access was gained with the help of sympathizers within, or of those who did not wish to face the severe privations of two years earlier. Little is known about what followed in the few days in which the Goths had Rome at their mercy. The stories of pillage related by Orosius are credible enough: it was rare that any Germanic people captured a city of any size, much less a treasure-house of gold and silver like Rome. But that Alaric should command the churches to be spared and human life to be respected must also be taken seriously. Rich mansions were an obvious target and several on the Aventine, Caelian and Quirinal were gutted by fire. In the area of the Forum, the Basilica lost some of its silver and it was reported that the Jewish treasure brought from Jerusalem by Titus was seized. But other riches were concealed, like the treasure hidden on the Esquiline, which included the wedding casket of the lady Projecta. That many Romans died and others were badly treated, despite Alaric's orders, can easily be imagined even without the testimony of Augustine.

The ordeal of Rome was brief, over within a week or even a few days. The Goths then headed south with their spoils and captives through Campania and into Calabria. Alaric had returned to the idea of an invasion of Africa and ships were collected together for an expedition which would sail via Sicily. Bad weather led to delay. Then, suddenly, after a short illness, Alaric died and with him the Gothic threat to Italy. Had he been able to seize Africa and control her grain-stores, he might yet have become the unquestioned military leader of the West and worn the mantle of Stilicho. He might also have gained for the Visigoths a settled kingdom in Italy. As it was, those of his followers who buried him beneath the bed of a stream near Cosenza could reflect that their people had still not found their promised land and that the road from the Danube still led upward. Alaric's Goths had shaken men's faith in the immortality of Rome and shattered a certainty born a thousand years before. But they were still homeless.

Athaulf was now acclaimed king of the Visigoths, a man who may already have realized that there was more to gain from championing the Roman cause than attacking the seat of Roman power. The famous report of Orosius on what Athaulf admitted to a Roman in his circle about a change in his attitude towards Rome is to be accepted as the first clear policy statement of a barbarian king towards integration of his people within the Roman Empire. The obliteration of the Roman name and its replacement by Gothia, ruled by the emperor Athaulf, was an abandoned dream. Since he could not transform the Roman Empire into a Gothic Empire, he would restore it to its former greatness by Gothic vigour. His change of attitude was due to the realization that the Goths were too barbarous to obey laws and without laws there could be no state. If the Goths were to live in the Roman world, they must live like Romans and their leader must rule like an emperor.

These *obiter dicta* were followed by a pronouncement of clear import. In January 414, on the advice of a Roman, Athaulf married the Roman princess Galla Placidia in a Roman ceremony at Narbonne. This lady had been captured in Rome in 410 and held as a hostage ever since. The Gothic king, wearing the woollen tunic of the Roman bridegroom, married the royal lady clad in Imperial robes and later the pair feasted to a wedding song delivered by a deposed emperor. It did not matter that many of the gifts of gold and precious stones showered on the bride had been plundered from Rome a few years before. Few Romans could resist wealth whatever its origins. Roman and Gothic were united in the match and later a child of the marriage was given the name of emperors, Theodosius. The union which had promised so much abruptly ended after only one year when Athaulf was assassinated by his own followers. In a very short time, the Visigoths were reduced to the most desperate straits they had endured since entering the Empire. Their main body was in southern Gaul, living there precariously and probably largely dependent on Roman subsidies. When the Roman commander Constantius ended that support and blockaded the Goths by sea, their position quickly became untenable. Many fled to northern Spain and then tried to cross to Africa. In 416 their resistance finally collapsed completely, and in return for food they agreed to act for Rome against the Vandals and their allies in Spain. Shortly afterwards, in 418, Constantius recalled them across the Pyrenees and settled them in Aquitania Secunda.[4]

At long last the Visigoths had their territory between the Garonne and the Loire, but they held it on Roman terms. There they were to remain for thirty years, largely inactive under weak leaders, until stirred by the Hun invasion of 451. The land they had gained was among the best in Gaul. Salvian lauded its vineyards, lush meadows and rich harvests as the image of Paradise. Precisely how the Goths were disposed in Aquitaine is not known, but they can hardly have been dispersed evenly across this immense region, for they still managed to maintain their cohesion over the following generations. The fact that Gothic kings used Toulouse in the far south of the region as their centre should indicate that the upper Garonne (where there were substantial late Roman villas) was one major focus of settlement. The great plain of the Saintonge and Poitou is another very likely region in which barbarian federates would have been established, though no direct evidence exists. They were apparently not assigned land in the hills of Auvergne and the Limousin, for it is not until after mid-century that we hear of them raiding here with serious intent.

Little is known of the history and internal organization of the kingdom which was ruled by Gothic kings from Toulouse and Bordeaux. It is fairly certain that throughout the long reign of the first king, Theoderic I, from 418 to 451, the *foedus* agreed with Constantius was respected by the Goths. That is to say, their military strength was never so great that they could openly attack Roman territory in Provence or Auvergne when a Roman commander was at hand to repulse them. Theoderic was a cautious monarch who was able to keep in balance the belligerence of his people towards their neighbours and the more personal ambitions of his nobles, some of whom

---

[4] M. Rouche, *L'Aquitaine des Wisigoths aux Arabes, 418–781* (Paris 1979). E. A. Thompson, *Romans and Barbarians: The Decline of the Western Empire* (Madison, Wis. 1982), 23–37.

were beginning to behave like the landed magnates on whose estates they had intruded. He was naturally attracted by the possibility of annexing the lower Rhone valley, but his several attempts to do so ended in failure against determined Roman resistance. It may have proved possible to extend Gothic territory northward, to the middle valley of the Loire: in other respects their realm retained its original bounds.

The Hun invasion of Gaul in 451 did not test Theoderic's loyalty to the Roman *foedus*, for the Visigoths had nothing to gain from the presence of a Hun army in Gaul. Goths formed the core of the mixed army which stopped the Hun onrush through Gaul on the Catalaunian plain and turned the invaders back towards Italy. Theoderic died on that battlefield, but his son of the same name adhered to the established alliance with Rome, still the only realistic path for the Goths to follow.

The material culture of the Visigothic kingdom in Gaul is unimpressive in its sum and quality, except in one notable feature. Settlement-sites are scarcely known at all in detail, the principal Visigothic centres being surviving late Roman towns. Germanic use of villa-estates is of course indicated in the historical record but this has been surprisingly poorly elucidated by excavation. Culturally and commercially, Aquitaine seems to have been relatively isolated in the fifth century. The luxury trade in metal goods between Italy and northern Gaul did not extend to the west, nor did coins from mints in Provence and northern Italy. The kingdom was cut off from the ports and workshops of the western Mediterranean to an amazing extent, and with predictable results. There is little in the sparse archaeological record to indicate a vigorous cultural life and virtually nothing to suggest the activity of innovative and original craftsmen. Stamped pottery derived ultimately from North African Red Slip Ware was produced in quantity in Aquitaine, but its inspiration lay in late Roman tradition and it was probably made by Roman craftsmen. It is striking that the external markets to which this material was distributed lay to the north and west: there was no outlet to the Mediterranean coast of Gaul. Metalwork and jewellery, the mainstay of archaeological chronology in other parts of the barbarian West, is astonishingly scarce, only three or four certainly Visigothic pieces being recorded, all of them imports into Aquitaine.

Few Frankish imports came in from the north, and no more Burgundian from the east. Belt-sets are known in considerable numbers but they are obviously derived from late Roman types in their construction and decoration. The great scarcity of brooches and decorated pins in Aquitaine suggests that Visigothic dress, especially the outer garments, was very different from that of the Franks and Burgundians. After half a century of domicile within the Empire, it would not be surprising if it was close to Roman provincial garb. Taken all in all, the absence of a distinctive Visigothic material culture in Aquitaine is best explained as the result of fairly rapid assimilation with the surviving Gallo-Roman order. Taking their lead from Athaulf and Theoderic, the leading Visigoths and their followings readily took to life in a province which still retained much of the character and material wealth of the late Roman world; hence their near-invisibility in the archaeology of the region.

When set against the poverty of metalwork and other small objects, the decorated marble sarcophagi of Aquitaine seem all the more exceptional. These are found at and close to major centres such as Toulouse, Bordeaux and Agen, as well as in Provence at Béziers and Narbonne, the majority being made of marble from St Béat in the upper Garonne valley. They have been variously dated, but a start in the mid-fifth century and a floruit about 450–525 accord best with stylistic details. They are not 'Visigothic' in any artistic sense, deriving their motifs from the repertoire of late Roman sculpture. Several bear rows of apostles below arcades; others combine such figures and scenes from the Bible with vine and ivy ornament. A number are covered by foliage, invariably in a distinctive flat relief far removed from the voluptuous curves of earlier sarcophagus sculpture. We do not know who was responsible for this unexpectedly rich series of reliefs, except that Germanic craftsmen can safely be excluded. Some unknown agency within the Christian community brought them into being in an area where an excellent marble was to hand. Later, about the end of the fifth century, workshops had been established at Bordeaux, Narbonne and probably elsewhere in Provence. Production continued into the sixth century, but to progressively poorer standards.

The prevailing impression, then, of the Visigothic kingdom

The Gothic Kingdoms

in the fifth century is one of isolation and cultural stagnation. There was little in the way of connections with Italy and those with Provence were limited and scarcely fruitful. The Franks and Burgundians left little impress on the Goths in Aquitaine and the Goths left little more impress on the land they occupied. The nomenclature of the region was not heavily influenced by the Gothic occupation. A number of place-names ending in -ens and having a Germanic personal name as their first element are usually associated with Gothic settlement, but not all of them necessarily record Gothic rather than later Merovingian Frankish landholders.

The defeat of the Huns in 451 marked the high-water mark of Visigothic power in Gaul. When Theoderic II succeeded his father after the battle on the Catalaunian Fields in 451, the Visigoths were the most powerful barbarian force in the West and it was not long before they had opportunity to extend their borders. Whether inspired by ambition or by genuine admiration, Theoderic took sides with Rome, acted indeed like a barbarian commander in Roman service. In 454, a Gothic force moved against the Bagaudae in the Ebro valley in north-eastern Spain at the behest of the emperor. Two years later Theoderic himself led his army to victory against the Suebi. Two years after that a Visigothic army under Cyrill was sent into Baetica, where it apparently stayed.

The Visigothic interest in Spain had begun, and it was shortly to receive a boost. In 406 Theoderic was murdered by his younger brother Euric and the new king soon turned his army in Baetica towards wider conquests, northward against what remained of the Roman provinces of Spain, and westward into Lusitania. Saragossa and Pamplona fell in or before 472, Tarragona and the other coastal towns at about the same time. Next year, the Goths swept on into southern Gaul and took Arles and Marseilles. These campaigns finally removed the last vestiges of Roman authority from the western provinces. Resistance was offered by Hispano-Roman aristocrats, but they could do nothing against the Gothic army. Euric and his generals continued the conquest of the rest of Spain, or most of it, without encountering major hindrance. By the time of Euric's death in 484, all of the Spanish peninsula, but for the Suebic enclave in the north-west, lay in Gothic control and a large

part of central Gaul could be wrested from Gallo-Roman proprietors. Euric recognized the value of the Roman administrative machine, even in its run-down state: both Romans and
Goths continued to be elevated to the highest offices, and some
aspects of Imperial protocol were still honoured. He was an
educated man, with a more than elementary knowledge of
Latin literature and a high respect for the law. The law-making
which began under Euric and was continued under his successor
would provide a written law to be applied not only in Spain
but in western Gaul. It may well have been at Toulouse, still
the major residence of the Visigothic king, that Euric's Code
was drawn up. The basis of the Code is much disputed. We
do not yet have the means of knowing whether it was rooted
in Germanic usage or whether it took its inspiration from late
Roman vulgar law. There are striking and suggestive analogies
between certain elements of the seventh-century East Roman
Farmers' Law and later Germanic law-codes, which may point
to a common origin in late Roman jurisprudence. But that does
not take us directly back to Euric's Code. It is at least likely
that Euric and his advisers relied to some degree on Roman
lawyers at his court, and their principal contribution may have
been in relating Gothic practice to Roman legal principles. The
legal difficulties which arose from the conjunction of Romans
and barbarians in old Roman territory now under Germanic
kings must in many respects have been severe. It is surely not
chance that so much of what survives of Euric's laws concerns
land, its ownership and occupation, its sale and inheritance.

In the last decade or so of the fifth century, the Visigoths
began to settle in numbers in northern Spain and quickly
expanded their hold on the peninsula.[5] By 500 they held sway
over much of Spain with the exception of the north-western
territory, which lay in the hands of the Suebi and the Basques,
as well as Aquitaine. But they were not to hold on to this
huge tract for long. In 507 the Visigoths under Alaric II were
crushingly defeated at Vouillé near Poitiers by the Frankish
army of Clovis and shortly thereafter had to abandon most of

---

[5] E. A. Thompson, *The Goths in Spain* (Oxford 1969); R. Collins, *Early
Medieval Spain* (London 1983).

their land in Gaul, retaining only a large part of Narbonensis. After 507 their future lay in Spain.

After Vouillé, the Visigoths elected Alaric's illegitimate son Gesalic to lead them against the Franks. For a time he continued the struggle, but Toulouse soon fell, followed by Narbonne. Gesalic pulled back into Spain and it was left to Theoderic, the Ostrogothic king, to halt the Franks in their advance through Provence. Theoderic was keenly interested in what was happening in Gaul. There was the possibility of extending the Ostrogoths' hegemony over their kinsmen there; furthermore Theoderic's daughter had been the wife of Alaric and his grandson Amalaric, unlike Gesalic born in wedlock, had an evident claim on the Visigothic throne. Not surprisingly, therefore, Theoderic was intent on removing Gesalic and when the Burgundians attacked Narbonne in 511 and drove Gesalic out, he deposed him. Gesalic struggled on for a time but his cause was doomed. For the next fifteen years, until Theoderic's death in 526, the Visigoths were under Ostrogothic suzerainty, their king Amalaric married to a Frankish princess, Clothild. She was a Catholic and her Arian husband's attempts to make her renounce her faith led to Frankish intervention. Clothild's brother Childebert I invaded Narbonensis in 531, seized Narbonne and drove Amalaric into Spain where he was murdered, probably by his own followers. The Visigothic nobles now elected an Ostrogothic commander, Theudis, to lead them. The absence of a strong ruling house had long been a weakness of the Visigoths. Like Germanic kings of a much earlier age, their leaders were required above all to be effective military commanders and not much more. If they failed in that, their rule was short.

Despite his Ostrogothic origins, Theudis did nothing to bring the Visigoths closer to their kin in Italy. He contracted a shrewd marriage with a wealthy Roman lady and raised a private army of 2,000 men from the slaves on her estate. This use of a substantial private following illustrates one of the principal difficulties facing a barbarian ruler in the vast spaces of Spain. The military organization of the Roman Empire had gone, and individual kings themselves had to organize, equip, feed and keep content a force large enough to maintain the peace in Spain and fend off attacks on her borders. Given the nature of

Visigothic society, it was inevitable that the fortunes of the army would be the recurring theme in the sixth and seventh centuries. Theudis, at least, had as much military success as failure. A Frankish invasion in 541 was beaten off and an attempt in 544 to seize a part of Africa around Ceuta briefly took the Byzantine army by surprise. Justinian's forces recovered quickly, however, and drove the Visigoths out.

Amalaric came into his own on the death of Theoderic in 526. He stabilized relations with the Ostrogoths, as well as defining clearly the Visigothic frontier in southern Gaul. From now on, the lower Rhone and its delta divided the Visigoths and the Ostrogoths. The major loss to the Visigoths was the great city of Arles, although it had held out for them in 508–10. What had been the coastal region of western Narbonensis under Rome now became Septimania, a province of the Visigothic kingdom containing the cities of Agde, Béziers, Nîmes, Narbonne and Carcassonne and a number of lesser strongholds. It was to be held in the face of Frankish pressure until the final collapse of the Visigothic kingdom in the eighth century. Amalaric also retrieved the treasure of the Visigoths which had been lost after Vouillé and which had been acquired by the Ostrogoths. But in other respects his reign was unproductive.

Theudis was murdered in his own palace in 548 and succeeded by a Visigoth, Agila, whose reign saw the Byzantine invasion of southern Spain and the establishment of an east Roman foothold on the Mediterranean coast. He was beset, too, by revolts: of the citizens of Cordoba and then of a noble, Athanagild, who based himself at Seville. He joined forces with the Byzantines against Agila and won a resounding success against him. Agila then went the way of so many Visigothic rulers at this period, slaughtered by his own men at Merida in 555. Athanagild succeeded him and immediately tried to push the Byzantines out of Spain, but without making much progress. His reign, to 568, is regrettably ill-covered by our sources, but it is clear that there were crises of several different kinds, threatening a breakup of the kingdom. Financial difficulties are hinted at by the coinage, and relations with the Frankish powers were in no way improved by the marriage of Athanagild's daughters to the rulers of Neustria and Austrasia. Athanagild's repute may have been unduly blackened by later Visigothic tradition, but it is clear that he left a weakened kingdom behind him in 568, the year in which the Lombards thrust into Italy.

The new king, Liuva, was elected at Narbonne and chose to base himself in Septimania, presumably because of renewed Frankish pressure on this most exposed province of the Visigoths. A year after his elevation, Liuva entrusted the governance of the Spanish possessions to his brother Leovigild, virtually his only known act. Shortly afterwards, certainly by 573, Liuva died and the kingdom was united once more under Leovigild, the most effective of Visigothic monarchs, though admittedly in an uninspiring procession.

With the reigns of Leovigild and his successor Reccared, the Visigothic kingdom in Spain reached the peak of its power and it is fortunate that for much of this period we possess an excellent source in the Chronicle compiled by a contemporary, John, a Catholic from Lusitania, who founded a monastery at an unknown site called Biclarum and eventually became bishop of Gerona. The written work of this little-known man is the most informative document on Visigothic Spain and one of the very earliest works of history produced by a scholar of Germanic origin in any part of Europe.

One of Leovigild's first acts was designed to make provision for the succession. His two sons were endowed with royal authority with the intention that one or both would succeed their father in due course. This was unusual foresight in a Visigothic king and it deserved more success than it was to enjoy in the longer term. Much time had to be devoted in the first years of the reign to exerting the authority of the king over the entire Visigothic realm, the unity of which had been seriously impaired by revolts in several regions, and to attacking the Byzantine province in the south. The invasion of Roman territory achieved little and may simply have convinced Leovigild that the Byzantines were too formidable an opponent, for the time being at least; at any rate he did not attack them a second time. His success in reuniting his own kingdom was much more impressive. Cordoba, in revolt against a succession of kings over several decades, was now recovered and peasants in the vicinity were defeated when they rebelled. Revolts on the north-western border, in Cantabria and Asturia, occupied Leovigild for the next three years. Wealthy landowners, presumbly of late Roman stock, were behind at least one of these movements, their aim being, perhaps, to achieve independence from both Visigoths and Suebi. They were ruthlessly put down and potential rebels or opponents were killed or exiled. Leovigild served notice on the Suebi that he intended to absorb their kingdom under his reign. The frontier against the Franks was secure throughout this time and once again the Visigoths were dominant over most of Spain. Their king marked these successes by founding a new city on the Tagus, Reccopolis, named after his second son Reccared.

But if Leovigild had secured his kingdom against external enemies and put down dissidents within, he still had to face a major threat from within his own family. The spark was provided by friction between the resilient Arianism of the Visigoths and the Catholic faith of their northern neighbours the Franks. Leovigild's elder son Hermenegild had been entrusted with the southern province of Baetica, presumably to guard it against encroachment by the Byzantines. Hermenegild was married to the young Frankish princess Ingundis, a Catholic who staunchly resisted brutal attempts to convert her to the Arian creed. In Seville, she joined with a monk, Leander (a brother of Isidore and later a bishop of Seville), in persuading her husband to enter the Catholic Church, in which they were eventually successful. This was not tantamount to a rebellion against Leovigild, but it clearly placed relations between father and son on a parlous footing. When Hermenegild refused to treat with his father and instead entered upon an alliance with the Byzantines, the breach was wide open and the kingdom was again at war with itself.

Hermenegild proclaimed himself king at Seville in 579 and began the minting of his own coinage. Exactly what territory he commanded is difficult to define, but it included Cordoba, Seville and Merida and thus much of Baetica and the southern part of Lusitania. Toledo, however, remained with Leovigild. Although he had allied himself with the Byzantines, he does not appear to have drawn them into the conflict. An embassy to the Burgundian king Guntram in 580 likewise bore no fruit in the form of military support. An alliance with the Suebi also did nothing to increase his forces. For a rebel occupying the richest parts of Spain and with more than one potential ally close at hand, Hermenegild seems to have been curiously reluctant to seize the initiative. Even when Leovigild was occupied with a campaign against the Basques in 581, his son did not take the chance to invade his domains or strike at his capital, Toledo.

It was Leovigild who made the decisive strike after successful operations against Basques. In 582, his army came south and took Merida and in the following year laid siege to Seville, still the residence of Hermenegild. The arrival of an army of Suebi under their king Miro did nothing to help the besieged, as Leovigild promptly cut them off and forced them to ally with him. Seville remained under siege through the following winter, Leovigild turning the screw tighter by seizing the old city of Italica nearby and repairing its crumbling defences. Seville fell in the summer of 538 and although Hermenegild made good his escape from there, he was captured shortly afterwards at Cordoba. His father at first treated him with mercy, but in 585, while in internal exile at Tarragona, he was put to death, most probably on Leovigild's orders. To the end he had kept to the Catholic faith, as did his wife Ingundis. She had escaped to the Byzantine province and was on her way to Constantinople when she died in Africa. The Arian king had won this contest, but the triumph of Catholicism was not far off.

One conquest was outstanding, that of the Suebic kingdom, and this was achieved with relative ease. Leovigild now enjoyed a prestige far above that of any his predecessors, and the succession to his son Reccared in 586 was unchallenged. Within a year, the new king was converted to the Catholic faith and convened the Arian bishops and clergy at Toledo to exhort them to follow his lead. There were resisters and Arian revolts broke out in Lusitania and Septimania. After Reccared's death in 601 there was a decade of internal conflict, finally resolved by the victory of the Catholic faction and the accession of their king Sisebut. The victory belonged not only, or primarily, to the Catholic Church. It was the Roman tradition that finally captured the Visigothic monarchs in the early seventh century, a tradition which owed most to the work and influence of a remarkable group of scholars and churchmen. The rise of Seville as the cultural centre of Spain accompanied the emergence of Toledo as the political capital and was due to the activity of two successive bishops, the brothers Leander and Isidore. It was the work of Leander that led to the eventual triumph of Catholicism in Spain. Isidore's writing and teaching in history and theology guided and informed kings as well as clergy. Although he is best known as the preserver of the learning of the Classical world, Isidore's impact on his own time was political, not least in the reign of Sisebut, the most Romanizing as well as the most cultivated of Germanic kings. From Isidore's day onward Visigothic kings could look to the Church for aid on civil matters, though the nobles retained a hold on the conduct of secular affairs. Patriotic confidence in the future of the kingdom was further strengthened by the move of the headquarters of the Church to Toledo. It was this phase of Visigothic power in Spain that was viewed as the ideal kingdom by the Middle Ages.

The record of cemeteries, so crucial to study of the migration period in other parts of western Europe, is neither extensive nor informative in Spain.[6] Burial traditions among the peoples who settled in the peninsula did not include the generous provision of grave-goods, so that both dating and the affinities of material culture are much more difficult to determine. About eighty cemeteries which can be assigned to the period of Visigothic settlement are known, barely half of which have been examined with any care. Only a handful have been excavated on a useful scale. By and large, the graves contain few artifacts, so that knowledge of even the basics of material culture is strictly limited. A further fundamental problem centres on the distribution of what are commonly termed 'Visigothic' cemeteries. The great majority of these lie in Castile, between the Ebro and the upper Tagus, with scattered instances between the Tagus and the Pyrenees and down the Mediterranean coast. Scarcely any lie in the fertile south or in the west. This distribution does not adequately reflect the political facts of Visigothic Spain. More plausibly it is to be explained by variation in burial practice. In the south, in the old province of Baetica, for example, the influence of a still strong late Roman cultural

---

[6] H. Zeiss, *Die Grabfunde aus dem spanischen Westgotenreich* (Berlin 1934). W. Hübener, 'Zur Chronologie der westgotenzeitlichen Grabfunde in Spanien', *Madrider Mitteilungen*, 11 (1970), 187.

substratum may help to account for the absence of 'barbarian' cemeteries. In several parts of Spain, inhumation burials without grave-goods are recorded, a substantial number of which can be assigned to the period from the fifth century onward. These may very well include the graves of Visigoths and other barbarian settlers. In this connection it is interesting that most of the known 'Visigothic' cemeteries were no longer in use after the late sixth century or at least contain no grave-goods that can be dated.

Visigothic and other cemeteries of the fifth and sixth centuries are not well recorded in Septimania. In Hérault the known instances lie on the valley floors; very few are known in the hill country. In Aude, they lie mainly between Carcassonne and Castelnaudary, again on river terraces. Fifth-century material is noticeably scarce. The great majority of the datable graves are sixth-century, with a few of the earlier seventh. The largest excavated cemetery is the row-grave cemetery at Estagel (Pyrenées Orientales) near Perpignan. Some cist-graves contain Gothic brooches, small, plain belt-buckles which could have been made and worn by anyone. Other material is simple, unostentatious and virtually impossible to assign to any ethnic group. Two buckle-plates with *cloisonné* ornament are, however, clearly Germanic, having a general similarity to Frankish work. Weapons were few, but scabbard parts indicate their presence in some graves.

Royal Visigothic graves have not, as yet, been examined, but there are glimpses of the panoply of seventh-century rulers in the treasures found at Guarrazar and Torredonjimeno. The former, now in Paris and Madrid, may have been concealed in the earth at the time of the Arab invasion in 711, at a villa site, whence the plough unearthed it in the nineteenth century. The bulk of the treasure was a group of eleven gold crowns (nine of which still survive), suspended by chains and, in three cases, with royal names hanging in single letters from their lower edges. These were plainly votive objects, not designed for use in court ceremonial. All are richly encrusted with agates, sapphires, pearls and crystals, and the gold is itself elaborately engraved. The three named persons are Reccaswinth, Swinthila and Sonnica, and the cache as a whole is part of the royal treasury of the later sixth and seventh centuries. There is much in the treasure that is reminiscent of Byzantine court art and of the elaborate ceremonial which that art served. This dependence on east Roman images of royalty is again revealed in the Visigothic coinage. In their coin-portraits, Leovigild wears an emperor's robe and brooch, Reccaswinth a diadem, and Wamba is shown with cross and sceptre; almost all the symbols of imperial authority are here.

The larger cities of Spain have been poorly studied with their post-Roman history in mind. One exception is Merida, which the written record informs us was a lively centre in the fifth and sixth centuries and which has been more than cursorily studied by archaeological means. The central area of Merida remained in use, though several of the old Roman buildings were converted to new purposes or entirely replaced. A church (of St Mary), a baptistery (St John) and the bishop's palace went up anew around the forum in the sixth century, the secular basilica being retained in use. More surprisingly, a pagan temple continued to stand in the same public place, though what it was used for cannot be guessed at; evidently it was not turned into a church. The *Lives* of the Fathers of Merida speak of further activity in the later sixth century, which is a helpful reminder to us not to assume too readily that urban communities at this date relied only on renovated Roman buildings. We would dearly like information about the contemporary urban centres of Seville and Cordoba, and, of course, Toledo. Not only new buildings were going up at Merida; sculptors were active too, working in a tradition which may have been inspired by the visible remains of the Roman past.

Barcelona, used as a base by several Visigothic kings including Athaulf, Euric and Amalaric, was later eclipsed by the southern cities in significance but remained a major centre of authority within north-eastern Spain. The north-eastern part of the walled city contained the most important of the structures used in the Visigothic period. Here lay the basilica and baptistery (partially below the present cathedral) and the palace, beneath the later royal residence. The area of the Roman forum was apparently abandoned in favour of this new focus and the move away from Roman urban manners was further reinforced by the placing of cemeteries within the city walls by the early seventh century. From then on, Barcelona was more of a fortress than a great city and it remained so until long after the Muslim conquest in the early eighth century.

It seems most unlikely that the early Visigothic kings took much care to repair and rebuild major structures. But there is one reminder that such a project was well within the capabilities of the craftsmen of the day. The great bridge over the Guadiana at Merida, nearly 800 metres long, was restored at the behest of Euric in 483 and this was recorded on an inscription, now lost but described in a manuscript of the ninth century. Other major buildings may have been kept in repair without any such record being made.

New ecclesiastical buildings are not known for certain in Visigothic Spain before the seventh century. The earliest dated church is that of St Juan de Baños (Prov. Palencia), whose dedicatory inscription places the building in the reign of Reccceswinth, at 661. This is a small aisled basilica, less than 20 metres long, with an enclosed sanctuary, a porch over the entrance and, originally, two chambers on each wing at the east end. Decorative treatment of the interior is minimal, being confined to narrow friezes of chip-carved ornament especially at the windows and door. The most striking feature is the use of finely dressed masonry blocks of large size, without mortar, and this St Juan de Baños shares with a number of other seventh-century churches in north-central Spain. The most imposing is San Pedro de la Nave in the Esla valley (Prov. Zamora), which was dismantled and moved to a new site in 1930. This is a cruciform building, the main basilica being flanked by opposed square chambers on the long sides. Closer to a truly cruciform plan is the mausoleum-chapel of San Fructuoso de Montelios at Braga, built during the lifetime of St Fructuoso in the mid-seventh century. Here the central vault is accompanied by three circular vaulted chambers and, on the west side, a square porch. Other cruciform churches, like Santa Comba de Bande (Prov. Orense) and San Pedro de la Mata are probably remnants of monasteries of which all other trace has vanished. The possibility that larger churches existed in the seventh century is hinted at by the survival of the Crypt of San Antolin in the cathedral at Palencia. Structurally, this has much in common with the known seventh-century buildings and thus could be all that remains of an early cathedral.

There are no grounds for believing that these skilfully built churches represent a continuance or a revival of Hispano-Roman techniques. It is inherently more likely that craftsmen from outside Spain were responsible for this sudden advance in the construction of masonry buildings. An obvious source for such expertise is north Africa; and the plans of the Spanish churches could support that connection. Also to be considered is the possibility of Byzantine influence from southern Spain, as is detectable in sculpture at this date.

Over 2,000 place-names of Germanic origin are known in Spain as a whole, most of them to be assigned to the Visigothic settlement, a few to the Alans and Suebi. Personal nomenclature was also influenced by the Germanic settlers. Names such as Alfonso, Fernando, Gonzalo, Elvira and Rodrigo are all Germanic in origin. Other personal names figure in the names of places such as at Bamba (Wamba), Guitiza (Witiza), Castro Adalsindo (Adalsindus) and Castelladral (Aderaldus). Common words in Spanish which are German in origin are fewer than one might have expected, but they are not confined to mundane tasks and objects as is sometimes alleged. Social relations, human emotions and warfare are also to the fore in the Visigothic linguistic inheritance. Modern Spanish, however, is still in essence the spoken Latin of Hispania in modernized form. Three hundred years of Visigothic rule did nothing to alter that. The relative fewness of the Visigoths amid the Hispano-Roman population will go most of the way towards an explanation. In the sixth century, German speakers probably numbered only between 100,000 and 200,000 among a total population of several millions (some have guessed up to 10 millions).

The Byzantine reoccupation of part of southern Spain is one of the half-forgotten episodes of early medieval Europe, passed over briefly even by Byzantine writers. The extent of the territory which the east Roman army was able to take over is disputed, but the only ancient source, the *Synecdemus* of Hierocles, names only six cities and alludes to one other within the western prefecture. These were Cordoba, Asidonia, Basti,

Carthago Spartaria, Malaga and Segontia. This list provides no support for the view that Byzantine Hispania extended into southern Portugal and Cantabria. Nor did it include the eastern coastlands north of New Carthage. Essentially it comprised the eastern part of Baetica and the southern coast as far west as Gibraltar. Inland, the Roman hold on even large centres was precarious. Cordoba was lost to the Visigoths in 572 and even Cartagena on the east coast had to put up new defences in 589. The entire episode of Byzantine occupation was over in seventy-five years and might be thought to be of no significance were there not increasingly clear indictions of cultural, artistic and ecclesiastical influences radiating from the south to touch not only the Visigothic capital of Toledo but also centres further north, especially in the late sixth and early seventh centuries.

An exceptional feature of the Visigothic kingdom among the barbarian powers was its treatment of the Jews in the seventh century. Persecution of any ethnic group was virtually unknown among the barbarian powers of the West and Visigothic policy towards so large a group can only be explained by the influence of Byzantine opinions. Jews were very numerous in the cities of Spain, especially in the south, and some of them had amassed enviable amounts of private property. After the conversion of the royal house to Catholicism, attention turned to them as outsiders whose religion excluded them from the nation-state and whose wealth made persecution of them profitable for the royal treasury. As early as 589, at the Third Council of Toledo, the baptism of the children of mixed Jewish and Christian marriages was enjoined, though the repeated enactment of this and similar measures later is sufficient indication of the ineffectiveness of such legislation. Jews, of course, continued to worship their god in secret and to bring up their families in their faith. All unconverted Jews were to be expelled from Spain under an enactment of 638, but even this failed to remove them all or to obviate the need for legislation which would turn them into model subjects of the king. The conditions under which the remaining Jewish subjects of the Visigoths lived in the seventh century steadily deteriorated, until the majority were ready to welcome the Arab invaders of 711 as liberators.

The Ostrogoths

The history of the Ostrogoths after their kingdom had been utterly overthrown by the Huns in the 370s is extremely obscure for over a century. The majority of Greutungrian Ostrogoths were bound in loyalty to their Hun masters after the disastrous defeat of 375 and largely remained so until the breakup of the Hun empire after Attila's death. The mixing of peoples north of the lower Danube was clearly a dominant feature of these decades and as a result the political and cultural history of the time is bewilderingly complex. The dates of events are poorly recorded.[7] There was movement of population and attempts were made to enter the Roman provinces by various groups. One such, under the leadership of the two *duces* Alatheus and Saphrax and comprising a band made up of Goths, Huns and Alans, crossed the Danube frontier in 376 and two years later made a decisive intervention at the battle of Adrianople. Later, in 380, they were settled by the emperor Gratian as federates in Pannonia and for a time discharged their duties reasonably faithfully. Other Gothic bands crossed the Danube after Adrianople, but a large proportion of the Ostrogoths remained under Hun dominance in the remains of Dacia, frequently appearing in battle alongside Huns and Alans. Some of their leaders achieved positions of authority under Hun kings, including Attila himself.

Ostrogoths formed part of the host which Attila took to Gaul in 451, three princes of their royal house commanding them. The defeat of the Huns and their allies in Gaul, followed in 453 by the death of Attila, led to a major redistribution of power north of the Danube. Hun domination of Pannonia ended very quickly at the battle on the river Nedao, a tributary of the Save, in 454. The centre of their territory was seized by the Gepids, who also took over part of Dacia. The Rugi rose to prominence in lower Austria and began to take over the province of Noricum. The Heruli occupied Moravia and extended their hold on land down to the Danube bank. The

---

[7] Wolfram, *History of the Goths*, 248–68.

Ostrogoths themselves retained much of Pannonia, accepting a role as federates in the area between Vindobona (Vienna) and Sirmium (Belgrade). But their rule there was uneasy and lasted under twenty years. The land was not sensibly farmed by its occupants, who became more and more dependent upon subsidies from Constantinople, and there were hostile neighbours on almost all sides. It seemed as though this branch of the Goths would not survive for much longer.

The leader who was to bring the Ostrogoths their most brilliant years had already been born, about 451.[8] The subking Thiudimir was presented with a son by a concubine, possibly not herself a Goth. He was named Theoderic, as were several other leading Goths of the period. In 459, the boy was sent to Constantinople as a hostage and he remained there until he was eighteen. The experience made him an exceptional man. Not only did Theoderic receive a Roman education but, in a favoured position at the Imperial court, he absorbed Graeco-Roman cultural values as no other barbarian ruler had done before him. But he did not abandon the warrior ethos of his forefathers. On his return from Constantinople, Theoderic assumed control of the eastern portion of Ostrogothic territory and immediately won an important victory over the Sarmatians. During the next decade, he built up his reputation as a forceful and ambitious ruler, leading his people to a new territory and federate status on the lower Danube, in the old province of Moesia, as close as could be to Constantinople itself. Moesia was well chosen as a base for power-play, against both eastern Rome and other barbarian groups about the lower Danube. The accidental death of his principal rival among Ostrogothic leaders, Theoderic Strabo (the Squinter), left Theoderic with an almost open field. In 484, Flavius Theodericus was elected to the consulship in Constantinople and in that year slew the son of Theoderic Strabo in the city. He now stood without challenge as the leader of the Goths in the east, powerful enough to march against Constantinople in 486, occupy its outlying districts and cut its aqueducts. But the attraction of carving out a kingdom in the west was still potent and Theo-

---

[8] W. Ensslin, *Theoderich der Grosse* (2nd edn; Munich 1959).

deric again turned his warriors in that direction, with the support of the Roman emperor, if not his direct commission.

The Ostrogothic invasion of Italy was a movement of people, not merely a military expedition. Not impossible estimates give a total number of 100,000 people, 20,000 of them fighting men. Not all the Goths in the Balkans joined Theoderic and not all those who took part were Goths: we hear of Rugi and even Romans in his army. The host set out after the harvest in 488, moved along the Danube valley, pushing aside an attempt by Gepids to halt them. They swung southward to approach north-eastern Italy, finding at the Isonzo bridge on the river Wippach the army of the barbarian king and defender of Italy, Odovacar. The Ostrogoths forced the crossing of the river and moved into northern Italy. It was now late summer, 489. For the next year, the armies of Theoderic and Odovacar struggled for mastery of northern Italy. The military victory was won by the Ostrogoths by the summer of 491, but not for two more years could Odovacar be removed from the scene, brutally, in the course of a banquet. Theoderic was not a forbearing opponent. He was now, unchallengably, the master of Italy and his army raised him to the rank of king. But not until 497 did the ruler of Constantinople recognize Theoderic as the ruler of the Roman west.

The kingdom over which Theoderic presided was still a wealthy realm.[9] The surplus produced by the land poured into the treasury of Ravenna, sufficient for programmes of building in addition to more mundane concerns. At Verona Theoderic repaired the city defences, the aqueduct, baths and a palace. Pavia saw building or restoration of a palace, amphitheatre, baths and defences. The royal residence at Ravenna was adorned with a new palace and splendid churches. These were surroundings fit for an emperor, not merely a barbarian king. The medallion of Senigallia might show Theoderic with the trimmed moustache and shock of hair of the Gothic warrior but his seal is that of an emperor, his left hand holding the orb surmounted by Victory and his right raised as though in *adlocutio*. But if Theoderic looked like an emperor, his

---

[9] Wolfram, *History of the Goths*, 286–90.

constitutional position was closer to that of a Germanic king. He was king of the Gothic army in Italy, not king of the Goths. He had received Roman citizenship and the consulship from the emperor and held the office of *magister militum*, the highest military rank of all. His kingdom was thus still part of the Roman Empire and Theoderic took some care to ensure that Italy remained a part of the Roman state, while leaving no one in any doubt about Gothic power to determine the course of events in the west. Romans recognized the truth of the situation and called Theoderic *dominus* or even *Augustus*, seemingly without effort. The Senate was held in honour; there were distributions of grain and games in the circus. Appointments to major posts within the bureaucracy were made by the king, but the emperor's power to nominate consuls and senators was still respected.

When we consider that the Ostrogoths were the masters of Italy for two generations, the physical remains of their presence in the peninsula are remarkably scanty. There are several reasons for this. As with the Visigoths in Spain, the main foci of Germanic power were long-established Roman cities like Ravenna, Milan and Verona, in which the leading urban functions could continue without any significant break, or at least any break which might leave a mark on the archaeology of those places. Away from the cities, the settlement of Ostrogoths on the soil will only be detected after detailed study, involving excavation, of late Roman agricultural settlements. This is work which has begun only since 1980 and the results are so far meagre for the fifth and sixth centuries. Even recognizably Ostrogothic cemeteries are far from common in Italy, and those that are known are relatively small and uninformative. The overall distribution of Ostrogothic material, however, is more revealing. Most of the graves, coin-hoards and other finds occur in northern and central Italy, and in Dalmatia.[10] North of the Alps in Raetia and Noricum, which formed part of the Ostrogothic realm, very few objects can be linked with their occupation. Within Italy, Gothic finds are non-existent in the

---

[10] V. Bierbrauer, *Die ostgotischen Grab-und Schatzfunde in Italien* (Spoleto 1975).

Figure 27 Eagle brooch, in gold with garnet cloisonné, *from the Domagnano treasure, Italy.*

south and very scarce south of Rome. The main concentrations lie around Milan and Pavia, together with Ancona on the Adriatic coast, reflecting the importance of these cities in the governance of the peninsula. The dominance of Ravenna, by contrast, is not evident in the surrounding area.

Single graves and small cemeteries aside, the archaeology of Ostrogothic Italy is distinguished by a few hoards, the most important being that found at Domagnano in the Republic of San Marino. The circumstances of burial of this magnificent treasure are not known in detail. It may have been included in the grave-goods of a leading Ostrogoth, or it may have been a cache of jewellery. The best-known piece from the treasure is the brooch in the stylized form of an eagle, but the jewellery as a whole superbly exemplifies the gold and garnet *cloisonné* work then approaching its greatest period of craftsmanship. The eagle brooch is without question one of the finest of all migration period jewels, simple in design and depending for its effect on the brilliance of its garnets laid over silver-gilt foils and contrasting with tiny squares of ivory in the tail and single cells of lapis lazuli at the wing-tips. The other surviving pieces (not all the treasure was recovered) are pendants from a necklace, a drop-earring and a brooch in the form of a bee – all, together with the eagle brooch, products of the same workshop. If from a grave, this fine set of personal jewellery was buried with an aristocratic Ostrogothic lady at a date about 500.

When Theoderic died in 526, the Ostrogothic kingdom was still a great power and so it continued for some years under the regency of his daughter Amalasuntha and her little son Athalaric. But only ten years after Theoderic's death, a Byzantine army had invaded Italy and was in possession of Rome. Justinian was ready to take Italy back to Roman control and wanted only a pretext to invade, and that was provided by the fall from power of Amalasuntha. For the next twenty-five years, Italy was enveloped in a hideous and destructive series of wars, recorded in immense detail by Procopius. Long before they were over, the kingdom which Theoderic had created had collapsed, though the Goths in Italy fought on under a succession of war-leaders until 552. The Italy over which Theoderic had ruled had been devastated and most of his people killed, enslaved or deported. As a people, the Ostrogoths had ceased to exist.

Figure 28 The mausoleum of Theoderic at Ravenna.

8

The Suebi and Vandals

The Suebi

The least-known of all the Germanic peoples who settled in Spain were the Suebi (Suevi or Sueves), who crossed the ice-bound Rhine with the Vandals, Alans and Burgundians on the last night of 406. For the next two and a half years, they and other barbarian bands devastated large areas of Gaul with no one to hold them in check. In the late summer of 409 a large company of Suebi, Alans and Vandals crossed the Pyrenees into Spain, which had been untouched by major barbarian assault for well over a century. A large tract of northern Spain immediately fell into their hands and only two years later the various invading groups divided up the Spanish provinces among themselves 'by lot', as the chronicler Hydatius tells us. They were apparently able to do much as they pleased in the matter. There is no reference to any treaty with representatives of Roman government in Spain or of any arrangement with surviving municipal authorities, if there were any. The old province of Tarraconensis in the north-east remained largely in Roman hands. The richest area, Baetica, south of the Guadalquivir, fell to the Siling branch of the Vandals, while the Alans, very surprisingly, took possession of Lusitania in the west and Carthaginiensis in the centre, the lion's share. The Asding Vandals and the Suebi were given the hilly and less advanced north-western province of Gallaecia. The entire arrangement is at first sight a strange one, even if allowance is made for the distribution of the land by lot. In terms of what these three

areas could offer, the division was not entirely fair. The huge
tract taken by the Alans included the sterile central plateau, a
virtual desert in places. Their best land was the plain of Lusitania and the coastal strip on the eastern seaboard. The Silings
acquired the most Roman parts of Spain and the cities of
Cordoba, Italica, and Cadiz, along with the major mineral
deposits of the Sierra Morena. The minerals of Galicia,
especially the gold and silver, also provided some consolation
for the Asdings and Suebi, whose share might otherwise have
seemed rather barren. However, events immediately after 411
suggest that the newcomers to Spain were content with what
they had gained. Only rarely do we hear of conflict between
the barbarian groups settled in the peninsula. The greatest
upheaval was caused by the Roman government itself when it
pitted the Visigoths against the Siling Vandals in 416,
destroying them in the process. The outcome had repercussions
for the peoples in the north: after attacking the Suebi in an
attempt to take over all Galicia, the Asdings moved south to
take over the land recently vacated. The Suebi were thus left
in possession of Galicia and thenceforward they maintained
themselves there largely untouched by the events of the wider
Spanish world. If we accept what Isidore of Seville says about
Galicia, that a part was still occupied by the remnant of provincial population, it becomes easier to understand why the Suebi
continued to raid and plunder within this region for so long
after their settlement there. Their main centres were, rather
surprisingly, the principal walled cities of the north-west: Braga
(Bracara Augusta), Astorga and Lugo. At Lugo, the Suebi lived
alongside Roman provincials, even as late as 460. In that year,
at Easter when the Romans relied on the sacred days to ensure
their safety, the Suebi fell on their neighbours and massacred
many of them. Outside the cities, Suebic settlement is scarcely
known at all, from either literary or archaeological sources.
No major cemeteries are recorded which can be confidently
ascribed to the Suebi and even occasional finds of Germanic
material are scarce in Galicia. Small quantities of Roman
material still found its way here, notably coinage. A small
hoard of gold coins found near Coalla in Asturias, consisting
of 9 *solidi* and 2 *trientes*, may have owed its burial, and non-
recovery, to the arrival of the Suebi in 411. After that date

material evidence bearing on their occupation of the soil is slight indeed. To some extent at least this is to be explained by the fact that they were not a large barbarian grouping. An estimate of up to 25,000 people in all may seem rather low, but it is not impossibly so. A population of that size, depending to a large extent on what they could acquire by plundering their neighbours, as we know the Suebi did, and settled in an agriculturally poor area, might well be virtually invisible in the archaeological record.

The history of the Suebic kingdom from 411 to its end in 585 is one of the least edifying episodes in the history of early medieval Europe, a brutal catalogue of raids, battles, cities destroyed, communities enslaved.[1] The *Chronicle* of Hydatius, our only major source, is lit by few shafts of the light of humanity and hope. From their base in the hill-country, the Suebi were able to threaten wide areas of Spain. In 439 they took Merida. Seville fell to them in 441, thus giving them control of the administrative centres of Lusitania and Baetica. A few years later they turned to the north and moved into the Ebro valley, taking Lerida and approaching the territory of Saragossa, though without seizing a permanent hold in the region. These moves were not viewed with equanimity by the Roman emperor, Avitus, or by the Visigoths of Aquitaine, who were persuaded to invade Spain and attack the Suebi. In 456 the Goths, aided by Burgundians and Franks, roundly defeated them at Campus Paramus near Astorga, attacked the Suebic centre of Braga and later caught their king Rechiarius and killed him. This defeat effectively ended Suebic authority in Spain outside the north-west. The Suebi continued to raid and plunder but their brief and brutal ascendancy was over. Some Suebi continued to live in their Galician fastness for over a century to come but they played no significant part in the course of Spanish history. In 585 their kingdom was finally merged with that of the Visigoths.

About the internal workings of the Suebic realm we know next to nothing. There appears generally to have been one

---

[1] E. A. Thompson, *Romans and Barbarians* (Madison, Wis. 1982), 161–87; R. Collins, *Early Medieval Spain* (London 1983), 20–4.

acknowledged king, though other leaders could lead raids into the territory of neighbours. Suebic rulers were considered important or dangerous enough to be sent embassies from Toulouse, or even Africa, but if any treaties were agreed they did not last long. Occasionally, marriage alliances were struck between Visigothic families and Suebic kings, but relations between the two peoples were not improved to any detectable extent. The Suebi were in matters of statecraft and diplomacy incorrigible: those very terms would scarcely have been intelligible to them. Before the massive defeat of 456, they did strike a series of gold *tremisses* (third of a *solidus*), most of them based on coins of the emperor Valentinian III (425–55), suggesting that they intended to take some part in the elementary economic system of barbarian Spain. But these issues seem to have petered out by about 460 and were not renewed later. The defeat at Campus Paramus damaged the unity of the Suebi for a considerable time. A series of warlords emerged after 456, little more than names to us: Framtane, Rechimund, Frumarius and Remismund. By the middle of the sixth century, a degree of unity had been restored, though by then the king of the Suebi ruled over no more than a part of Galicia.

The Christian faith had been accepted by Suebic leaders, through what agency we do not know. Rechiarius was a Catholic, unlike his predecessors who had all been pagans. What lay behind his surprising conversion is quite unfathomable. He was the first of the Germanic kings settled in the Empire to become an orthodox Catholic and we do not know how this came about. A king of the Suebi does not seem a likely object of the proselitizing zeal of Hispano-Roman priests, such zeal always being under strict control, especially where barbarians were concerned. Did he then come to the Catholic faith as a result of some more personal contact, through a wife, perhaps, or some other associate? The truth is beyond our reach. We can be fairly certain, however, that the conversion of Rechiarius, by whatever agency it was achieved, did not lead to the widespread acceptance of Christianity by his people. Hydatius would certainly have reported that if it had occurred. In fact he is wholly silent about the religion of the Suebi, eloquently so. When the Suebi did become Christians, it was Arian Christianity that they embraced and they were introduced to it about 465 by someone with evident Gaulish connections, a bishop with the unlikely name of Ajax.

The Vandals

After the mass crossing of the Rhine at the end of 406, the Vandals thrust southward through Gaul. Within three years their main body had reached the Pyrenees. In the early autumn of 409, they, the Alans and the Suebi swept across the mountain passes into Spain and found there lands that were poorly equipped to resist. After two years of revelling in these rich provinces, the Asding Vandals settled in Galicia and the Silings in the southern province of Baetica. At the instigation of Rome, Wallia and his Visigoths fell on these settlers in the south (above, p. 161) and threatened to remove them from the map entirely. But in 419 or 420 the Asdings moved south to join their brethren and some form of joint kingdom was built in Andalusia. We know little about this Vandal settlement in southern Spain and there may be little to know. It may have been in essence a barbarian army settled on Roman soil, living largely off the land and what could be plundered from nearby provincials. Shipping was to hand in the harbours and unlike most German invaders of the Empire they quickly learned the arts of seamanship and piracy. In 426 they were bold enough to raid Mauretania and the Balearic islands. Two years later the port and naval base of Cartagena was in their hands. When even the ample resources of Baetica began to run low, the wealth of Africa beckoned across the narrow strait. Threatened by an Imperial expedition to Baetica in 422, and encouraged by the *comes Africae* Bonifatius to move themselves bodily to Africa in his support, the Vandal leaders Guntheric and his illegitimate brother Gaiseric (or Geiseric or Genseric) prepared a great fleet for the largest single sea-borne movement of barbarians of which we know. Guntheric died suddenly as these preparations were going forward and Gaiseric was left as sole leader of the enterprise. In him the Vandals had one of the most effective of all barbarian leaders of the migration period. Militarily able, politically ruthless and diplomatically skilful,

Gaiseric outmatches all those German kings who led their people into fresh territory in the fifth century. He was not only a warrior-leader of massive authority; a century after his death, he would be spoken of as the cleverest of men. His conquest of north Africa, unlike most of the barbarian invasions of the fifth century, did not result in the easy accommodation of barbarians within the provincial order. For Gaiseric was more vigorously intent on pillage than most kings, and more determined to inflict defeat on the Roman Empire. A devoted Arian (according to one story, an apostate from the Catholic faith), his hatred of the Catholic Church was extreme. No bishop, priest, church or treasure was to be spared in the Vandal invasion.

In May 428, the Vandal nation and its Alan associates assembled on the Strait of Gibraltar, 80,000 we are told, of which number perhaps about a quarter were capable of bearing arms – by no means a formidable army when set against the paper-strength of the African provincial garrisons. But those provincial armies had not faced a major external foe for centuries and the frontier system along which they were deployed stretched for over 3,000 kilometres from the Atlantic to the Nile. Reinforcements of any kind could not be expected from Italy and Sicily as the Vandal fleet was already beginning to dominate much of the western Mediterranean. These weaknesses of the Roman forces still do not completely explain the rapid progress of the Vandals. A paralysis of will seems to have afflicted the Roman command when the Vandals arrived on the coast around Tangier. If opposition was offered, it was quickly brushed aside. Within two years only three minor cities in the coastal areas had been able to hold out against the invaders: Carthage, Cirta and Hippo Regius. The Vandals had been greatly helped in their eastward sweep by not having to spend much time on looking for supplies. The unprotected estates and the myriad farmsteads of the coastal belt provided all they needed, so that their energies could be directed against the towns, churches, cemeteries and villas. There may have been exaggeration about the savagery of the Vandal host as it drove across this peaceful land, for the massacres and looting may have appeared all the more horrifying in the rich and peaceful land in which they took place. But there is no doubting the horror and destruction which the Vandal host left behind it.[2]

The invaders were largely in control of the Mauretanian provinces and Numidia inside two years. Rome's offer of a *foedus* was the best that could be done in the circumstances, but it was far from enough to satisfy Gaiseric. The ancient and wealthy province of Africa Proconsularis, with its grain-lands and rich villa-estates, was his next target, even though this was forbidden by the *foedus* of 435. Carthage fell to the Vandals with surprising ease in 439. This provided them with an excellent base for naval operations in the western Mediterranean and in 440 a Vandal force landed in Sicily and threatened Italy. Again Gaiseric was bought off by a treaty. But opportunities to raid widely in the Mediterranean, from Spain to Greece, were too tempting to ignore. In 455, Spain and Italy were invaded and Rome itself sacked. Within the North African provinces there were naturally enough widespread confiscations of Roman land and other property. But many Roman proprietors were able to hold on to their estates, while some of the Vandals were seduced by the pleasurable life-style of an estate, adopting the manners and tastes of their Roman neighbours. Most of the Vandal settlers may have been settled after 439 in the area around Carthage. Others took possession of the fertile plain around Cherchel and Tipasa, and of the broad lands about the great cliff-stronghold of Constantine. There is no archaeology of Vandal Africa and it is unlikely that the subject will ever be extensive. A very small amount of Germanic metalwork has been recovered from the coastal regions, but it tells us little about those who carried it there. The splendid belt-fittings found at Ténès near Cherchel are more probably those of a late Roman officer than a Vandal.[3] The best hope of identifying Vandal occupation would seem to lie in study of late Roman levels within a well preserved coastal city. For those communities, or many of them, continued through the

---

[2] C. Courtois, *Les Vandales et l'Afrique* (Paris 1955) is the best short account of Vandal Africa. See also, H.-J. Diesner, *Der Untergang der römischen Herrschaft in Nordafrika* (Weimar 1964).

[3] J. Heurgon, *Le trésor de Ténès* (Paris 1958).

period of Vandal occupation, in altered circumstances. At Cherchel the forum was now flanked by timber booths instead of stately colonnades. At Carthage, houses were still being built in the sixth century and at Tipasa and Hippo Regius the old cities still housed communities after 500. But everywhere in Africa the divide between Vandals and the provincial population was wide and it never looked like being reduced. The Vandal regime in Africa did not soften during the century of its existence. It struck no roots into the soil and when the end came, it came quickly. In 533, a Byzantine army under Belisarius invaded Africa and within only a few months Vandal power was overthrown. It left virtually nothing behind it.

9
Franks, Alamanni and Burgundians

The Franks: from Gaul to Francia

Although the Franks receive their first mention in the historical record after the middle of the third century, it is possible that, like the Alamanni, the new grouping originated early in the third century or even late in the second.[1] The name, which is from the same root as the modern German word *frech* (meaning insolent, impudent), means 'courageous', 'bold', the kind of name that might well have been used by war-bands to describe themselves. For that is the likeliest origin of the Franks, groups of adventurers combining to attack the lower Rhine frontier as internal stresses weakened the effectiveness of the Roman forces. Several small tribes occupied the region between the Rhine, the Weser basin and the North Sea, some of them already mentioned in Roman sources of the first century: the Bructeri, Ampsivarii, Chamavi and Chattuari. These no doubt provided many of the early Franks, but other groups probably contributed warriors or were included under the general name by Roman writers. These included the Chauki and Frisians of the northern coastlands. The later Franks had very indistinct notions about their own origins, resorting to myth to give their

---

[1] E. Zollner, *Geschichte der Franken* (Munich 1941); P. Périn and L. -C. Feffer, *Les Francs* (2 vols; Paris 1987); E. James, *The Franks* (Oxford 1988).

ruling house some semblance of antiquity. Archaeology throws virtually no light on the origins and early history of the Franks, there being no distinctive cultural traits which define a bloc of people lying to the east of the lower Rhine. This state of affairs continues throughout the fourth century, when on several occasions Franks were in possession of parts of the Rhineland. Even in the first half of the fifth century, Franks are all but invisible in the archaeological record, and this in a region which has been studied in greater depth than most parts of Europe. It is a sobering reflection on the inability of archaeological material to reveal major episodes of population-change.

The military power of the Franks developed apace after the mid-third century. Along with the Alamanni and others, they raided Gaul freely between 250 and 275, the most devastating invasion being that of 274–5, in which the barbarians swept across all of Gaul. The Franks operated on sea as well as on land, raiding the Channel coasts and using the river-routes to attack far inland. One source reports that they invaded eastern Spain, and there seized ships with which they invaded Africa. This is not incredible, especially if the Frankish force included elements from the northern seaboard. The revival of Roman military strength from Diocletian's reign onward (AD 284–305) stabilized the Rhine frontier against the Franks. Groups of defeated Germans were settled on the land of northern Gaul at the end of the third century, there to till the soil and provide unspecified military service to the Roman army. These settlers, *laeti* as they were called, had a very humble status within the Empire, being only half-free and tied to the land on which they worked. At higher levels, Franks were able to enjoy far more rewarding service in the Empire. Several regiments of Franks are listed in the *Notitia Dignitatum* (early fifth-century list of commands and posts), while some leading commanders in the fourth-century armies were Frankish or part-Frankish by birth (above, p. 60).

The burials of Germanic warriors, among them no doubt Franks, have long been known in northern Gaul.[2] These graves

---

[2] H.-W. Böhme, *Germanische Grabfunde des 4. bis 5. Jahrhunderts zwischen unterer Elbe und Loire* (Munich 1974).

stand out from the main mass of Gallo-Roman burials of the late fourth and early fifth centuries, containing weapons and other war-gear, as well as rich grave offerings of pottery, glass and bronze. At Vermand and Monceau-le-Neuf, such graves lay in large inhumation cemeteries, but they also occur in small warrior-cemeteries or as isolated graves. The main concentration of these graves is between the Rhine and the Seine, though others lie east of the Rhine and the personal equipment they contain is also found in the northern coastlands. Some lay close to Roman forts like Oudenburg and Gellep, or other centres like Cologne. The cemetery of warriors and their families at Furfooz, near a hilltop stronghold in the Ardennes, may represent a small group of Germans established there to protect that place and its environs. Other graves, like those at Vert-la-Gravelle and Abbeville-Homblières, lay in rural locations and may have been connected with late Roman villa estates. Although not all these warriors need have been Franks, many probably were; their presence is a reminder of the mingling of provincial and barbarian populations at this date, leading to the creation of a mixed culture which was to provide the basis for the developed culture of the Franks.

There is no sign at this early date of any unified Frankish power. We hear of kings of the Franks but none of them appear to have ruled effectively or for long. Ambitious leaders seem to have found service with Rome far more remunerative. The military frontier on the lower Rhine was in ruins shortly after 400 and certainly by 420. In this region, power passed into the hands of Frankish leaders between 420 and 440, though Roman authority in the person of Aëtius was not yet moribund. He operated against the Franks in northern Gaul on several occasions, struck treaties with them and recruited aid from some of them in the Roman cause, as against the Huns in 451. A major victory over the Franks at Vicus Helena near Arras probably not long after 440 indicates how far the Franks had spread to the west by mid-century. After the Roman victory, the Frankish king Chlodio was recognized as a federate leader and left in possession of the region around Tournai, there to create a significant enclave of Frankish power. It is likely that this pattern, or something like it, was repeated elsewhere, for example in the Rhineland and in the Moselle valley about Trier.

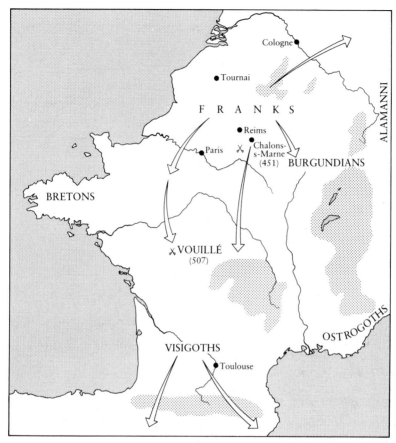

Figure 29 The Germanic kingdoms in Gaul.

The emerging picture is one in which minor kings founded their own power bases and later began to contend for paramount rule. The petty kingdom of Tournai made considerable progress between 450 and 480, first under Chlodio and then under Childeric. Childeric had apparently maintained the federate status of his Franks, while increasing his influence in western Gaul, to at least the Somme valley. The contents of his burial vault (he died in 481–2) reveal not only his wealth but also his adherence to a structure of power which was still late Roman in outline. His successor Chlodovech, or Clovis as he is more generally known, was to pursue a more ambitious path.

The Rhineland Franks have left remarkably little trace behind them of their activities in the fifth century. It is possible that they were far from numerous and tended to congregate in fairly limited areas at first. It might have been expected that one of those areas was around Cologne, once the leading city on the lower Rhine and a target for Frankish assaults in the fourth and early fifth centuries. Cologne still possessed its circuit of walls and some at least of its major buildings were presumably still usable. And yet there is scarcely a sign of Frankish presence in Cologne in the fifth and early sixth century. Not until the burial of aristocratic or royal personages in the north-east corner of the city in the sixth century is there any certain indication that Cologne numbered Franks amongst its population. Stray finds of Frankish metalwork and pottery within the walled area remain very scarce until the seventh century. This blank picture is modified by finds in the environs of the city. Frankish burials of the late fifth century are known at several locations, for example at the villa of Köln-Müngersdorf. But it still seems strange that so little was made of Cologne itself by the new masters of the region. One possibility is that a relatively limited part of the city was occupied by Franks and the place has so far eluded detection.

At one site on the lower Rhine, continuity between a later Roman site and its community and incoming Franks is attested with unusual clarity. This is the late Roman and Frankish cemetery at Krefeld-Gellep, sited close to the Roman fort and *vicus* (township) of Gelduba.[3] The inhumation of the late Roman dead continued here into the fifth century, a large proportion of the graves containing no grave-goods of any kind. About 400, a few graves contained the remains of military belts, knives and occasionally weapons. One object from a fourth-century grave, a silver disc-brooch with a setting of blue glass surrounded with granulated ornament, is a Germanic piece, perhaps brought to the lower Rhine by a high-born barbarian. Probably at least some of the occupants of the burials with military grave-goods also came from east of the

---

[3] R. Pirling, *Das römisch-fränkische Gräberfeld von Krefeld-Gellep* (Berlin 1966, 1974, 1979).

Rhine, to serve in late Roman units at Gelduba. During the fifth century, there was a steady increase of graves containing only Frankish artifacts, and by the end of that century two distinct cemeteries existed side by side. Throughout this long period, continuity of burial, and thus of settlement, was maintained. In the sixth century, princely burials appeared in the cemetery. The earliest is a superbly furnished warrior-grave, the equipment including a north Italian *Spangenhelm*, *spatha*, shield, javelins and knives, and parts of a saddle and reins. A massive gold finger-ring adorned with exuberant filigree work is set with a Roman intaglio. The richness of the gold and garnet work in the grave marks it out as the resting-place of a Frankish leader of some consequence. A *solidus* of Anastasius I (491–518) fixes the date after 500 and the other goods all belong to the first half of the sixth century. Another burial, in a large chamber once covered by a mound, contained the remains of a cart or burial-wagon, a rarity in a migration period grave, while a third, a double burial, was distinguished by its weaponry and parts of scale-armour, an even more exceptional find in western Europe at this date. These rich graves extend over most of the sixth century, beginning about 525. They seem to indicate important changes in the political structure of this lower Rhine region consequent upon the emergence of a dominant noble group, perhaps a single family. After 600, these clear social distinctions are no longer evident in the cemetery, even though it continued in use until the eighth century.

When Clovis succeeded his father Childeric in 482, the Franks were disposed in a number of separate enclaves across northern Gaul from the Channel to the Rhine. When he died, most probably in 511, the Frankish kingdom was unified, in control of most of Gaul, well on the way to being the most powerful Germanic power in the West and recognized by the other major powers of the time. His long reign was a succession of conquests, few of them easily won. First, and probably easiest, was the absorption of the last independent Gallo-Roman enclave, around Soissons. The bringing together of the several Frankish minor kingdoms up the Rhine was the obvious next step and it was achieved early in the 490s. This brought Clovis up against the Thuringians, expanding west from the

Elbe basin, and the Alamanni on the upper Rhine. His campaigns against the former were inconclusive, but he was able to push the Alamanni southward towards the Alps and out of the immediate way of the Franks. The final conquest of the Alamanni came later in the sixth century. The Burgundians were a tougher proposition, but Clovis had at least one success against them and had their assistance in his next and most important venture. For some years during the 490s, the Franks had mounted campaigns against the Visigoths in the south-west, without lasting success. Relations between the two kingdoms remained uneasy until, in 507, Clovis invaded Visigothic territory and won a clear victory at Vouillé, near Poitiers, killing the Visigothic king Alaric II. This signal success decisively turned the attention of the Visigoths towards Spain, but it also alerted Theoderic to a major change in the balance of power in the West. He dispatched an Ostrogothic force into southern Gaul to support his Visigothic kinsmen. But Clovis was undeniably the controlling force over the greater part of Gaul, and this must have had some influence on the decision of the Byzantine emperor Anastasius to make overtures to him and honour him with the consulship. In the aftermath of Vouillé, Clovis was quick to consolidate his position against the remaining Frankish leaders in Gaul, notably in the Rhineland, where reflections of closer connections with other Frankish regions are evident in the archaeological remains. When Clovis died in 511, after a reign of thirty years, there could be no doubt that the dominant power in western Europe was Francia.

The archaeology of the early Franks is distinguished by a striking number of royal and aristocratic graves, which provide an invaluable chronological framework as well as exceptional insight into the tastes and cultural outlook of noble Franks. The earliest royal burial was found at Tournai in 1653 and the splendid contents were illustrated and published not long after discovery by Chiflet, an Antwerp physician.[4] This was a fortunate circumstance, as most of the objects were stolen from the Imperial Art Gallery in Paris in 1831 and never recovered. A

---

[4] J. J. Chiflet, *Anastasis Childerici I Francorum Regis* . . . (Antwerp 1655). M. Kazanski and P. Périn, 'Le mobilièr funéraire de la tombe de Childéric Ier', *Revue Arch. de Picardie*, 3–4 (1988), 13.

signet-ring inscribed CHILDERICI REGIS leaves little room for doubt about the identity of the dead man and thus establishes a vital fixed point in early Frankish archaeology. The king was surrounded by a treasury of gold and other precious objects: two great swords with scabbards inlaid with garnet, gold buckles and belt-mounts, a gold torc, a crossbow-brooch, a hundred gold coins and twice as many silver pieces. Most striking of all perhaps are the 300 golden bees, symbols of eternal life, apparently sewn on to a richly brocaded cloak, a strong reminiscence of Roman Imperial authority. The Imperial echoes around this grave are unmistakable; and yet Childeric and his greater son Clovis were rulers of the very people who would extinguish the last vestiges of Roman power in the West.

A series of very splendidly furnished burials occurs in the Rhineland, all dating from the sixth and earlier seventh centuries and sharing much in common in the character of their contents. Others, somewhat later in date, occur in Rheinhessen, for example at Flonheim near Alzey. The occurrence of the burials in or near the Rhine valley, and in most cases within or close to major centres of late Roman authority, is notable as yet another indicator of the continuing attraction of Roman places, though not necessarily demonstrating direct continuity. The graves and their contents make it clear that the Rhineland was not merely a frontier province of a Frankish world which had its creative centre in northern France. The nobles for whom these burials were furnished could command the skill of the best craftsmen of the day and acquire, by one way or another, fine objects from widely scattered areas of Europe. A number of individual finds from the Rhine valley had hinted as much from the nineteenth century. Evidence which has come to light since 1955 provides a new basis for understanding Frankish power in the Rhineland and the socio-political structure which underpinned it.

From the end of the century is the warrior-burial at Morken on the little river Erft.[5] The position of this grave is of great interest for it lay within the ruins of a Roman villa and beneath

---

[5] K. Böhner, *Das Grab eines fränkischen Herren aus Morken im Rheinland* (Bonn 1959).

a later church, accompanied by other graves with humble furnishings. The Morken coffin contained the dead man, his *spatha* and belt. The noble possessed a *Spangenhelm* very similar to that from Gellep and almost certainly from the same Ostrogothic workshop. It had seen considerable use in battle and bore traces of a hefty blow on one side. The skull of the dead warrior also showed signs of the scars of battle. The rest of the grave-furniture was dominated by weaponry: shield, javelin, spear, *franciska* (throwing-axe); but more domestic objects were included: a bucket, glass, pottery vessels, a whetstone and a feather cushion. A fragment of silk textile is another sign of long-distance contact with the Mediterranean world.

The most superbly equipped grave – and perhaps most surprising of the series so far known – is a women's burial beneath the medieval Cathedral of Cologne, within the north-eastern corner of the Roman city. Close by lay the burial of a young boy, close in date and probably a near relative.[6] In the magnificent ornaments of the woman's grave-goods are some of the most impressive achievements of craftsmen working in the Frankish realm. The confident use of garnet *cloisonné* combined with deeply set filigree anticipates in the most striking fashion the work of Lombard jewellers in seventh-century Italy. The two graves are not only close together in date but there are close similarities between their respective furnishings. Coins in the woman's grave extend down to a half-siliqua of Athalarich of 526–34, giving a mid-sixth-century date to both interments. The woman, in her later twenties, had been laid to rest in fine garments and bedecked with ornaments. Vessels of glass and bronze were set at the foot of the grave along with a drinking-horn and three leather flasks. The boy, no more than six years old, had laid on a wooden bed surrounded by the paraphernalia of the warrior in miniature: *Spangenhelm* (with horn plates), *spatha*, *franciska*, *ango* (javelin), spear, arrows, shield and knife. He too had vessels for food and drink, and a small drinking-horn. Nothing in the Cologne graves helps to identify their occupants. We may guess at a princess or queen of the

[6] O. Doppelfeld, 'Das Frauengrab unter dem Chor des Kölner Doms', *Germania*, 42 (1964), 3.

Franks in Cologne, perhaps buried with her son, of the time of Theudebert, about 550.

At least one Frankish burial can be securely identified as royal and its occupant given a name. Beneath a small Merovingian basilica at St Denis, north of Paris, a grave containing a fine limestone sarcophagus had been placed over interments of the fifth century.[7] Within lay the body of a woman of mature years, probably in her forties. The corpse wore a fine linen shift and over it a knee-length silk dress, violet-blue in colour, belted at the waist. White linen stockings and fine leather shoes over them were held in place by cross-straps fastened by an armature of small buckles. Over the dress she wore a cloak of red-brown silk, lined with linen and with its cuffs ornamented with red satin embossed with gold thread. The jewellery is of comparable quality and brilliance. A gold and silver belt-buckle and plate lay across the lower chest, a gold and garnet disc-brooch at the throat and another on the chest. Gold ear-rings and hair-pins set off the lady's blonde hair and a long gold pin lay across the breast. Dress apart, grave-goods were virtually absent, the exception being a small glass flask wrapped in linen. On the left hand she wore a gold signet ring giving clear indication of her identity. The ring is inscribed ARNEGUNDIS REGINE (the latter word a monogram). The inscription puts beyond any reasonable doubt that this is Arnegunde, the second wife of Clothar and mother of Chilperic I, who would have died about 570–75, a date which is supported by the jewellery.

The settlements of the earliest Franks in the Rhineland and northern Gaul are now beginning to emerge, though well excavated sites are still few. It is likely that the majority of the sites occupied in the fifth and sixth centuries lie buried beneath villages still in existence today. Those sites that have become available for excavation may in many cases have been marginal to the main distribution of settlement or otherwise vulnerable to shifts in the occupation of the land. They may, therefore, not be fully representative of the range of settlement forms which existed in the migration period. The individual sites so

---

[7] A. France-Lanord and M. Fleury, 'Das Grab der Arnegundis in St. Denis', *Germania*, 40 (1962), 341.

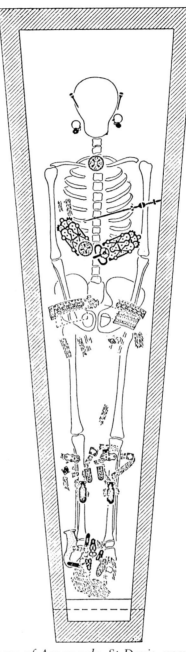

Figure 30 The grave of Arnegunde, St Denis, near Paris: a Frankish royal lady of the later sixth century.

far identified are relatively small. Nothing like the extensive villages of northern Germania has been encountered, though that does not mean that they did not exist.

The record of Frankish settlement west of the Rhine now extends back to the fourth century. At Neerharen-Rekem, 7 kilometres north of Maastricht, lay a small Roman villa, destroyed and abandoned in the third century.[8] After 350, a Germanic community established itself, or was established, here and it continued until the end of the fourth century. This was not a single farmstead of Frankish *coloni*. The buildings were mainly *Grubenhäuser*, but a number of large rectangular halls also existed. The site would not look out of place east of the Rhine or even on the northern coasts. A few kilometres away, at Donk, lay another German settlement of the later fourth century. It begins to look as though Franks were settled in the valley of the Meuse before 400 in greater numbers than has been recognized hitherto, and more detailed survey will increase the known record of sites. The valleys of both the Meuse and the Rhine are deeply covered by alluvium and this will mask settlements of this period, as of others.

Further south, in the hills of the Ardennes, there are other clear signs of German settlers in the later fourth century. About the middle valley of the Meuse lie a number of hilltop strongholds dating from the late Roman period. One, at Furfooz, has long been thought to have a military cemetery associated with it, and in some of the graves there were German objects indicating that at least some of the occupants had come from east of the Rhine. Another of these hilltop fortifications, at Vireux-Molhain, has been more recently examined, with even clearer results.[9] This was reoccupied in the late fourth century with a small garrison, perhaps twenty-five strong. The burials in the cemetery are predominantly military graves and among the equipment are throwing axes and other non-Roman weapons. In the few women's graves are two brooches of certain Germanic origin. The Germanic presence at Vireux-Molhain is

[8] G. de Boe, 'De opgravingscampagne 1984 te Neerharen-Rekem', *Arch. Belgica*, 1 (1985), 53.

[9] J. -P. Lemant, *Le cimetière et la fortification du Bas-Empire de Vireux-Molhain, Dép. Ardennes* (Mainz 1985).

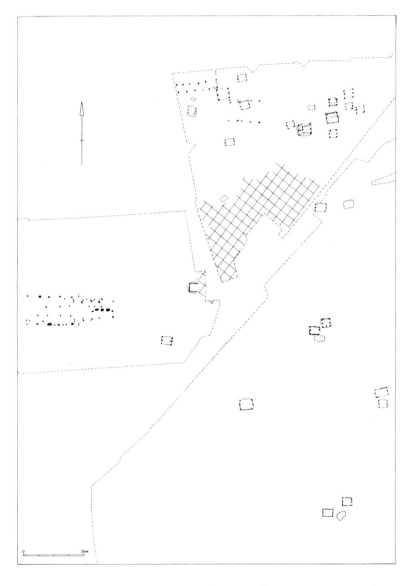

Figure 31 The settlement at Neerharen-Rekem, near Maastricht, a Germanic settlement of about AD 400 within the Roman provinces.

unusually well dated by coins in the graves. The main period of occupation was at the end of the fourth century and the first decades of the fifth century. A *solidus* of Honorius in mint condition is the latest coin, this suggesting an end to the military occupation about 430.

There are signs on other sites of a close relationship between the earliest Frankish settlements and the late Gallo-Roman pattern. At Berry-au-Bac in Picardy a late Roman settlement may have formed the focus for a group of Frankish buildings, mainly *Grubenhäuser*, but including larger halls. The possibility of continuous settlement here from late Gallo-Roman to Frankish is real, as it is at a number of late Roman villa sites in north and central Gaul. Frankish cemeteries frequently lie on or near the sites of Roman villas, and in many cases give way in turn to an early medieval village with a focus on a Carolingian or later church. The sequence of villa, cemetery and church is so widespread in Gaul that either continuous occupation or the deliberate choice of old sites must be invoked to explain it. Unfortunately, the suggestive sequence has yet to be fully elucidated by archaeological means.

Later Frankish settlements are unimpressive in their planning and component structures, but may not be representative of what once existed. One of the most fully excavated villages is that at Gladbach in the Neuwieder Becken, where a cluster of *Grubenhäuser* lay around at least one substantial rectangular hall with several rooms. Other substantial hall-like buildings are known in the Rhineland, at Rhode and Hochlamark, but these in no way approach the northern long-houses in scale. At Brebières in the Pas-de-Calais an agglomeration of *Gruben-häuser* dating from the sixth and seventh centuries was chiefly concerned with base trades and may have been an ancillary settlement to the royal villa at Vitry-en-Artois nearby.[10] More substantial structures seem to have existed at Vitry itself, and at Juvincourt-et-Damary in the Alisne, so that the prevailing picture of rather squalid hovels is fairly certainly false. As yet, chieftainly residences have not been located, though they clearly existed. The most distinguished probably lay within Roman

[10] P. Demolon, *Le village mérovingien de Brebières* (Arras 1972).

towns and cities, where the circumstances of survival are far from favourable.

The death of Theoderic in 526 removed the final block to Frankish expansion over the remaining parts of Gaul. First, the weakened kingdom of the Burgundians was attacked in 532–4 and its king Godomar captured and killed. The chequered history of this people was thus brought to an end, though they retained their own code of law and their leading families were not deprived of their lands. And all sense of Burgundian unity was not lost for ever. Only Provence under its Visigothic rulers remained, and not for long. Here the Franks were aided by the revival of east Roman power in the western Mediterranean. Belisarius was at this time ending Vandal rule in Africa and on the point of invading Italy. The emperor Justinian recognized the strength of the Franks and was happy to enlist their aid with money. When Belisarius captured Rome, the Ostrogothic king Witigis saw the intervention of the Franks as his only hope of averting disaster and offered them an even larger sum than the emperor for their services. He also offered all that part of Provence that the Goths had under their control. The offers were received and the Franks thus advanced their frontier up to the Alps. The new territory gained was partitioned by the surviving descendents of Clovis.

The geography of modern France was now virtually complete. The ambition of the Frankish kings, however, was not yet satisfied. Now Italy seemed to offer rich prizes. In 539 Theudebert led an army of Franks, Burgundians and others into the north Italian plain and destroyed there first a Gothic force and then the Imperial army, both of which had expected the Franks to come as allies. But no long-term success resulted from this incursion. The Franks were soon forced by famine and disease to pull back. Their leader could claim one gain: Justinian recognized the Franks as the rulers of Gaul and the name of a Frankish king appeared on coinage for the first time. Theudebert did not abandon his ambitions of conquest in Italy and even, some believed, of attacking Constantinople. But injuries sustained during hunting put paid to all such projects in 548. By then, the power of the Franks was evident to all. Thenceforward, though frequently weakened by internal strife which could be savagely pursued, the kingdom of the Franks was one of the principal players in the power politics of Europe and the Mediterranean. Its true origins lay not east of the Rhine, but in the ruins of the Roman West, a fact acknowledged by its greatest king, Charlemagne, who had himself crowned emperor of the Romans in 800 and who saw his residence at Aachen in northern Gaul as a New Rome.

The Alamanni

The Alamanni are first named in our sources in AD 213, when Caracalla campaigned successfully against them beyond the upper German frontier. The name implies a confederacy: 'all men', 'everybody'. The area occupied by the new grouping had been held by the Hermunduri and Suebi in earlier days, and these tribes presumably made up a large part of the new grouping. But elements from other peoples, displaced in the disturbances of the late second century, probably also made their contribution. The weaknesses that began to show in the frontier between Rhine and Danube from the early third century may have prompted the Alamanni to step up their offensive action. In 233, they again attacked the frontier line in strength, breaching it and causing widespread damage. Over the next twenty years they kept up the pressure and finally caused the now exposed salient to be abandoned by Rome in 260.[11]

Very little is known of the internal organization of the Alamanni in the third and fourth centuries. The confederacy was evidently a loose one, for we hear not only of several kings ruling at the same time, but also of numerous local princelings. Even in the fifth century, a centralized power seems not to have emerged among the Alamanni, the broken country of south-western Germany which they occupied not being conducive to political unity. Their settlement of the region between the Rhine and Danube abandoned by Rome was not achieved for some decades after the fall of the frontier. By about 300, a piecemeal takeover of the land had begun, as had the regular employment of Alamannic soldiers in the Roman forces. But attacks on the

[11] R. Christlein, *Die Alamannen* (Stuttgart 1978).

Roman provinces continued in the fourth century and intensi-
fied after 350. The emperor Julian faced Alamannic war-bands
in eastern Gaul, defeating them several times, most decisively
at a battle near Strasbourg in 357. But the Alamanni's military
power continued to wax in the late fourth century and they
remained a formidable force east of the upper Rhine and in
the region north of the Alps. They did not, however, move far
into Gaul and settle there, and as the fifth century progressed
their bounds were increasingly constricted by the rising power
of the Franks. In the longer term, this would mean that they
never founded an enduring kingdom, nor created a recognizably
distinct enclave between the two great rivers and the Alps.

   In 406–7 Alamanni played an important part in the massive
invasion of Gaul and about that date small numbers of them
began to settle in Alsace and in the Pfalz. The rise of Frankish
power to the north compelled them to look southward for new
territory, along the Rhine and into the Alpine valleys. By the
mid-fifth century they were able to raid deep into eastern Gaul,
south into Italy and east into Noricum. Their defeat by Clovis
in the Rhineland in 497 seems to have been a temporary setback
at most, and by 500 they were taking possession of the more
fertile parts of the Alpine region from Augst, near Basel, to
Windisch (Vindonissa), near Brugg. They felt the attraction of
the north Italian plain at this time but were not strong enough
to settle there in force. The plain of Raetia was the last of their
major acquisitions, early in the sixth century. Thereafter, their
activities were limited by powerful neighbours, particularly
the Franks, with more centralized seats by authority. By 536
Alamannic territory was under the control of a commander
answerable to the king of the eastern Franks, and this uneasy
suzerainty was maintained until the end of Frankish rule in
Germany. Alamannia retained its territorial identity until
Charles Martel ('the Hammer'; *c.*688–741) absorbed it in his
empire early in the eighth century. But in all other respects
Alamannic identity had long before been submerged in the
power of the Franks.

   Early Alamannic settlement in south-western Germany has
been greatly illuminated since 1970. The military employment
of Alamannic warriors and their chiefs by Roman commanders
is well attested in the historical sources. It is now clear in the

archaeological record on the upper Danube frontier which faced the Alamanni themselves. The fourth-century cemetery at Neuburg contains a significant number of military graves which include Germanic material in their contents.[12] Three chronological divisions exist within the cemetery. In the first, dating from 330 to 360, Germanic troops serving in a mixed garrison attached to a small fortification are in evidence. In the next phase, from 360 to 390, the Germanic connections of the equipment are even clearer and they point to the Elbe valley as the origin of its bearers. Finally, from the late fourth to the early fifth centuries, the links were with the lower Danube and the northern Balkans. There are indications elsewhere on the upper Danube frontier of Alamannic groups on Roman service, at Günzburg, for example, and other forts north of Lake Constance.

Settlements which were entirely independent of Rome have also begun to appear, notably a series of hilltop strongholds which were probably the seats of the Alamannic *regales* and *reguli* (petty rulers) mentioned by Ammianus Marcellinus. The most fully studied is the Runder Berg at Urach.[13] Here, an ovoid area 70 metres long and 50 metres across was surrounded by a substantial timber rampart in the late third or early fourth century. Within lay many timber buildings of fourth-century date and other buildings occupied the lower slopes of the hill. The latter may have housed craftsmen dependent on the lord of the stronghold above. Centres of local power like this may have existed in some numbers in the fourth and early fifth centuries. The Reissberg near Bamberg was certainly occupied by German settlers during this period, as was the Gelbe Burg near Dittenheim, though its defences are at present dated to the fifth century. The prevailing pattern of Alamannic settlement at this time is far from fully recorded and may be irrecoverable in detail. Many of the early sites of occupation probably continued in use into more stable times and now lie deeply buried beneath medieval and modern villages. This means that the lesser settlements so far uncovered may be untypical and thus

---

[12] E. Keller, *Das spätrömischen Gräberfeld von Neuburg an der Donau* (Munich 1979).
[13] Not fully published. Short account in Christlein, *Alamannen*.

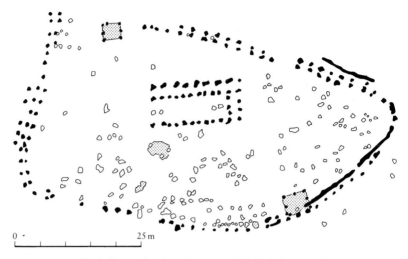

*Figure 32 The hilltop chieftainly stronghold of the Runder Berg, near
Urach, Germany: an Alamannic noble residence of the fourth century
and later.*

no reliable guide to the main development of Alamannic land-
taking. Those settlers who moved into lands which had until
about 260 formed part of the Roman provinces of upper Germany and Raetia may further have been influenced by Roman
provincial land-use. Certainly, some Roman villas in the old
agri decumates (upper Germany between the upper Rhine and
Danube) did attract attention from incoming Alamanni. The
Praunheim villa, near the Roman town of Nida (Heddernheim),
was occupied by barbarians, who seem to have constructed
dry-stone walls within the old structure, and the villa at
Holheim was also partially restored by its German occupants.
At Baldingen, a series of Roman gold coins, relative rarities on
late villa sites, and a Roman military brooch, may indicate a
group of Germans who had settled here after service with the
Roman armies. It must be seen as likely that the immigrant
Alamanni encountered and cohabited with Roman provincials
in these areas. The total removal of the earlier population after
260 can scarcely have occurred.

The Burgundians

The Burgundians belonged to the relatively shadowy world of the east Germanic peoples, little known to the Roman Empire.[14] Pliny had ranged them, along with the Goths, in the Vandalic group of peoples and Ptolemy located them east of the Semnones between the Oder and the Vistula. Bands of Burgundian warriors took part in the raids on the upper Danubian provinces in the later third century and some were able to settle in the Main–Neckar area by 290. But the main grouping remained in eastern Germania, on the Oder and to the east of it. Archaeologically, this region is characterized by an independent culture, the Lebus-Lausitz or Luboszyce culture, with connections towards the south-east and the Przeworsk culture of southern Poland and adjacent Russia. Warrior burials dominate the record of cemeteries, richly furnished chieftains' graves being generally rare. An elevated social group is, however, evident in a number of rich women's graves and the hoard of gold rings found at Cottbus.

The Main–Neckar Burgundians steadily increased their influence during the fourth century and were probably joined by other westward-moving groups. In the crossing of the Rhine in 406–7, Burgundians under Gundohar seized a tract of land around the Worms, Strasbourg and Speyer and won recognition of their presence there from Honorius. They joined forces with the Gallic usurper Jovinus to attack southern Gaul in 412–13, and in 435 Gundohar led them in a search for new territory in Gallia Belgica, an expedition which Aëtius promptly brought to an end. In the following year, a Burgundian force of 20,000, again under Gundohar, was surrounded by an invading Hun army and wiped out. This disaster, which effectively ended Burgundian expansion in Gaul, provided the germ for the epic poem relating the legend of the Nibelungen, which beneath its chivalric veneer recounts a confusion of several stories of the time of Germanic expansions along and west of the Rhine.

Archaeological testimony to the Burgundian settlement on

---

[14] L. Schmidt, *Die Ostgermanen* (Munich 1941), 129–94.

the Rhine and Neckar is scarce. A number of later fourth- and fifth-century burials is known and in some of them material elements from far to the east put in the occasional appearance. But specific assignation to the Burgundians is always difficult to demonstrate. The cemetery at Lampertheim illustrates the problem well. The fifty-six graves here recall the furnishings and burial rites much further east, perhaps in the upper Elbe basin. But the dead in the cemetery could as well be Alamanni as Burgundians. Other graves with eastern objects occur at Gross-Gerau and Gerlachsheim, but again we cannot be sure about the origins of their occupants. At least one Burgundian princeling, Hariulf the son of Hanhavold, found his way into high Imperial service, in the emperor's bodyguard, as his tombstone of about 400 at Trier informs us. There will have been others who took this path to fortune. But about the Burgundian enclave we know hardly more than where it lay and that while residing there the population was converted to Arian Christianity before the disastrous defeat of 436.

The Burgundians were still numerous and powerful enough to earn federate status in 443 and along with it a new area of settlement in Sapaudia, by which is meant southern Switzerland and the adjacent part of eastern France, where their presence might assist with the control of the Alpine passes. They served Rome as faithfully as any other federates in the fifth century, fighting against Attila in 451 and against the Suebi in 456. But on returning from Spain they took possession of a large area of central Gaul around Lyons and Vienne and later consolidated their hold here after being briefly pushed out by Majorian. By the end of the fifth century they had taken over much of eastern Gaul as far south as the Alpes Maritimes.

Later there were to be opportunities for enlarging their realm. This region of Gaul had been little affected by the events surrounding the collapse of Roman authority in the early fifth century and had not been settled by any sizeable barbarian grouping before the Burgundian entry. Several of the late Roman towns and castella at places like Aventicum (Avenches) Lousonna (Lausanne) and Eburodunum (Yverdon) still contained a thriving and active Roman provincial population. Churches were maintained and burial of the dead was still being conducted outside the walls of the main strongholds.

Romance dialects were spoken and the motifs used on fine metalwork were those of the late Roman world. It is, then, no surprise that there are frequent signs of close relationships between Burgundian settlers and the surviving provincial population. Burial-places were shared, as is seen at Sezegnin-Avuzy near Geneva and at Monnet-la-Ville in the Jura. It is a safe deduction that such mixed communities also shared their settlements. The Burgundian nobility seem to have recognized from an early date the advantages to be gained from co-operation with Gallo-Roman landowners, some of whom were to achieve positions of high authority in the kingdom. The kings were concerned to establish good relations with the Church and its bishops. Orosius reports that the Burgundians embraced the Catholic faith early in the fifth century, but if they did there was a later switch to Arianism. Possibly some were Catholics shortly after their entry into the Empire and later adopted the faith of many of their Germanic neighbours.

The area settled by the Burgundians was broadly that bounded by the Rhone to the south, Lakes Geneva and Neuchâtel to the east and the Saône to the west and north.[15] The distribution of cemeteries suggests a denser concentration of settlement about the two lakes and a looser scattering on the upper Saône. But this pattern is misleading. The fertile plain between Rhone and Saône will obviously have attracted early settlers and there was indeed a clear tendency for the Burgundians to expand into the area of Lyons and Vienne before 460. Lyons itself was occupied by the Burgundian king in 470 and during the years 465–75 there was a move further south into northern Provence. To the north, particular targets were the area of Langres (held by 485) and Nevers. Auxerre and a part of its territory was briefly in Burgundian possession before it was handed to the Franks under the terms of a treaty. Of the several urban centres in their territory, Lyons and Geneva enjoyed especial favour. The imposing Roman past of Lyons made it the obvious centre for kings whose admiration for Rome was keen or keener than any other barbarian people.

---

[15] R. Moosbrugger-Leu, *Die Schweiz zur Merowingerzeit* (Berne 1971), vol. B, 14–20.

But Geneva was also prominent. Gundobad had a residence there and about 500 renewed its Roman defences. There was also an important church here, now revealed beneath the basilica of St Pierre.

The material culture of the settlers in the Burgundian realm is mixed and it reveals very clearly the mingling of the early intruders with a lively Gallo-Roman population. Few distinctive traits are evident before the late fifth century when certain types of belt-sets and buckles began to figure. Richly ornamented brooches and other dress-ornaments were not common (or at least were not placed in the graves) and large weapons and items of war-gear are much less frequent than among the grave-goods of the Franks and Alamanni. Inhumation was the rule from the beginning, but a small number of cremations appear in some cemeteries (e.g. Monnet-la-Ville), marking the continuation of renewal of links with the area of Burgundian settlement east of the Rhine. Sumptuously furnished burials have not yet been recorded, though these may lie close to or in churches which have not been examined on any scale. Aristocratic groups are indicated by a few cemeteries, including that at Charnay near Chalon-sur-Saône with its series of rich graves. This cemetery and others like it may represent the deliberate plantation of warriors in strategic positions on major routes. Certainly the Burgundians continued to perform their function as a buffer against expansionist neighbours. In 454 and again in 472 they pushed the Alamanni out of the Saône valley and kept the Visigoths from crossing the Rhone between 469 and 475 and seizing territory on the east bank. The last thirty years of the fifth century saw the peak of Burgundian power, under Chilperic I and Gundobad. After 500, the main threat came from the mounting strength of the Franks, a fact recognized by some Burgundians who were prepared to listen to overtures from Clovis and thus assist a Frankish takeover. The border with the Franks was briefly stabilized early in the sixth century, but in 532 the Burgundians suffered a major defeat at the hands of the Franks at Autun and soon afterwards lost their independence to the heirs of Clovis. The kingdom was swallowed up in the empire of the Franks, though the Burgundian inheritance was still to be recalled in medieval France. As federates the Burgundians had performed their task well. As independent

Germanic rulers they were much less successful. The land they occupied was hemmed in by the Alps to the east and by powerful neighbours to the north and west. The brief success of the kingdom was probably due at least in large part to the wealth and vigour of the surviving Gallo-Roman landowners. When their world began to collapse, the Burgundians went down with it.

The known cemeteries, and especially those in the western Alps, are very closely related to the pattern of Roman roads, notably those between Lakes Geneva and Neuchâtel and the road running from Yverdon to Solothurn around the northern flank of Lake Neuchâtel. Nothing illustrates more clearly the link between the Burgundians and the Gallo-Roman settlement-geography. These cemeteries are most probably mixed in their ethnic character, the provincial population taking over features of Burgundian burial rites. The individual objects which reveal this most clearly are the so-called Daniel buckles, rectangular buckle-plates with a scene of a human figure set between two monstrous creatures. Several of these buckle-plates also bear Latin inscriptions and a few at least were probably reliquaries. The surviving use of Latin on such minor objects as well as on tombstones and other stone panels is merely a reflection of the relative strength of Latin learning and education in the kingdom until well into the sixth century, encouraged by the Gallo-Roman senatorial families which still took an important part in the direction of the administrative order. The Burgundian kings came closer than any other Germanic monarchs to the furtherance of late Roman provincial administration.

10

The Northern Peoples

The Saxons and Frisians

Although first mentioned in the second century, the Saxons came to serious notice in the later third, when they appeared as sea-raiders along with the Franks. Ptolemy had located them between the Elbe and the base of the Jutland peninsula, but in the later Roman period their name seems to have been generally applied to the inhabitants of the lower Weser and Elbe valleys and the adjacent coastlands. The tribe of the Chauki may have been gathered up into an enlarged grouping before the fourth century and there were certainly connections with other peoples in the region, including the Anglii. The sea-raids on northern Gaul and Britain continued in the fourth century, intensifying in the later decades, and into the fifth, when settlement began in south-eastern Britain and in Gaul. Saxons also seem to have moved southward by land into the area between the Rhine and the Ijssel in Holland. The increased Saxon interest in Britain from the early fifth century seems to have taken most of the pressure off the lower Rhine, from this quarter at least. But the Saxon people remained a strong force in northern Germany until they were finally brought under Frankish control by Charlemagne in the eighth century.

The political organization of the early Saxons is scarcely known. The names and activities of no great leaders are recorded and there is little sign of any strong centralized power. The Saxons of the third and fourth centuries seem to have been organized in war-bands, constantly forming and reforming for

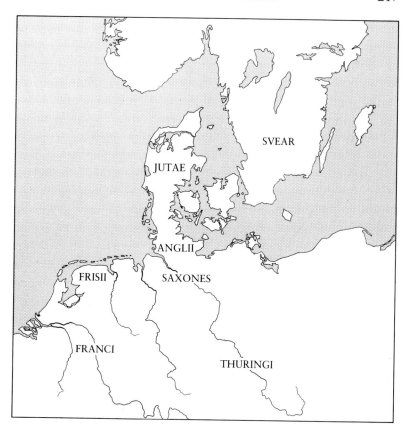

Figure 33 The northern Germanic peoples: AD 400–700.

particular enterprises. It is highly likely that the name 'Saxon' was applied by terrified provincials to any group of warriors who appeared from the northern seas. There will have been little inducement to make enquiries about their precise tribal affiliation. The loose structure of the Saxon confederacy probably continued through the fifth century. This was a period of great change in the northern coastlands. Many settlements were abandoned in the first half of the century and not reoccupied. This was partly due to migration to Britain and elsewhere, partly to a major redistribution of settlement in the Saxon region. This is also seen in the record of some of the great cremation cemeteries. Many came to an end before 450; others began in the fifth century and continued until the eighth or later. The best studied of the latter is the cemetery at Liebenau, near Nienburg in the Weser valley.[1] This began about 400 and was still in use in the mid-ninth century. The rites of inhumation and cremation were both followed in the disposal of the dead, both grave forms containing fairly rich furnishings, in contrast to the simple urns of many Saxon cemeteries. The grave-goods at Liebenau are of outstanding interest as they reveal close connections with the Thuringian area to the south and with the Merovingian Franks to the west. The links with Francia are evident in other Saxon cemeteries, but here they are revealed with unusual clarity. Political connections, sealed by the interchange of gifts, may be suspected in addition to trade. The Liebenau graves are untouched by Christian practice until the eighth century at the earliest. Eleven separate horse-burials lay in the cemetery, presumably those of mounts belonging to leading warriors. The latest human graves date between Widukind's baptism in 785 and the middle of the ninth century.

The movement of Saxons and others to Britain in the fifth and sixth centuries was followed by reorganization of the northern mainland peoples. The Angles disappeared from the scene, their land in Angeln deserted for a time and then colonized by Danes and Slavs. The Frisians extended their territory to the east and the Varini, hitherto shadowy but known to Tacitus four centuries earlier, tried to take over land left untenanted by migration. The Saxons who remained in northern Germany were still a powerful people, well able to extend their borders to the south and south-west. During the seventh century they occupied Westphalia, part of Hessen and the valleys of the Ruhr and Lippe. The last brought them to areas already disputed with the Franks and there their advance was halted. In the following century, they were defeated and subjected by Pippin the Short (first of the Carolingian dynasty, 714–68) and Charlemagne.

The settlement of Saxons in Gaul is often forgotten, perhaps because until the 1970s there was little archaeological evidence

---

[1] A. Genrich, 'Der Friedhof bei Liebenau in Niedersachsen', in *Ausgrabungen in Deutschland, 1950–75* (Berlin 1975), 17.

for it. But it did occur and in certain areas was of considerable significance. The most enduring Saxon settlement in Gaul was that in the Calvados around Bayeux, the Saxones Baiocassini, established in the fifth century and twice mentioned by Gregory of Tours in the context of relations with the Bretons.[2] Chilperic sent them off to fight against the Bretons under Waroch, by whom they were heavily defeated. Later, in the late sixth century, Fredegund made them reinforce the Breton army against her enemy Guntram and again they suffered heavy casualties. Recognizable Saxon material is now appearing in the region occupied by this group of northerners. Sixth-century graves at Giberville in the Calvados contain not only hand-made Saxon pottery, but also disc-brooches and at least one square-headed brooch. Another cemetery in the Calvados, at Sannerville, has produced fifth-century Saxon pottery and brooches with Saxon affinities. Another group of Saxons had penetrated to the western coast of Gaul and established themselves on islands at the mouth of the Loire. It may have been one of the leaders of this group, one Adovacrius, who campaigned in the Loire valley in 464. They maintained an independent existence until the late sixth century and were then converted to Christianity by the bishop of Nantes. Yet others, perhaps the most numerous group, took land in the coastal plain between Boulogne and Calais and extended south to the Somme. These, too, have begun to appear in the archaeology of the region, for example in the fifth- and sixth-century graves at Nouvien-en-Pontieu (Somme). After the late sixth century, they were submerged in the regional cultures of Merovingian Gaul.

We hear little about the Frisii in the later Roman Empire, the name Saxones being applied to the peoples of the coastland of Holland as well as northern Germany. But a Frisian identity was maintained and in the fifth century they again emerge, though into a twilight. The coastal lands were affected by a major marine transgression in the fourth and fifth centuries and this brought about a marked decrease in population. On their southern borders, on the lower Rhine, the rising power of the Salian Franks was a mounting threat: by the sixth century

---

[2] Gregory of Tours, *History of the Franks*, V, 19; X, 9.

the Frisii could be called a people under Frankish control. However that may be, there is no doubt about the extent of Frankish cultural influence among them, and the political weakness of the Frisii, as well as their restricted space, may have been a spur to their more adventurous sons to seek their fortune in trade far from their homeland.[3] For others, migration beckoned, to Britain, according to Procopius, and to northern Gaul. Culturally, there were natural links with the Saxon area in the Elbe and Weser coastlands. In the late fourth century, cemeteries of mixed cremations and inhumations began to appear in Friesland, the grave-forms and furniture being broadly similar to those east of the Ems. Rich graves do not commonly occur, an exception being a woman's burial in the cemetery at Zweelo which contained a composite silver disc-brooch and an equal-armed brooch, along with a necklace of amber beads and another of glass beads. This dates to about 450. The Zweelo cemetery began with inhumations aligned north–south, later replaced by east–west interments among which lay horse-burials.

The detailed history of Germanic settlement in southern Britain is a well-developed subject of its own and one which cannot be adequately summarized in a book of this kind.[4] But the migration of settlers from the northern coastlands into the Roman provinces of Britannia had such an impact on the island, and on the later history of western Europe, that it may not be ignored entirely. The historical record of the migration of northern Germans into Britain and the subsequent emergence of Anglo-Saxon polities there is far from impressive, especially for the earliest phases. Interpretation of the two main accounts, those of Gildas and Bede, is fraught with difficulties, too often made light of in the past. The contribution of archaeology, for so long centred on excavation of cemeteries and the stylistic analysis of metalwork, has since the 1960s begun to offer more broadly based approaches to early Anglo-Saxon studies, most tellingly in the field of settlement. The clarification of chron-

---

[3] S. Lebecq, *Marchands et navigateurs frisons du haut moyen âge* (2 vols; Lille 1983).

[4] J. Campbell (ed.), *The Anglo-Saxons* (Oxford 1982); J. N. L. Myres, *The English Settlements* (Oxford 1986) is dated in its approaches.

ology, both of pottery and metalwork, which has been won since the 1970s in northern Germany and Denmark in particular, has had major repercussions for studies of early Anglo-Saxon England, establishing for the first time beyond reasonable doubt the beginnings of Germanic settlement in the east of the island. There is much still to be achieved, but at least a reliable framework for the subject now exists.

The migrants to Britain came from the coastlands about the Elbe and Weser estuaries, from Schleswig-Holstein, especially the region of Angeln, from northern Holland and from at least parts of the Jutland peninsula. This much is revealed by the historical sources and substantially supported by archaeology. The stimuli to migrate were probably various, including a deterioration of living conditions in the coastal areas, a rising population and, not least, a growing awareness of the opportunities for material advancement now opening across the North Sea. As elsewhere in the western provinces, the defenders of Roman Britain relied to some extent on barbarian units and barbarian officers from the later third century onward. The formal ending of Roman rule by 410 did not mean the end of all efforts to protect Britain from external attacks, the most serious of which came from sea-borne Saxons and others. It was a natural reaction of those who assumed power in Britain after 410 to continue to employ Germanic troops and perhaps to increase their numbers. For their part, the Germans who were recruited will have seen no significant break with the practice of the past: they were joining a provincial army just as their predecessors had done. But after a generation or so, the breakdown of central power in Britain would have allowed the German forces a much freer hand in dictating the course of events. Against such a background, the accounts of Gildas and Bede make general sense, even though much is unexplained and probably inexplicable. The employment of imported Germanic troops, at first in small numbers, later reinforced, was effective early on, but soon the incomers demanded greater rewards and then broke out in a destructive mutiny. Later on, the Germans went home. This is the essence of Gildas's account, of the mid-sixth century, and it formed the basis for Bede's fuller narrative of about 730. There are puzzling features here, not least the Saxon return to their homeland, but it is likely that Gildas had access to at least one fifth-century source and what he says seems to reflect a tradition which rests on a foundation of fact, and one, moreover, which is entirely credible within the circumstances of fifth-century Britain.

Archaeological evidence for the earliest settlement of northern Germans in Britain has been greatly enlarged since 1960.[5] The earliest Anglo-Saxon cemeteries and settlements appear to lie in the region between the lower Thames and Norfolk, with indications of others in Lincolnshire and Kent. On the northern shore of the Thames estuary at Mucking, a group of Germans was established at a date which cannot have been long after 400, evidently under the supervision of officers who wore uniforms of late Roman style.[6] The early pottery from Mucking is very close in character to that from late deposits at Feddersen Wierde, suggesting that some of the migrants had arrived on the Thames direct from the north German coast. Whether they did so entirely on their own initiative or were settled there as an act of policy on the part of the late Romano-British authority (whatever that may have been) is unclear. The fact that troops with equipment of late Roman type were present suggests the latter case. In East Anglia, two particularly striking instances of early Anglo-Saxon settlement present themselves. Outside the walls of the small Roman town of Caister-by-Norwich lay a large Germanic cremation cemetery, in which the earliest burials date from about or shortly after 400.[7] Of several possible explanations of the presence, the likeliest is that these Anglo-Saxons were established at this place and given land on the surrounding territory by those responsible for the security of the town and its community early in the fifth century. The occurrence of other early Germanic cemeteries close to Roman towns and cities in eastern England, for instance at Leicester, Ancaster and Great Chesterford, demonstrates that this was not an isolated case. At West Stow in Suffolk, however, the

---

[5] H. W. Böhme, 'Der Untergang der römischen Herrschaft in Britannien', *BRGK* 68 (1987), 86.

[6] H. F. Hamerow, 'Anglo-Saxon settlement, pottery and spatial development at Mucking, Essex', *BROB* 37 (1987), 245.

[7] J. N. L. Myres and B. Green, *The Anglo-Saxon Cemeteries at Caister by Norwich and Markshall* (London 1973).

early Anglo-Saxon presence was apparently not related to an existing Romano-British settlement.[8] Here, a village community came into existence early in the fifth century and survived for two centuries or more. It lay at a distance from any Roman town or sizeable villa, though it may possibly have lain within the bounds of a villa-estate. Precisely how and why this group of Germans was settled here is still obscure, but there is no doubt that they were here about the time that Roman authority in Britain was coming to an end.

It is not surprising that Kent figures prominently in the account by Bede (but not in that of Gildas) of the Germanic migrations into Britain. His indication is that Kent was settled by Jutes and that the Jutes came from Jutland. The claim of a Jutish Kent has for long been debated, but there is now sufficient archaeological testimony to connections between Jutland and Kent, especially in jewellery and bracteates, to treat Bede's assertion with respect. Kent lay close to a northern Gaul that was increasingly Frankish in its material culture and some reflection of that proximity is to be expected in the archaeology of the region. And it is clear enough, in the Frankish radiate and bird-brooches of cemeteries like Faversham and Lyminge, in imports of glass from the Rhineland and even Frankish pottery flasks. Frankish weaponry, too, puts in an occasional appearance. But there is no demonstration of a movement of Franks into Kent. Contact between Gaul and Kent was maintained at a high level, especially in the sixth century, reaching a peak under the first Kentish king to embrace Christianity, Aethelbert, whose reign covered the half-century from the 560s to 616. He married Bertha, a Frankish princess who brought her Christian faith with her to the most advanced English kingdom of the period. In doing so, she probably played a part in influencing the direction of Pope Gregory's mission, which carried Augustine to Kent in 597, there to initiate the conversion of Germanic England.

The emergence of the kingdom of Kent (the name is derived from the Germanic *Cantware*, the *Cantiaci*, the Romano-British

---

[8] S. E. West, 'West Stow: the Anglo-Saxon village', *East Anglian Archaeology*, 24 (1985).

inhabitants of the region) was followed in the seventh century by others, most of them tiny by the standards of mainland Europe and several far from stable.[9] Connections with the Continent were maintained by several of these minor states, particularly Kent and East Anglia, and not only with the adjacent parts of Europe. The magnificently furnished burial at Sutton Hoo in Suffolk (of about 625) reveals connections with the graves at Vendel and Valsgärde in Sweden (below, p. 231), and contains coins from Frankish Gaul and a Byzantine silver dish of some age, perhaps a diplomatic gift. Few, if any, parts of the Germanic world were completely isolated and most were bound by political and other ties to a much wider world than is often imagined.

Scandinavia

A region of which written sources have very little to relate is southern Sweden and the Baltic islands of Gotland and Öland. Such events as are mentioned at all are raids and battles, like the Swedish attack on Frisia or the expansion of the Svear of Uppland. The overall tenor of life can only be established with the aid of archaeological evidence. Unlike most of the areas of Europe dealt with in this book, Sweden and the adjacent lands were not subject to major intrusions of people from outside. But the period from 400 to 700 was none the less one in which there was a considerable degree of cultural change. In part this was due to external forces, but the main motor of change was internal. The land was rich in agricultural products and its potential was increasingly realized in the fifth and sixth centuries by its largely nameless leaders. The turbulent decades which witnessed the end of Roman rule in the West released a stream of gold into northern Europe, some of booty, some payments for military service. A large proportion of this gold, for reasons that are still obscure, reached Sweden, Öland and Gotland in the form of ingots, spiral rings, *solidi* and magnifi-

[9] S. Bassett, *The Origins of the Early Anglo-Saxon Kingdoms* (Leicester 1988).

cent worked ornaments, some of them of majestic scale. A single gold ring, from Trolleberg, weighs 1.255 kg and one hoard, found at Tureholm in Södermanland in 1774, amounted to 12 kg. The Golden Age of Sweden is not mis-named.[10]

The land was settled by a variety of small groups and the tribal units which were known to the literate south were few. The most powerful was the tribe of the Svear or Sviar which

Figure 34 Gold hoard from Tureholm, Sweden.

[10] *Sveagold und Wikingerschmuck* (Mainz 1968).

had its centre in Uppland in eastern Sweden, a people who had been mentioned centuries before by Tacitus as strong in men, ships and war-gear. These are probably the same people who were known in the fifth and sixth centuries (the *Suehans* of Jordanes) as possessors of fine horses who hunted animals for their furs which were exported to the Mediterranean world. Jordanes also reports on northern peoples (the *Screrefennae*) who were nomadic hunters, without settled homes and agriculture. Also in southern Scandinavia lay the East and West Gotar, probably the Gautae of earlier writers, and linked by some with the early Goths, though on weak grounds. Western Norway was also brought within the same cultural orbit as the rest of southern Scandinavia from the fifth century. We hear at this time of a king ruling over a group of tribes including the Rugii (whose name survives in Rogaland) and Harothi (Hordaland), evidently an early stage of state-formation similar to that of southern Sweden. In most areas of southern Scandinavia there was an evident quickening in economic progress as the resources of the land were more systematically used. In several regions there was a marked population increase and a filling up of the landscape by farms and small hamlets. Fortified settlements appeared across Sweden in their hundreds, testifying to ever-present raiding and warfare of an acquisitive aristocratic society.

The growing political importance of Uppland and Mälar in the migration period is evidenced by the siting of three huge mounds at Gamla Uppsala (Old Uppsala), to the north of the modern city.[11] These lie within a region of rich inhumation burials and large hoards of gold, and there is later literary evidence that this place was a focus of surviving heathendom as well as the royal power of the Svear. The three mounds lie in a row with hundreds of smaller mounds nearby. A low platform-mound to the east of the row is evidently not a burial-monument: its traditional name is the 'Thing-mound' or council-mound. To the north lie the remains of the eleventh-century church of Gamla Uppsala built after the ultimate

---

[11] S. Lindqvist, *Uppsala Högar och Ottarshögen* (Stockholm 1936); M. Stenberger, *Det forntida Sverige* (Stockholm 1964).

triumph of Christianity in Sweden, the cathedral of the first archbishop. Two of the large mounds were examined in the nineteenth century, not thoroughly but with reasonable care. The burials located within it were much less spectacular than might have been expected, being cremations furnished with a few objects of gold, bronze and glass, all of them damaged in the funeral pyre. But the dating is fairly secure: about 500 for the eastern mound, half a century later for the western. The central monument, which has never been examined, is usually considered to be the earliest and to cover the founder-burial or burials of the fifth century. If the suggested dates are broadly correct, the men commemorated here were members of the ruling Ynglinga dynasty who figure in both Norse and English sources. The central mound would thus be the tomb of Aun, who died of illness in the fifth century, the eastern the grave of Egil and the western that of Adils. One of Aun's sons, Ottar, is recorded to have fallen in battle a few miles to the north of Uppsala at Vendel. Here too there is an exceptionally large mound, long known as Ottar's mound (Ottarshogal). This was excavated early this century and in it was found a worn *solidus* of the later fifth century. Construction of the Vendel mound is thus likely to have been about 500 or a little later, in line with local tradition about its occupant. There are more huge mounds in other parts of southern Sweden, often sited in areas of good land and close to route-ways. One of the largest of all is Anundshogen at Badelunda in Västmän on the edge of Lake Mälar. This is 15 metres high and overlooks a cemetery of the largest ship-shaped monuments in Sweden, one of them over 50 metres in length. That this was a political centre in the migration period is hinted at by the fact that a 'Thing' was held here in medieval times.

Gamla Uppsala was a focus of religion as well as of kingly power. Adam of Bremen, writing in 1070 when pagan religion was still a force, describes the heathen temple at Uppsala thus: 'A gold chain surrounds the temple, hanging about the steep roof and gleaming from afar to those drawing near; all the more as the sacred place itself, set in an open space, is surrounded by mounds so arranged as to form an amphitheatre.' Within the temple stood three images of gods, Thor, Odin and Freyr, and in a grove nearby hung sacrificial victims both human and animal. Every nine years great ceremonies took place in this ancient sanctuary, hallowed by age and the graves of kings. Beneath the twelfth-century church, part of a timber structure framed on massive uprights was found in 1926. This may well be the temple described by Adam, destroyed and symbolically replaced by the church of 1150. This, then, was the heart of the land of the Svear and it would retain its power until the end of paganism in the twelfth century. But long before that other centres of power had emerged in Uppland, at Vendel and Valsgärde and probably elsewhere. A unified state or kingdom had not yet emerged and was not to do so before the ninth century.

The economic development of southern Sweden and the Baltic islands from the late Roman period will inevitably have been accompanied by competition for resources and the wealth they afforded. Alongside the treasure it is not surprising to observe the spread of fortifications among the settlements of the period. In the coastlands of the west, in Södermanland and Östergotland, on Öland and Gotland, an enormous number of stone-built hill-forts testify to local insecurity and to the likelihood of long-distance raiding by sea. The great majority of these forts are small, with a single wall round them. Some now show no trace of internal buildings; a small number have planned structures covering most of the interior. The largest stronghold, Graborg on Öland, is roughly circular, 210 metres in diameter and with a defensive wall up to 9 metres high. Most are a good deal smaller than this and may be the strongholds of individual families, offering refuge for retainers and stock in time of crisis. The most fully examined fort, Eketorpsborg on Öland,[12] began as a refuge in the later fourth century, but after 400 developed into a highly ordered community settlement with buildings of roughly equal size radiating from the inside of the perimeter wall and a further group of structures in the centre, providing dwellings, storage and animal stalling for a sizeable unit of people. The degree of social organization and forward planning evident here is very unusual and argues for

---

[12] U. Näsman, *Eketorp. Fortification and Settlement on Öland/Sweden. The Monument* (Stockholm 1976).

a strong local or regional leadership which was long maintained on the island.

The gold found in southern Scandinavia was substantially, probably mainly, provided by Roman coinage.[13] Of roughly 700 gold coins of the fifth and sixth centuries, about 280 have come from Öland, 250 from Gotland and 150 from Bornholm. Most of the coins which reached Öland and Bornholm were of the emperor Leo (457–74), whereas those on Gotland were struck for later emperors, from Anastasius to Justinian

Figure 35 Aerial view of the fort of Eketorpsborg, Öland.

[13] J. M. Fagerlie, *Late Roman and Byzantine Solidi found in Sweden and Denmark* (New York 1967).

(491–565). The prominence of hoards is clearly significant. A high proportion of the coins reaching the north was hidden away by its new owners in uncertain times and not recovered. It may be surmised that the coins reached the Baltic lands from the Oder–Vistula coastal regions, where similar hoards are known, though in smaller numbers, originally as tribute and military payments to northern leaders and their warriors who had taken part in the campaigns of the period 370–450. On the Swedish mainland the coins are found in smaller numbers. An important concentration is evident at Helgö, a trading centre on Lake Mälar, where about 80 coins have been found to date, including a hoard of 47 and another of 21 *solidi*.

External trade and the widest oversea and overland contacts are evident on this small island in Lake Mälar, earlier called Helgö, the Holy Island.[14] Several groups of large rectangular buildings here stood on terraces along with smaller huts and workshops. Helgö was occupied over many centuries from the late Roman Iron Age to the Middle Ages, and the material now recovered from its many phases of activity is vast, particularly from the period 500–800. Imports from many quarters of Europe and beyond are the most revealing aspect of the site. Aside from the familiar gold *solidi*, there is glass from the Frankish world, metal ornaments and brooches from various parts of northern Europe, a bronze ladle from Coptic Egypt, a bronze figure of the Buddha, made before 700 in northern India, and an elaborate bishop's crozier of Irish origin dating from the following century. The goods came from east and west, across the North Sea, the Baltic and over the wide plains of eastern Europe to this emporium on its inhospitable crag in a northern lake. How was this traffic organized and who lay behind it? It must be emphasized that Helgö was not at any date an agglomeration of farmsteads. Nor can it be seen as the forerunner of a town in any sense that would be comprehensible to medieval or modern man. It is not enough to see it as one of that number of trading sites, such as Dorestad or Quentovic, which emerged from the realignment of trade patterns consequent upon greater political stability from the later seventh

---

[14] W. Holmqvist et al., *Excavations at Helgö* (4 vols; Stockholm 1961–72).

century onward. For Helgö was also concerned with manufacturing, particularly of metal objects, for local markets. The functions of the place were thus complex and almost certainly altered over the centuries of its life. It may have begun as a local market centre, added manufacture of certain goods, and later became involved in long-distance commerce. Even this does not cover all the likely functions of Helgö. We might expect a cult-centre here and the Irish crozier might be a relic of a mission to a well-established pagan centre. And it is not impossible that it possessed at least limited administrative functions within the Mälar valley. As for who brought Helgö to its position as a trade and manufacturing centre, the archaeological evidence, extensive as it is, is so far silent and is likely to remain so.

Richly furnished graves occur in Sweden from the later Roman period onward, but not until the seventh century do we encounter anything as lavishly equipped as the royal graves of the Franks. The two cemeteries of Vendel and Valsgärde in Uppland, along with other burials in eastern Sweden, give glimpses of a ruling dynasty of which the material culture of the preceding period has betrayed scarcely a trace.[15] Close by the site of the medieval church at Vendel lay a group of at least fourteen ship-burials, many of them damaged and plundered before the thirteenth century. Vendel lies only 2.5 kilometres north of the Ottarshogel (above, p. 227) and thus may well be the burial-place of later members of the same ruling group. The earliest known ship-burial in Scandinavia is that of a woman at Augerum in southern Sweden; it dates from the second half of the sixth century. In the later burials at Vendel and Valsgärde we encounter the rite in its developed form and with accompanying grave-goods of unparalleled richness in the northern Germanic lands. One grave at Valsgärde (no. 6) will give some idea of the splendour which surrounded these rulers in life and in death. A ship some 8 metres long bore the dead man to the other world. Beneath the corpse were feather cushions, at its side a formidable array of weapons: two long

---

[15] H. Stolpe and T. J. Arne, *La nécropole de Vendel* (Stockholm 1927); J.-P. Lamm and H. -A. Nordstrom (eds), *Vendel Period Studies* (Stockholm 1983); G. Arwidsson, *Valsgärde* (3 vols; Uppsala 1942, 1954,1967).

Figure 36 Helmet from grave XIV at Vendel, Sweden.

swords, three shorter blades, two shields, a helmet, lance, spears and a box of tools. Vessels of glass, wood, bronze and iron along with other furnishings of the festive hall such as firedogs, a spit and flesh hooks represent the princely feasts of Germanic story. Near the prow lay two horses and their saddles, a deer and a dog. Carpets of birch-bark covered the grave-offerings and over all a mound of earth and stone had been heaped up. Another of the wealthiest graves, no. 12 at Vendel, reveals the cultural and ceremonial linkages across the northern world. A splendidly decorated iron helmet with embossed bronze plates is a remote descendant of the helmets used by late Roman troops.

Many small farming settlements of the Roman and migration periods are also evident in the landscape of southern Sweden and the Baltic islands. One of the most fully investigated is Vallhagar on Gotland.[16] This consisted of five or six farmsteads set within walled fields and closes, each comprising a central dwelling and a small number of associated buildings. The social unit represented at Vallhagar was probably a small group of interconnected families, each with its own economic focus, but linking up with its neighbours for certain joint purposes. The place was occupied from around 400 to the mid-sixth century, though earlier farms existed on this site and close by. The community was supported by mixed agriculture, with the rearing of stock predominating over the growing of crops. Cattle and sheep were the main standby, with pigs and fowls also present. Half-wild russ horses were periodically rounded up and their flesh eaten. The crops grown at Vallhagar included emmer wheat and Einkorn, barley, rye, spelt and flax. The imports that reached Gotland from many quarters in the migration period reached the Vallhagar farmers in small quantities, presumably in exchange for agricultural products. They included glass vessels from the Rhineland, and pottery and metalwork from several parts of the western Baltic.

The emergence of early states in Scandinavia followed a different pattern from that in much of the rest of Germanic Europe. The relative geographical remoteness and small size of

---

[16] M. Stenberger and O. Klindt-Jensen, *Vallhagar* (Stockholm 1955).

these states did not mean that they were insignificant or negligible. Their power to attract wealth from the eastern Roman world and later from western German powers was not inconsiderable. By the late sixth century, if not earlier, their ruling houses had connections not only with the lands across the Baltic, but with the Franks and the dynasts of eastern England, the last-named so startingly revealed at Sutton Hoo. In these wide-ranging contacts is foreshadowed the expansion of the Vikings from the eighth century onward.

11

The Gepids and Lombards

The Gepids

The most shadowy of all the major Germanic peoples of the migration period are the Gepids, and we cannot pretend to be able to do more than sketch their history.[1] They did not succeed in establishing an enduring state or even a stable settlement within defined boundaries; no later chronicler was moved to record their history and traditions, if indeed such were current among the Gepids themselves. They first appeared after 260 when they were attacking Dacia along with the Goths. But they failed to seize possession of part of that province when it was abandoned by Rome a decade later, thus tending to confirm the Gothic tradition that Gepids were lazy and lacking in initiative. The area in which they did settle lay on the north-west flank of Dacia, east of the river Tisza, and there they remained until they were subjugated by the Ostrogoths early in the fifth century. In the following decades their warriors were increasingly drawn into service with the Huns; the Gepid king Ardaric was more favoured by Attila than any other vassal leader. In the Hun attack on the Balkans in 447, the Gepids were the staunchest allies of Attila. On the Catalaunian Field in 451 they formed the right wing of the Hun army. But after Attila's death they led a revolt against his sons, still under the

---

[1] L. Schmidt, *Die Ostgermanen* (Munich 1941), 529–64; I. Bona, *The Dawn of the Dark Ages* (Budapest 1976).

leadership of Ardaric, and together with allied Sarmatians, Suebi and Rugii, crushed the Huns on the river Nedao in 454. This success gave the Gepids a homeland in the eastern Carpathian basin, the status of allies of Rome, and a modest subsidy in gold. But the old enemy, the Ostrogoths, were still at hand and more than a match for the Gepids. Theoderic's forces thrust them out of the Danube lands in 504 and it was not until 537 that the Gepids were allowed to settle around Sirmium, when the Goths were intent on their own struggle with Byzantium. But this hold on the Danube valley was precarious, for the Byzantines were still keenly interested in the security of this stretch of the river and looked to the Lombards, not the Gepids, to ensure it. In 546 Audoin and his Lombards were given the task of occupying the old provinces of Pannonia and holding them as allies of Byzantium. This involved driving out the Gepids, which was achieved over the next five years. At the battle of the Asfeld in 552, the Gepid army was dispersed and never again were they to play any formative role in shaping events.

Although Gepid tenure of any one territory was relatively brief, it is possible to define the archaeology of their settlement to some extent. The area which has produced the most convincing evidence for their presence is the valley of the Tisza and the region immediately to the east. The eastern boundary may have been the great frontier earthworks erected by the Sarmatians in the fourth century against the Goths and Vandals. The richest burials are concentrated in the area of Szentes and these probably indicate a major centre of power here. Settlement sites are now beginning to be recognized. These suggest that the single farmstead or hamlet was widespread, while extensive and nucleated settlements were virtually unknown. In the Transylvanian hills, earlier hilltop fortifications were occasionally reoccupied by Gepid groups, but in the Tisza valley defended sites are as yet unknown. The material culture of the fifth- and sixth-century Gepids is related to that of the contemporary Lombards, though there are distinctively Gepid metalwork ornaments.

In 567 the nomadic Avars fell upon the Gepid homeland, destroyed what was left of Gepid power and at the same time threatened the Lombards so seriously as to force them to

Figure 37 Reconstruction of the horse-gear found in a richly furnished Gepid(?) burial at Apahida, Romania.

migrate to Italy. At least some splinters of the Gepid people survived this shock. A Byzantine general encountered Gepid settlements across the Danube in 600 and a group of them took part in the Avar attack on Constantinople in 626. But after 567 the Gepids were a spent force and soon disappeared from history altogether.

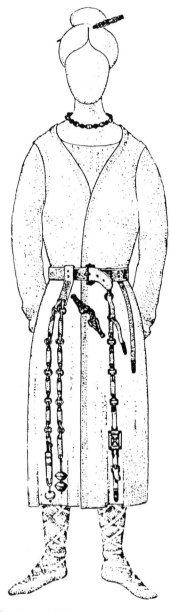

Figure 38 Dress of a Gepid lady, reconstructed from grave furniture found at Szentes-Nagyhegy, Hungary: sixth century AD.

The Lombards

The Lombards had played little part in the invasions of the Roman provinces before AD 400. During the earlier part of their recorded history they had occupied the lower and middle Elbe valley, a relatively small tribe but respected for their warlike prowess. It was not until the fifth century, after the considerable movements of Goths, Alamanni and Franks, that they moved south, to settle in northern Austria north of the Danube on land earlier held by the Rugii. This was about 486–7. There they remained for several decades as adherents of the Heruli. In the early years of the sixth century the Lombards crossed the Danube and settled in the old province of Pannonia, alongside several other Germanic groups, and began to establish themselves as a major power.[2] Their king Wacho (*c.*510–40) maintained good relations with Byzantium and also made marriage alliances through his daughters with the successors of Clovis. Arian Christianity made advances among them during the settlement in Pannonia and in general Lombard leaders were assimilated into the nexus of military service which had its centre in Italy. A *foedus* was struck between Wacho's successor Audoin and Justinian shortly after 540, the emperor requiring assistance against the Franks and the Ostrogoths. In 552 Lombards took part in the final Byzantine campaign in Italy. That glimpse of the lush valley of the Po was not forgotten. It was not long before uncertainty in Pannonia reinforced the attractions of northern Italy. The nomadic Avars began to intrude upon Lombard territory from the east and the new Lombard king Alboin found less support from Byzantium than he might have hoped for. Alboin decided that the best hope for the future lay in conquering part of Italy, and in 568 a large army headed westward towards the head of the Adriatic. This host included not only Lombards but Gepids, Sarmatians, Pannonians, Noricans and even Bulgars, according to the principal narrator of Lombard history, Paul the Deacon. Several of these groups were to leave their mark on the nomenclature

[2] J. Werner, *Die Langobarden in Pannonien* (Munich 1962).

of Italy. Others joined this extraordinary train either at the beginning or *en route*: Bavarians, Thuringians, Taefali and Saxons. Behind them the land they had left was taken by the Avars and the exposed northern Balkans fell to the Slavs and Bulgars.

Alboin's forces broke into Italy in May of 568, seized Aquileia with ease and then went on to take the other strongholds of the plain of Venetia. Within a year they had occupied most of the Po valley, including the old Imperial capital of Milan. Pavia held out against the invaders for three more years. Otherwise the Byzantines and their allies could only hang on to Alpine redoubts like Susa and Aosta and to well-fortified cities in the plain, including Cremona, Mantua and Padua. Lombard success in the north was thus rapid and the invaders were soon able to sweep southward through the Apennines into Tuscany and on to Rome by 575. Other bands began to occupy the

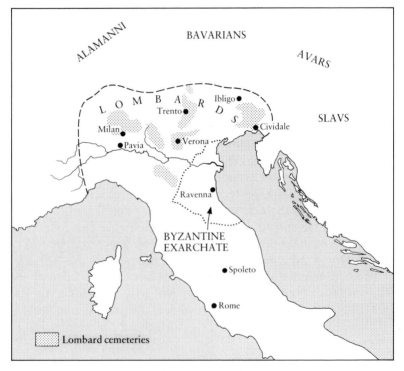

Figure 39 Lombard Italy and its neighbours.

eastern coastlands at about the same time, and by 580 Lombard *duces* were installed in Campania and beginning to look further south. Alboin had been murdered in 572 and his successor Cleph came to the same end after only two years. For a decade after this the Lombards had no king, power residing in a number of allied *duces*, traditionally thirty-five of them, six of whom in the north were regarded as of higher station. At the head of the confederacy was Zaban, who had his base at Pavia. It is unlikely that there were as many as thirty-five *duces* at one time. There were clearly more than six and probably fewer than twelve.

War-bands of the *duces* found rich pickings in late sixth-century Italy.[3] The cities provided them with comfortable lodgings; the countryside and its estates lay largely at their mercy. Many landowners were removed and killed for their land; others were kept on mainly to provide for their *hospites*. The Lombards had arrived in Italy as invaders, not as *foederati* of Rome and for a generation at least that is how they behaved. No orderly system of government was installed to replace that shattered by the invasion of 568. To the churchman and landowner of the sixth century the Lombards were a plague to rank with those of the Old Testament. As Pope Gregory was later to write, 'What is left of delight in the world? On all sides we see war, on all sides we hear groans. Our cities are destroyed, our strongholds razed, the countryside desolate. There is no one to till the fields; no one almost to keep the towns . . . Some have gone into slavery, some are left limbless, some slain.'

But the Lombards were not invincible. Attacks on eastern Gaul on several occasions between 568 and 575 all came to naught, while defeats in 571 and 575 at the hands of the Gallo-Roman general Mummolus were particularly severe. The Byzantine armies in Italy began to recover about 580 and later the Slavs and Avars began to push into the north-eastern province of Istria as the Lombards had themselves done. In 584, in the face of these dangers, the monarchy was re-established,

---

[3] W. Menghin, *Die Langobarden* (Stuttgart 1985) for most aspects of Lombard Italy; also C. Wickham, *Early Medieval Italy* (London 1981), 28–46.

Authari the son of Cleph being raised to power. Under him and his son Agilulf (590–616) the Lombard kingdom took shape and the framework of a state replaced the war-bands of the *duces*. But beneath the new order lay an essentially military organization, the main unit of which was the territory ruled by a *dux* and controlled by his army. Hence the prominence of Lombard terms like *gastaldus* (estate manager), *arimannus* (soldier), *adelingus* (noble or lord) in the documents of the day. The destruction of the Roman landed class and the concomitant expropriation of land meant that a substantially new social order came into being in Lombard territory. Lombard Italy was more fundamentally a Germanic kingdom than the Italy of Theoderic.

The Lombards had entered Italy as Arian Christians or as pagans. They must soon have encountered Catholics in their dealings with Rome and Ravenna, and their conversion to the Catholic faith must have appeared to many, as it did to Pope Gregory, a desirable step towards their integration in the political world of Italy. An instrument was to hand in the form of Theudelinde, a princess of the Bavarians, but related through her mother to the Lombard royal house. The connection with Bavaria offered the hope of alliance against the Franks and Theudelinde's acceptability in all ways is underlined by her marriage to Authari and to Agilulf in succession. Her influence was of enormous value to the Catholic Church, in the founding of churches, monasteries (like that of San Dalmazzo at Pedona) and in supporting missions and, on occasion, refugees like Colombanus in flight from the Franks. There were limits to what she could achieve. Authari forbade the baptism of Lombards according to the Catholic rite and Agilulf did not abandon his Arianism, despite allowing his son Catholic baptism. And Theudelinde's influence did not extend to control of Agilulf's policy towards the Byzantines.

His reign was to see major extension of Lombard territory in the north and in central Italy. From his first year as king he began the consolidation of Lombard power, which existed still in scattered nuclei and was in some areas far from secure. First, in 590 he reached an accommodation with the Franks after a determined eastward thrust of a Frankish force had threatened to sweep the Lombards away. Missions were sent to the Austrasian court and met with quick success, mainly because the Franks will by then have realized that they could achieve little that was permanent in Italy. In the next few years, furthermore, children were to occupy the three Frankish thrones of Burgundy, Neustria and Austrasia, giving further reason to draw back from adventures far from home. Agilulf had more than Franks to worry about. Several of the Lombard *duces* were in rebellion against him and one or two had transferred allegiance to Rome. Gaidulf, the *dux* of Bergamo, seems to have aimed at taking the Lombard throne for himself and twice had to be taken prisoner, his treasury being confiscated on the second occasion.

The struggle with the Romans could then be entered upon with greater vigour, the main objectives now being the fertile lands of Latium and Campania, with Rome and Naples as the final prizes. But there was still resistance in the valley of the Po and not until 593–4 could Agilulf make a strike against Rome. The hill-country of Tuscany was also to prove a far from easy target, and even at the end of his reign Lombard power there was still largely in the hands of an independent duke. The Lombards penetrated the Campagna in 593, but there was no siege of Rome, perhaps because of Pope Gregory's intervention, or perhaps because a pestilence still had the environs of the city in its grip. Naples, too, was spared. There is nothing to indicate that Agilulf mounted a determined campaign to seize and absorb these southern territories. The Lombard dukes in the south were left to prosecute their own ambitions and these were never formulated into a coherent plan of total conquest. The whole of Italy was thus not to fall to the Lombards. It was in the north that Agilulf strengthened the foundations of his kingdom, doing so with Roman forms and symbols of authority around him and with Roman advisers at his side. One inscription hailed him as 'by the grace of God most glorious, king of all Italy' and his son Adaloald was in 604 presented as king in the Roman circus at Milan before envoys from the Frankish court. Although a heroic warrior-figure in some respects, Agilulf had a clear view of the importance (even the inevitability) of the Roman cultural inheritance and its political significance. In so mixed an area as northern Italy about 600, some appeal to a stable past was sorely needed.

It did not matter that many elements of that past no longer possessed real power.

Agilulf's forces were not able to dominate central Italy to any lasting effect and a truce with Pope Gregory, backed by the promise of tribute from Rome, was probably accepted with some degree of relief. Gregory was also instrumental in the agreement of a truce with the Byzantines in 598, though this did not last more than three years. Then Agilulf resumed his conquests in the north, steadily taking those towns which still held out for the Byzantines: Cremona, Mantua and Padua. After further intermittent fighting, a more or less stable position was reached. The Empire accepted that it could not hope to recover what had been lost and the Lombards mounted no great campaigns to extend their power across the peninsula. When Agilulf died in 615, he was followed by his son Adaloald, baptized a Catholic as a boy. Arian Christianity was still strong, however, and tensions between Arians and Catholics could lead to, or represent, political divisions. But a sharp division between 'progressive' Catholics and 'traditionalist' Arians is surely false. Adaloald was deposed by an Arian group in 626 and replaced by Arioald his brother-in-law, though the intention was not thereby to restore the Arian faith. Another Arian, Rothari, *dux* of Brescia, inflicted a major defeat on the Empire and extended Lombard power to Genoa and the western sea. Following reigns, however, saw the advance of Catholicism, especially after Grimoald (662–71). In the final quarter of the century the Lombard conversion to Catholicism was completed and a more enduring peace established with the Empire. The final Byzantine throw had been an attack from the south on the duchy of Beneventum in 662, beaten off by Grimoald without much difficulty. By 680 the long wars were over.

There were major developments in Lombard society and law in the seventh century. The Edict of Rothari, issued in 643, is, surprisingly, the most extensive and most ordered expression of Germanic custom which emerged from any of the Germanic kingdoms, apart from the laws of the Visigoths. And the Edict is essentially a *Germanic* code of law, its Romanity being limited to language and to certain aspects of property. Its main concerns – set out in 388 titles – were with land, inheritance, marriage, compensation for injury, the court, military affairs, slaves and legal procedures. Within this framework, Lombard custom was carefully set out, in some cases with emendation, as for example in increasing the monetary compensation for wounding in order to reduce the emphasis upon the feud.

Lombard government was centred on the king, who exercised supreme authority in legal, administrative and military spheres. He was elected by the assembly of freeman, nominally at least, though several seventh-century rulers took their thrones after machination culminating in marriage. The assembly aided the king in upholding the law and in taking major decisions of state. To the principal posts of government were appointed members of the court, generally members of the *gasindi*, the king's personal entourage. The territorial possessions of the crown were governed by *gastaldi*, who wielded power on a temporary basis and who were answerable directly to the king. Gradually, *gastaldi* came to administer an increasing number of estates as Lombard territory was extended, though the royal patrimony was also dispersed to churches, monasteries and to favoured individuals, so that it did not remain concentrated on the king. The old Roman provinces had by the sixth century given way to Lombard duchies, based largely on the territories of certain of the larger cities. Some of the duchies on the frontiers were larger than the rest and might indeed embrace entire Roman provinces; this was true of the duchies of Trent and Friuli and, in the south, those of Spoleto and Beneventum. The two last often operated independently of the king (or even against him), not least because of their remoteness from the Po valley. The *duces* who ruled these lands were appointed by the king, usually for life, though dispute or delinquency often led to a fall from favour. The effective autonomy of the more powerful *duces* was based on their domination of the people who inhabited their territory. Some could thus establish a dynasty within which the succession could scarcely be challenged. These kingdoms in miniature naturally imposed severe restrictions on the rule of Lombard kings and, in especial, helped to ensure that the conquest of Italy would only be partial.

Within the order of the people as a whole, three main groups distinguish themselves: freeman, the half-free or *aldii*, and slaves. In the early days of the settlement in Italy, the freemen were landowners and soldiers (*arimanni* or *exercitales*). Men who lost their land through any cause might restore their fortunes by being recruited as *gastaldi* (estate managers) and could later acquire land from the king. The half-free *aldii* were tied to the land, like the *coloni* of the late Roman Empire, and though they were technically free they were wholly under the charge of the landowner for whom they laboured. Within the ranks of the slaves there were a remarkable number of divisions, including ministerial slaves who managed the master's household and estate, stewards in charge of cultivation, swineherds and common farm-labourers. The position of Romans within Lombard society has provoked much debate and many features of their status remain uncertain. For the Romans who lived in Lombard Italy have left scarcely a trace in the written record, even as late as the eighth century. Yet they can hardly all have been enslaved by the invaders as some nineteenth-century scholars believed. Nor can they have been exterminated or expelled, though no doubt there were many casualties, especially in the late sixth century, as Paul the Deacon relates. Much more plausible is the idea that in the areas which quickly fell under Lombard control there followed a rapid mixing of Roman and barbarian, especially among the population settled on the land. That certainly seems to be suggested by the admittedly limited archaeological evidence. There is evident cultural mixture in the common artifacts found in cemeteries and on settlement-sites, which hints strongly at association between craftsmen and consumers of different origins. It is also striking that most of the Lombard loan-words in Italian are for mundane things (for example *bica* – a sheaf; *melma* – a mire). So far as it goes, the evidence is that the Lombards gave up their own language at a relatively early date, perhaps by the end of the seventh century, a further sign that integration with the Roman population was both rapid and full.

A thorough restructuring of society in the areas of Lombard settlement probably did not therefore take place. A considerable survival of Roman landowners may be suspected down to the eighth century, and Lombard nobles seem to have moved into the cities and lived there like the municipal elites of the Roman Empire, alongside and increasingly mingled with Roman families. There is some evidence that the northern cities attracted

Lombard aristocrats from an early date, presumably for military reasons. A century after the invasion of 568, it must have been difficult to make any real distinction between Lombard and Roman in the cities and on the great landed estates.

The Lombards entered a land in which there were many walled cities and towns, and it has already been remarked that the progress of their conquest is measured by their seizure of the major cities of the Po valley and the hill-country on its flanks. The fate of those cities in the sixth and seventh centuries was various, though probably few were utterly destroyed or abandoned. In the tenth century more than 75 per cent of the old Roman cities were centres of population and, to some extent, of authority. A general urban continuity is one of the most notable features of Ostrogothic and Lombard Italy, though it was a process marked by both change and diversity. The cities most at risk were those in the more marginal situations. The city of Luni on the coast of Liguria could not maintain its forum and surrounding public buildings after the fourth century, and by the sixth century simple timber structures occupied the heart of the place. Even in the eighth century activity and occupation seem to have been concentrated in a limited part of the site, around the cathedral. Other cities shifted their sites, usually to more defensible positions, as in the case of the move of Volsinii to Orvieto. Some of the smaller cities retained their attraction simply because they *were* small and thus easier to protect. The largest, Milan and Aquileia, were too large to survive the major recession in trade from the fifth century and went under.

A feature which still strikes the visitor today is the survival of the ancient street-plan in so many of the larger cities. In Brescia, Cremona, Bologna, Verona, Piacenza and Lucca the modern plan preserves the Roman layout to a quite extraordinary extent, supporting the idea that the ancient streets did not go out of use in the fifth and sixth centuries. The ancient focus of a city might well, of course, alter. The forum gave way to the royal palace or the cathedral, the latter often being built away from the earlier centre. Churches began to dominate the town-plan, as in Milan and Pavia, and nothing illustrates the continuing wealth of cities so well as the continuance of church-building. The impression gained from Lucca, the best-recorded city of the period 500–1000, is of a densely settled core, about the royal palace and the cathedral, with much building outside the Roman walls. A striking proportion of the inhabitants were landowners or craftsmen associated with the landed interest, a fact which underlines the general similarity with the cities of the Roman world, themselves the residences of the landowning elite. Probably no cities developed into major commercial centres before the eighth century at the earliest, not even a great centre like Milan. It follows that the structure of Lombard administration was urban-based, as was the Church, the development of rural monasteries not beginning in earnest before 700.

The peak of Lombard power was attained under Liutprand, whose long reign from 712 to 744 was marked by skilful diplomacy in disturbed political circumstances. The papacy was at loggerheads with the Byzantine state and was backed by widespread support among the Italian communities. Liutprand seized upon the occasion to attempt a unification of Italy under Lombard control and marched on Rome. The *duces* of Spoleto and Beneventum were ranged against him on the side of the Pope, and Liutprand promptly changed tack, allied himself with the forces of Ravenna and laid siege to Rome. He succeeded in holding down the rebellious *duces*, and Byzantine rule was affirmed in Rome; but further attempts at a unification of Italy came to nothing. After Liutprand's death in 744, the strength and political will of the papacy began to rise. The possibility of combating the Lombards by appealing to the Franks was grasped and the revival of a strong Frankish monarchy after Charles Martel offered circumstances favourable to a realignment of power in Italy.

Pope Gregory III had failed to enlist Frankish aid against Liutprand in 740, but after the death of Charles Martel in the following year Frankish interest in Italy grew. The Lombard king Ratchis recognized the mounting danger to his kingdom and had to make way for his more determined brother Aistulf in 749. Aistulf set about his task with a will, taking over the Duchy of Spoleto, occupying Ravenna and demanding tribute from Rome. The Pope prevailed upon the Franks to intervene and Pippin III invaded Italy in 755 and defeated Aistulf. Lombard rule in the peninsula was all but over, though under the last monarch, Desiderius, at least the kingdom still held together. In 773 Pippin's son Charles, without marked enthusiasm, invaded Italy, defeated a Lombard army and took the Lombard centres of Verona and Pavia. The most powerful Germanic state had finally won control of the heart of the old Roman Empire, and its king could later claim the place of emperors in Rome itself.

The main areas of Lombard settlement are sketched out by the distribution of inhumation cemeteries. The main concentration of these occurs north of the river Po from Piedmont to Friuli, between Lake Maggiore and Lake Garda. To the south a markedly thinner scatter of cemeteries runs up into the hills of the Romagna but scarcely beyond. In this same region several groups of place-names attest Germanic settlers: Gepids, Suebi and Burgundians as well as Lombards. Names which are most plausibly linked with Lombards are commonest immediately west of Lake Garda and in the northern plain of the Po. The general picture is thus outlined with fair clarity. But when we seek information on individual settlement-sites, our sources fail us almost totally. Excavation of a distinct settlement which can be assigned to Lombards has yet to be carried out and identification of such sites is still at an early stage. The Lombard invasion of Italy was carried out by a number of war-bands, the leaders of which were eager to seize strong-points and cities and use them as their headquarters. Colonization of the surrounding land came later and would in all probability be in the hands of a population very mixed in ethnic origin. Several of the commoner place-names reflect this phase of colonization very well. Names in *braida* (plain) and *sunder* (a separate holding) are eloquent of land-taking, while *gehagi* and *gastaldi* relate to administrative arrangements in a reordered landscape. *Sala*, too, meaning an estate-centre, may also point to reorganization of land-holding, not merely to renaming of older holdings. Several of the small Lombard cemeteries, representing the burial-places of single families, are to be seen in this context of land-taking in the late sixth and earlier seventh centuries (for example in the region of Brescia).

The greater part of the population is likely to have been centred on walled towns and other strongholds, or more specifically on the courts (*curtes*) of their leaders which were based there. This is certainly suggested by the rich graves in the area of Cividale and by the large warrior-cemeteries of Castel Trosino and Nocera Umbra. There are no clear indications of intensive Lombard settlement outside such core areas, though it is worth noting that from the mid-seventh century recognizably Lombard cemeteries became less and less easy to identify, as burial customs were increasingly influenced by Christian practice. As is to be expected, Lombard burials and place-names do not occur in the hinterland of Ravenna and the cities which adhered to Byzantium. Nor do they appear in the vicinity of Mantua and Cremona, which only fell to Agilulf nearly twenty years after the invasion.

The significance of cities in the ruling order is underlined by the burial practices of leading families. Queen Rodelinde ordered a church to be built on the site of a Lombard cemetery outside the walls of Pavia, the church known as Santa Maria ad Perticas ('at the stakes'). The siting of the church is of particular interest as it occupied a peculiarly significant burial-place, the stakes referred to in the dedication marking the graves of dead warriors. Yet the cemetery lay outside the walls in the Roman manner. The topographical arrangement of Lombard cemeteries is even more striking at Cividale.[4] This small Roman town in Friuli was a favoured early centre of the Lombards, and a remarkable series of their cemeteries lay outside its walls on both sides of the river Natisone. One of the most significant of these is a group of more than 250 graves outside the Porta San Giovanni, of which at least 127 were Lombard interments, women and children as well as men. It is unfortunate that a large proportion of the burials were brought to light in the early nineteenth century, before clear records of the graves were kept, for it is clear that both male and female burials contain objects which are to be ranked among the earliest Lombard material in Italy, dating from 568 to about 590. In all probability these are graves of those who took part in the invasion. Other cemeteries at Cividale belong to a more settled phase of Lombard rule. Outside the church of Santo

---

[4] Menghin, *Langobarden*, 149–56; M. Brozzi, 'Zur Topographie von Cividale im frühen Mittelalter', *JRGZM* 15 (1968), 134.

Stephano in Pertica, close to the walls, a small group of burials is to be linked with a leading Lombard family of the years about 600. The presence of gold-leaf crosses in these graves is a plausible indication of Christian burial close to an extramural church.

Other richly furnished burials were placed near churches within the walls, including the cathedral, the most imposing being the so-called grave of Gisulf within a now vanished church in the north-eastern sector of the town. This splendidly equipped burial in a sarcophagus contained several marks of high rank, quite possibly those of a *dux* or a member of ducal family. But despite the name 'Gisulf' scratched on a tile in the lid of the sarcophagus, the burial is not that of the *dux* of that name, being some thirty or forty years later in date. All these graves, and others from Cividale, are a sufficient indicator of the attraction of the city for noble families from the earliest period of Lombard occupation and of the close association between churches and the interment of nobles from at least 600 onward. What is evident at Cividale is probably also true of Verona, Brescia, Milan and the other cities of the north, but there the remains of the relevant burials have either been destroyed or not yet revealed.

Just as churches could attract burials, so burials could determine the siting of churches. As the Christian rite of burial spread through all levels of Lombard society, so churches were built in, or on the edge of, existing cemeteries. This is attested by the remains of a church in the large cemetery at Castel Trosino (below, p. 252) as well as being reported for us at Pavia by Paul the Deacon.

Paradoxically the best-known Lombard cemeteries are not in the main area of Lombard settlement but in central Italy in the duchy of Spoleto. These are the extensive cemeteries of Nocera Umbra and Castel Trosino, both of which were associated with strong hilltop fortifications in strategically important positions.[5] Nocera Umbra is an outstanding stronghold on an

---

[5] A. Pasqui and R. Paribeni, 'Necropoli barbarica di Nocera Umbra', *Monumenti Antichi della Reale Accademia dei Lincei*, 15 (1918), 137–362; R. Mengarelli, 'Necropoli barbarica di Castel Trosino', *Monumenti Antichi della Reale Accademia dei Lincei*, 12 (1902), 145–380.

impregnable, rocky height overlooking the Via Flaminia, the main link between Ravenna and Rome. The graves are eloquent of the dominance of warriors in this community, some of the weapons and war-equipment recalling the earlier Lombard material in the Danube lands. Consonant with the obvious military importance of the place are a few graves of men of high rank. One of these contained a folding chair of iron, a mark of authority which harks back to Roman practice, as well as a saddle with golden mounts. Another warrior-grave held the remains of a fine helmet composed of overlapping iron plates, among other gear appropriate to a horseman of high rank. Yet another rich burial had at its feet the horse and hound of the dead warrior. Nocera Umbra gives us a vivid glimpse of warrior-nobles in a forward position above the road to Rome. They were established there by the end of the sixth century and the position was still held at least half a century later.

Castel Trosino was also in Lombard hands by the late sixth century, having earlier played a role in the Gothic wars. The fort overlooked the Via Salaria, which ran from Rome to Ancona on the Adriatic and was apparently held by a Lombard garrison throughout the seventh century. The cemetery, the largest so far known in Lombard Italy, contained well over 200 interments, many of them in stone-walled vaults or small chambers. A high proportion of burials contained no grave-goods and this was particularly marked close to the church, suggesting the advance of Christian practice. There are other signs of contact with the Roman population of the area. Several of the women's graves contained large disc-brooches which were derived from contemporary Roman dress, while other burials had jewellery based on Byzantine models. The picture of a community in which Germanic and Italian populations were mingled is rather stronger here than at Nocera Umbra; the emphasis upon a purely warrior-dominated society so much the less, at least by the later seventh century. Even at so late a date, Romanization in material things was still possible and it may have been at work in less tangible ways.

12

The Thuringians and Bavarians

Central Germany also saw the emergence of new peoples at the end of the Roman period and later, though the written sources for this region are exiguous. Several tribal groups had occupied the area between the upper Elbe basin and the Danube, including the Hermunduri, Marcomanni and, later, the Rugii.

A group of richly furnished burials in the area of the confluence between the Elbe and the Saale in central Germany clearly represents a base of local power in the late third and early fourth century. The best known of these graves are those from Hassleben and Leuna, but there are others, all apparently dating from a limited period to either side of 300.[1] The grave-chambers of some members of the group were unusually elaborate, large graves lined with planks being provided. The grave-furniture included Roman imports, conspicuous among which are bronze and silver vessels. Some of the Leuna graves contain the accoutrements of horsemen, and the sacrifice of a horse is attested near one grave in the form of the skull and feet of an animal, a ritual practice well known on the steppes as well as in other parts of Germania. Weaponry was not normally present in the graves, though sets of three arrows, with heads of silver or bronze, were occasionally provided, probably serving as marks of rank. Fine Germanic ornaments are in evidence,

---

[1] W. Schulz, *Leuna. Ein germanischer Bestattungsplatz der spätrömischen Kaiserzeit* (Berlin 1953); W. Schulz, *Das Fürstengrab und das Grabfeld von Hassleben* (Berlin and Leipzig 1933).

especially at Hassleben, along with pottery vessels and drinking-horns. The Leuna and Hassleben chieftains and their entourages were earlier seen as owing their wealth, and perhaps their status, to successful warfare on the Roman frontiers in the later third century. It is more probable that their acquisition of Roman goods and their level of affluence was due to service with the Roman armies in that turbulent period. We hear of sizeable German contingents being employed in the armies of more than one third-century emperor, desperate for manpower. These warriors would have returned home enriched by their service in Gaul and elsewhere, taking with them perhaps the Roman gold coins which are found in some numbers in central Germany about this date.

The Thuringians (Thuringi, Thoringi or Toringi) are first mentioned about 400, but had probably developed a separate identity during the previous century, the Hermunduri possibly providing the core of the new grouping.[2] Not until after the middle of the fifth century is it possible to speak of a recogniz-able archaeological culture in their heartland, which was the region about the confluence of the Saale and the Elbe, along with the valley of the Unstrut to the west. Although they figure rarely in the historical sources for the fifth and sixth centuries, the Thuringians were a force to be reckoned with for over a century. They did not attempt to move south towards the Danube in the later fifth century, probably because they had sufficient territory to support themselves, and this left them vulnerable to Frankish expansion east of the Rhine from the time of Clovis onward. About 530, most of the Thuringians were made subject to the Franks and thereafter they rapidly declined in influence. Some of them accompanied the Lombards to Italy in 568; others were absorbed by the Bavarians. As with the Burgundians in Gaul, little more than their name survived on the map of central Europe to record their existence.

The emergence of the Bavarians is among the most obscure episodes of the later migration period.[3] There was no mention of this people until about 550 and by then they were settled

---

[2] B. Krüger (ed.), *Die Germanen*, vol. 2 (Berlin 1983), 502–48.
[3] L. Schmidt and H. Zeiss, *Die Westgermanen. Die Baiern* (Munich 1940), 194–206.

south of the old Danube frontier. The fact that they were not mentioned by the biographer of St Severin, that well-informed source on the middle Danube in the fifth century, is clearly significant. The Bavarians were not recognizable until after 488 and probably not until after 500. Where they originated is still a matter for debate. Two theses are proposed. One argues that they migrated from Bohemia to the region south of the Danube, the other that they were an amalgam of elements in the Danube valley. The matter is still disputed. In the disturbed sixth century, it is highly likely that migrant groups moved into Raetia and Noricum from the north, and also along the Danube from the east. The region also held the remnants of a provincial population, much of which was absorbed in the new grouping. The Bavarians lay east of the Alamanni and west of the Slavs. They had close connections with the Lombards and some of them took part in the Lombard invasion of Italy in 568. After that was achieved, they were exposed to the Avars and thus were prepared to accept the protection of the Franks in the late sixth century. They remained between the Germanic and the Slav worlds until they finally submitted to Charlemagne late in the eighth century.

Conclusion:
From Antiquity to Today

Consciousness of the separate identity of the Germanic peoples was a slow development, and little headway was made in the medieval centuries. The works of the early inhabitants of northern Europe, especially megalithic graves and fortifications, were evident in the landscape and had to be explained. But even to literate observers like Saxo Grammaticus, the thirteenth-century Danish scholar, these seemed to be the work of demons and giants; hence, 'giant's grave' or 'giant's tumulus', or later 'heathen's ditch'. Ancient objects found in the ground were for long regarded as of magical or natural origin. Even as late as the sixteenth century, Mathesius, the friend and biographer of Martin Luther, could come down in favour of their being natural phenomena.

The great advance came with the rediscovery of Tacitus' *Germania* in the monastery at Hersfield in 1451 and its printing in Venice in 1470 and Nuremberg in 1473 in the edition of K. Celtis.[1] Even before it was printed the Italian humanist Piccolomini had issued a rough commentary on the work in 1458 and this was translated into German in 1526. The *Germania* provided a fund of information on the early Germans of a wealth and variety that would have astonished a medieval reader, but more than that its praise of certain aspects of Germanic society encouraged the rise of a nationalistic

---

[1] The *Germania* had been known to and used by Rudolf of Fulda in the ninth century, and Adam of Bremen in the later eleventh.

approach to the interpretation of the ancient past. For the first time, the ancient Germans could step out of the shadow of Rome and it was all the more satisfying that they should be introduced to the full light of European history by a Roman author of the highest repute. It is not surprising that several very rash works followed on the publication of the *Germania*, claiming far more for the Germans than could be deduced from Tacitus' text. Even descent from the heroes of Troy was mooted, in emulation of the origin of Rome itself. More important than these outbursts was the commentary published by Beatus Rhenanus in 1519 and the same scholar's compilation of ancient references to the early Germans which appeared in 1531. There was renewed interest in Caesar's writings at this time and the *Annales* of Tacitus and the work of Velleius Paterculus were now circulating. The geography of ancient Germany, and particularly the positions of the tribes mentioned by Tacitus, was the subject of a study by P. Melanchthon in 1557, while an attempt at an all-embracing historical account of the Germans was made by Philipp Cluverius (Klüver), *Germaniae Antiquae Libri Tres*, in 1616. Moves towards establishing the archaeology of the early Germans were understandably tentative. The easily identifiable Roman remains and objects, especially inscriptions, tended to claim most attention. Distinctively Germanic material was scarcely to be separated from the remains of other peoples: Celts, Slavs, even the Scythians. But the first glimmerings of archaeological awareness can be seen in the work of J. Aventinus, whose *Chronicle of the Origin, Descent and Achievements of the Ancient Germans* of 1541 was an account of the lineal ancestors of the Germans of medieval Europe. The beginnings of the first collections of antiquities in central Europe also brought this problem to the fore. A major prehistoric collection was formed by the Electors of Saxony at Dresden in the later sixteenth century and a catalogue was compiled as early as 1587. There were other early collections of antiquities at Vienna, Munich, Prague and Berlin. But comparative study of artifacts was very difficult before the late seventeenth century and even then the absence of any sure chronological indicators for virtually all of the material meant that an attribution to the Cimbri or Boii or Wendi was the most that could be offered.

Towards the end of the sixteenth century, growing curiosity about visible monuments and other antiquities led to the first excavations, chambered tombs and other megalithic monuments being a particular target. These undertakings gave rise to various learned speculations about the peoples who had constructed these works, notably in such books as *Bevolkerts Cimbrien* of J. -D. Major (1692) and M. T. Arrkiel's *Cimbrische Heyden-Religion* (1691). The early eighteenth century saw an increased flow of writing on the monuments of northern Europe, but little real advance in understanding what they were. Too much was attributed to the Germanic peoples known from the Classical sources, such as the Cimbri, Chatti and Langobardi, quite simply because they were the earliest recorded inhabitants of those regions. The immense time-scale of European prehistory could not be grasped or measured in any way, so that Palaeolithic handaxes, Bronze Age weapons, Iron Age pottery and migration period jewellery were thrown together hugger-mugger, not to be adequately separated and placed in their proper chronological context until the nineteenth century.

The growing professionalism evident in historical research in the eighteenth century owed much to the foundation of academies such as the Prussian Academy of Frederick I's reign and the Göttingen Academy of 1751. In Scandinavia there were similar foundations. Frederick's sister Lovisa Ulrika, the Queen of Sweden, established the Vitterhetsakademi in 1753, its objectives including the study of antiquities as well as history and rhetoric. The Norwegian Royal Society, founded in 1760, actually organized excavations and established a museum. In Denmark, the Royal Society was also concerned with records of discoveries, and a succession of members of the royal house were involved in the conduct of excavations. The first volume of the *Proceedings of the Danish Royal Society* contained a report by the court chaplain Erik Pontoppidan on excavations conducted by him on the site of a prehistoric burial monument in the park of the royal palace. The report is a model of intelligent observation, clear record and sober interpretation, the whole presenting an appealing picture of an honest man wrestling with evidence too complex for him to understand, but successfully avoiding the wilder flights of fancy indulged in by his immediate predecessors.

A masterly overview of the early Germans at the time of the Roman Empire was included in Edward Gibbon's *Decline and Fall of the Roman Empire*, the first volume of which appeared in 1776. Gibbon shows an interest in the German peoples themselves, not merely as enemies of the civilization of Rome. He was impressed by the vigour and strength of the barbarians, though he was not burdened with illusions about the noble savage. He often displays a balanced detachment when writing about barbarians which had scarcely been evident earlier. Thus he can remark that 'the ravages of the barbarians were less destructive than the hostilities exercised by the troops of Charles the Fifth, a Catholic prince, who styled himself Emperor of the Romans.' Gibbon had a high regard for Tacitus and depended heavily upon the *Germania* for his account. There seemed to be little more to say about the individual tribes, so that he confined himself to a general statement, with several characteristic observations of his own. On the absence of money in Germania, for example: 'Money, in a word, is the most universal incitement, iron the most powerful instrument, of human industry; and it is very difficult to conceive by what means a people, neither actuated by the one nor seconded by the other, could emerge from the grossest barbarism.' Gibbon understandably overemphasizes the lawlessness of the early Germans, their inability to combine effectively against Rome, their shortcomings in equipment and organization for war. He shows no deep interest in the relation between the tribes described by Tacitus and the later confederations which invaded the Roman world. Nevertheless, Gibbon's chapter on the Germans is a recognizably modern and relatively objective treatment, far more so than many that were to appear in the nineteenth century.

Johann Gottfried Herder, a contemporary of Gibbon, gave in his *Ideen* (1784–91) an interesting account of the impact of the Germans on the Roman Empire. He saw their tribal barbarism as wholly inadequate to the role they aspired to play within that world. But like other writers of the day, including Goethe, Herder had virtually nothing to say about the Germans before the great migrations. An early sign of changing times came in 1780. In that year Graf Ewald Friedrich von Hertzberg, a minister in the Prussian government, delivered a lecture to the Royal Academy of Sciences in Berlin in which he lauded the virtues of the Germanic peoples and their superiority over those of the Romans. Over the next decades there was a steady rise of interest in Germanic antiquity, fostered and encouraged by the foundation of a number of regional historical societies. These provided the meeting-places for historians, philologists and archaeologists which were essential if real advances were to be made. The advances were not long in coming. The great undertaking, still in operation, of the *Monumenta Germaniae Historica* was founded in 1819 and its first volume appeared in 1825. In 1836, Gustav Klemm published his *Handbook of German Antiquity*, a many-sided study of Germanic culture, society and religion based on the ancient sources and upon the still limited archaeological record. That record was to develop significantly in the next few decades. Levezow published his pioneer study of Germanic and Slav antiquities in the region between Elbe and Vistula in 1825. Lisch performed the same service for Mecklenburg in 1837. In the following year Giesebrecht confronted the major problem of dating early Germanic material found in graves in northern Germany. All of these were intelligent attempts at interpreting the antiquities now being found in the earth in ever-increasing quantities. But without an overall cultural and chronological framework their contribution was inevitably minor. A major advance came about mid-century.

In 1855 John Mitchell Kemble wrote to the Secretary of the Society of Antiquaries of London concerning a number of mortuary urns found at Stade in northern Germany, his letter being later published in *Archaeologia* volume 36. Kemble remarked on the striking similarities between the vessels he saw at Stade and other urns found in eastern England. His observation was soundly based and thus began the modern study of early Anglo-Saxon pottery and metalwork, which provides a primary source of information on the Germanic settlement of England. Archaeological studies in England and Germany were not yet so advanced that the full implication of Kemble's observation for the chronology of Anglo-Saxon pottery could be grasped. Shortly afterwards, however, discoveries were made in southern Denmark (after 1864 in Germany) which provided important chronological data as well as illuminating the material culture of the Germanic peoples during the life of the later Roman Empire.

Peat-bogs at Nydam, Thorsbjerg and Vimose began to yield up extraordinary quantities of objects, especially weapons, items of armament, brooches and other personal ornaments, pottery, textile garments, leather shoes, and Roman coins. The Nydam deposit contained an even more remarkable feature, a trio of boats, one of which was recovered virtually intact, now to grace the Schloss Gottorp Museum in Schleswig. These great discoveries of what were plainly votive deposits, ably recorded and illustrated by C. Engelhardt in four fine monographs,[2] revealed in the most startling fashion the contacts between the Germanic world and the Roman Empire in the third and fourth centuries AD and thus opened the way to the establishment of a firm chronology for Germanic cultural material of the later Roman Iron Age by providing a well-dated archaeological 'horizon'. These peat-bog deposits revealed clearly to Engelhardt and to J. J. A. Worsaae, the most influential northern prehistorian of the time, that the northern Iron Age was not a brief phase which closed the prehistoric era but a lengthy and formative period which linked the preliterate Nordic world with that of the Viking sagas. In 1865 these two scholars suggested for the first time that the Iron Age could be divided into three distinct phases, corresponding broadly to the Roman Iron Age (*c*.AD 200 to *c*.AD 450), the migration period (*c*.450 to 700) and the Viking Age (*c*.700 to *c*.1000). The scene was thus set for major progress and steady refinement in chronology as archaeological techniques began to develop in the late nineteenth century.

A pioneeering work of migration period archaeology was published in 1848 by the brothers Wilhelm and Ludwig Lindenschmidt. This was *Das germanische Todtenlager bei Selzen in der Provinz Rheinhessen* (The Germanic Burial-place

---

[2] C. Engelhardt, *Thorsbjerg Mosefund* (Copenhagen 1863); *Nydam Mosefund* (Copenhagen 1865); *Kragehul Mosefund* (Copenhagen 1867); *Vimose Fundet* (Copenhagen 1869).

at Selzen in the Province of Rheinhessen). This modest little monograph was the first orderly and clear publication of a Germanic cemetery and it set standards that were not surpassed until well into the twentieth century. An overall plan of the graves was provided and a range of individual burials and their contents was illustrated, in watercolour, as they were recorded in the ground. A selection of the grave-goods was discussed and analogies quoted from other sites in Germany and Switzerland. The Lindenschmidts were fortunate in finding two coins of Justinian among the grave-goods, so that they were able (correctly) to assign the cemetery to the sixth century. The publication of the Selzen cemetery marks the beginning of modern studies of Germanic migrations. For the first time there was clearly demonstrated the possibility of dating burials (and thus other deposits) to the post-Roman period. Comparative studies, of which Selzen was the first exemplar, could thereafter establish links with the material of other sites and regions, thereby laying the foundations of a dating scheme on which much of our present knowledge of the period rests. Ludwig Lindenschmidt went on to further major studies of migration period archaeology, as well as to a major role in the founding of the Römisch-Germanisches Zentralmuseum in Mainz.

Philological studies also came to the fore at this period, one of the principal fascinations of its exponents being the light which language might be made to throw on early relations between Germans and Celts. To the grave detriment of the subject, several of these early accounts were shot through with Celtomania or an equally powerful German reaction to it. In their most extreme form these views were informed by national sentiment rather than by dispassionate linguistic scholarship, as for example when d'Arbois de Jubainville argued that the Germans had at one time been subject to the Celts and as their bondsmen had taken over many loan-words. The more neutral view of Holtsman, whose *Celts and Germans: A Historical Enquiry* was published in 1855, seems equally inexplicable. He sugested that the Celts of continental Europe and the Germans were the same people, while the insular Celts of Britain and Ireland represented a quite different branch of the Indo-European family-tree. The German reaction to such propositions was understandably abrupt, and a natural prejudice in favour of German integrity in matters of language and of race was strongly reinforced by these exchanges. By the end of the century in Bismarck's Germany that prejudice had hardened into something even less amenable to open debate.

In many respects study of Germanic history and archaeology made great strides in the later nineteenth and early twentieth centuries. Archaeologists were increasingly confident of their ability to date material and the sites from which it came. Studies of individual peoples and of the land they had inhabited proliferated. Standards of source criticism rose considerably. Karl Müllenhoff's *Deutsche Altertumskunde* of 1880, a commanding survey of the whole field, was the best work of synthesis that had appeared to that time. But the scholar who left the deepest impress on how the subject was to be studied over the following half-century was Gustav Kossinna. In 1885 he made his approach clear in a famous lecture delivered before the German Anthropological Institute at Kassel. In Kossina's thesis the original German homeland had been Mecklenburg, Schleswig-Holstein, Denmark and the west Baltic islands, and southern Sweden. In that region German culture had developed entirely without external influence since the Mesolithic and from this enclave Germans had extended control over the lands to east, west and south. The title of Kossina's most popular book, published in 1912, neatly encapsulated the doctrine: *German Prehistory, a Pre-eminently National Discipline.* Its direct appeal to German nationalism ensured its popularity and its later editions could be adopted almost as a political text by the National Socialist Party. The leaders of the Third Reich took Germanic antiquity, or at least Kossinna's version of it, very seriously indeed, encouraging the formation of a Reichsbund für deutsche Vorgeschichte (Imperial Association for German Prehistory) and effectively barring any suggestion that early Germanic culture might have drawn on that of neighbouring peoples.

Already by the middle decades of the nineteenth century the idea of a racial supremacy enjoyed by the northern peoples had emerged from the studies of physical anthropologists who tirelessly, and in some cases obsessively, spent their time measuring the cephalic index of early populations. The long-headed (dolichocephalic) northerners were clearly marked out from the broad-headed (brachycephalic) peoples of the south and endowed with a virile and energetic identity; tall, blond, blue-eyed. Morally as well as physically, the Nordic race was seen as superior to all others. But where had it come from? Early linguists had looked to central Asia and western India for the original homeland of the Indo-European peoples. But the

Figure 40 An idealized German warrior, with dress and equipment based on material from the Thorsbjerg votive find.

findings of the anthropologists did not produce any encouraging signs of a suitably impressive physical type in those regions. By the 1860s a European homeland was being sought for the Nordic race. Germany, Scandinavia and western Russia all had their proponents. The Scandinavian hypothesis was later aggressively advanced by Karl Penka in a series of works which influenced not only scholarly opinion but also the public perception of the origins of northern European man. Before the end of the nineteenth century, the link between an original, superior Aryan race and the Germanic peoples of historic times was firmly embedded in the popular imagination. Its legacy was to affect more than the fanatical adherents of National Socialism in the following half-century. Gordon Childe, a prehistorian with strong Marxist sympathies, accepted many parts of the Aryan thesis, not least the outstanding mental capacity and cultural inventiveness of the Aryans. Those who used the idea of an Aryan ancestry as a support for political demands in the twentieth century could claim, if they wished, to have the support of a wide spectrum of scholarly opinion. The Third Reich did not invent the Aryans, nor the idea of a Nordic super-race. Both notions were firmly established before 1900 and formed parts of an orthodoxy most Europeans would now find embarrassing as well as bogus.

The search for a national cultural unity led many writers and thinkers to the remoter German past. Widespread dissatisfaction with the divided state of Germany after the Napoleonic wars found a variety of outlets in politics, art, literature and popular culture. National monuments were erected, partly as expressions of nationality, partly to provide foci for a popular, secular religion. Many of these monuments were Classical in form, though Germanic themes were to the fore in the associated decoration and symbolism. The most notable was the Valhalla built by King Ludwig I of Bavaria overlooking the Danube near Regensburg between 1830 and 1842. This took the form of a Greek temple, 120 metres in length and 50 metres high. Within were two halls, their ceilings and walls adorned with Germanic gods and the symbols of their power. On the eaves along one side stood personifications of the German states gathered about a victorious Germania; on the other, Arminius the Cheruscan leader who had triumphed against the

legions of Rome in the Teutoberg forest. Much more enduring
in its fame was a monument begun as Ludwig's Valhalla neared
completion. This is the *Hermannsdenkmal*, the monument of
Arminius, set high on a hill within the Teutoberg forest itself.
The creation of Ernst von Bandel, this was begun in 1841, but
its construction was delayed by lack of funds in the disturbed
years of the 1840s; it was eventually finished in 1875. Unlike
the Valhalla, this was to be a Gothic conception, a symbol of
the force and power of youthful Germany. The massive pedestal
supporting the figure of Arminius was intended to contain a
Hall of Fame celebrating famous Germans, though this element
was never completed. The statue of the hero is that of an
armoured medieval warrior, wearing a winged helmet and
holding aloft a huge sword, its impact somewhat reduced by
the unconvincing proportions of the figure itself. In its upland
landscape, however, the monument is still impressive. It was
disliked by the Nazis, Hitler believing that the Gothic was an
outmoded style which had no place in his New Order. But of
all the monuments to the Germanic past, the *Hermannsdenkmal*
has the most secure place in the affections of twentieth-century
Germans and is still today much visited. A later monument
erected on the banks of the Rhine between 1874 and 1885, the
Niederwalddenkmal, was not to enjoy anything like the appeal
of the Arminius statue. Built to commemorate German unity,
this was a huge statue of Germania in Classical guise, its
massive pedestal bearing friezes depicting Peace and War, and
the rivers Rhine and Moselle.

But national feeling ran along other courses and found
expression in darker shades. The almost mystic vision of the
German nation as a *Volk*, at one with the land it inhabited, had
become embedded in political ideology during the nineteenth
century. Historians and archaeologists strove to make their own
contribution to *Germanentum*, by finding material evidence of
its antiquity. The heroic past was seen by many scholars as
providing not only a proud heritage but also hope and guidance
for the future. The glories of the Germanic past offered moral
and social values which other peoples had lost or never known.
The Germans of antiquity had emerged in the northern lands
of Europe, purifying and saving mankind from the decadent
Mediterranean empires. The qualities of the northern warrior

Figure 41 The Hermannsdenkmal, *Germany.*

were lauded to the skies; the power of the sword was the only true power. It was a short step to endow the German warrior with a unique, superhuman strength. The superiority of the Nordic peoples was attested by their victorious progress over Europe and in particular by their defeat of the most ambitious of the ancient empires, that of Rome. Proof of that superiority was supplied not only by history, but by studies of racial types (a matter of precise measurement at that time and much in vogue) and of archaeological cultures. The developing disciplines of physical anthropology and of field archaeology provided abundant material to support theories of a steadily ascendant Germanic culture, morally as well as materially superior to that of other races.

The creation of a heroic German past was followed by its exploitation by the National Socialist Party in the 1930s with seeming inevitability.[3] With high levels of government support, programmes of research were devoted to establishing the antiquity and dominance of the Germanic race over the widest possible area of Europe. There were excavations, often of high quality, on prehistoric sites, many conducted under the supervision of the SS. Indeed, Himmler hoped that a Germanic excavation would be close to every SS *Standarte* in the Reich, to serve as a cultural centre of German greatness. There were innumerable studies of how the racially pure Germans of prehistory had extended their cultural dominance over less favoured races like the Slavs or the Celts, had beaten off the Romans, and finally invaded and destroyed their empire. Much archaeological publication of the period, though depressingly predictable in its conclusions, was excellently done; many of the regional surveys which appeared during the Third Reich laid important foundations for further study. In 1940, the largest general survey of the Germanic peoples attempted to that date emerged under the editorship of H. Reinerth. It represented the culmination of fifty years of writing on the early Germans from a strongly nationalist base and it proved to be the high-water mark of that historical tide. Understandably, since 1945 the

---

[3] G. L. Mosse, *Nazi Culture: Intellectual, Cultural and Social Life in the Third Reich* (London 1966).

emphasis on a heroic Germanic warrior-culture has all but disappeared. Cultural interchange with the other peoples of Europe has been assigned a much more prominent role. The impact of Rome on a barbarian society has been more subtly interpreted and the lineaments of that society more clearly defined. Large-scale excavation of settlements and related studies of their environment have revealed a population which exploited the land and its resources with marked expertise, and which developed social and economic structures which proved to be remarkably durable. The five centuries from the rediscovery of Tacitus' *Germania* to the extensive archaeological projects of today have seen great change in appreciation of the place occupied by the early Germans in European history. The end of that long process is not yet in sight, but we may fairly claim to hold a vastly better vantage-point than that of any previous generation.

Sources

The more important and accessible of ancient sources are listed below. Recent editions do not exist for all of them. Only the most reliable of early editions are noted here.

Ammianus Marcellinus, *Roman History*, ed. W. Seyfarth (Berlin 1968–71).
    A selective translation is available in Penguin Classics (1985).
Ausonius, *Opera*, ed. H. Schenkl (*MGH AA* 5:2).
Caesar, *Commentaries*, ed. R. du Pontet (Oxford 1900).
    Translation available in A. and P. Wiseman, *The Battle for Gaul* (London 1980).
Cassiodorus, *Variae*, ed. T. Mommsen (*MGH AA* 12).
Chronica minora, ed. T. Mommsen (*MGH AA* 9 and 10).
Eugippius, *Life of St Severin*, ed. R. Noll (Berlin 1963).
Gregory of Tours, *History of the Franks*, ed. O. M. Dalton (Oxford 1927).
    Translation also available in Penguin Classics (1974).
Hydatius, *Chronicle*, ed. A. Tranoy (Paris 1974).
Isidore of Seville, *History of the Goths, Vandals and Suevi*, ed. D. Coste (Leipzig 1909).
    Translation by G. Donini and G. B. Ford (Leiden 1970).
John of Biclarum, ed. T. Mommsen (*MGH AA* 11).
Jordanes, *Getica*, ed. T. Mommsen (*MGH AA* 5:1).
Notitia dignitatum, ed. O. Seeck (Berlin 1876).
Orosius, *History against the Pagans*, ed. C. Zangemeister (Vienna 1882).
    Translation by R. J. Deferrari (Washington, DC 1964).
Paul the Deacon, *History of the Lombards*, ed. O. Abel (Leipzig 1939).
Procopius, *The Gothic Wars*, ed. D. Coste (Leipzig 1922).

Sidonius Apollinaris, *Opera*, ed. C. Lutjohann (*MGH AA* 8).
Symmachus, *Opera*, ed. O. Seeck (*MGH AA* 6:1).
Tacitus, *Germania*, ed. R. Hoops (3rd edn; Heidelberg 1967).
   Translation available in Penguin Classics (1948).

Select Bibliography

The following list includes the more accessible of the studies cited in the notes, together with suggestions for further reading.

Ament, H. 'Der Rhein und die Ethnogenese der Germanen', *Präh. Zeitschrift*, 59 (1984), 37.

Arrhenius, B. *Merovingian Garnet Jewellery: Emergence and Social Implications* (Stockholm 1985).

Bachrach, B. S. *A History of the Alans in the West* (Minneapolis 1973).

Beck, H. *Germanenprobleme in heutiger Sicht* (Berlin/New York 1986).

Birkhan, H. *Germanen und Kelten bis zum Ausgang der Römerzeit* (Vienna 1970).

Boeles, P. C. J. A. *Friesland tot de eelfde eeuw* (The Hague 1951).

Böhme, H. W. *Germanische Grabfunde des 4. bis 5. Jahrhunderts zwischen unterer Elbe und Loire* (Munich 1974).

Böhner, K. *Die fränkischen Altertümer des Trierer Landes* (Berlin 1958).

Bolin, S. *Fynden av romerska mynt i det fria Germanien* (Lund 1926).

Burns, T. *History of the Visigoths* (Bloomington, Ind. 1984).

Campbell, J. (ed.). *The Anglo-Saxons* (Oxford 1982).

Capelle, W. *Das alte Germanien. Die Nachrichten der griechischen und römischen Schriftsteller* (Jena 1929).

Christlein, R. *Die Alamannen* (Stuttgart 1978).

Collins, R. *Early Medieval Spain* (London 1983).

Cunliffe, B. *Greeks, Romans and Barbarians* (London 1988).

de Vries, J. *Altgermanische Religionsgeschichte* (Berlin 1969).

Diesner, H.-J. *The Great Migration* (London 1982).

Eggers, H.-J. *Der römischer Import im freien Germanien* (Hamburg 1951).

Ekholm, G. 'Die Zeitstellung der Hemmoorer Eimer', *Bonner Jahrb.* 143–4 (1938–9), 311.

——'Scandinavian glass vessels of oriental origin from the first to the sixth century', *Journ. Glass Studies*, 5 (1963), 29.

Ellis Davidson, H. R. *Gods and Myths of Northern Europe* (Harmondsworth 1964).

Engelhardt, C. *Thorsbjerg Mosefund* (Copenhagen 1863).

——*Nydam Mosefund 1859–63* (Copenhagen 1865).

——*Kragehul Mosefund* (Copenhagen 1867).

——*Vimose Fundet* (Copenhagen 1869).

Ensslin, W. *Theoderich der Grosse* (2nd edn; Munich 1959).

Ewig, E. *Frühes Mittelalter. Rheinische Geschichte*, vol. 2 (Dusseldorf 1980).

Fagerlie, J. M. *Late Roman and Byzantine Solidi found in Sweden and Denmark* (New York 1967).

Gelzer, M. *Caesar: Politician and Statesman* (Cambridge, Mass. 1968).

Gimbutas, M. *The Balts* (London 1973).

Godlowski, K. *The Chronology of the Late Roman and Early Migration Periods in Central Europe* (Cracow 1970).

Goffart, W. *Barbarians and Romans, AD 418–585: The Techniques of Accommodation* (Princeton 1980).

Grünert, H. (ed.). *Römer und Germanen in Mitteleuropa* (Berlin 1976).

Haarnagel, W. *Die Grabung Feddersen Wierde*, vol. 2 (Wiesbaden 1979).

Hagberg, U. E. *The Archaeology of Skedemosse* (Stockholm 1967).

——(ed.). *Studia Gotica* (Stockholm 1972).

Halbertsma, H. *Terpen tussen Vlie en Ems* (Groningen 1963).

Haseloff, G. *Die germanische Tierornamentik der Völkerwanderungszeit* (3 vols; Berlin 1981).

Hatt, G. *Nørre Fjand: An Early Iron Age Village in West Jutland* (Copenhagen 1967).

Horedt, K. and Protase D. 'Das zweite Fürstengrab von Apahida', *Germania*, 50 (1972), 174–220.

Hougen, B. *The Migration Style of Ornament in Norway* (Oslo 1967).

Hvass, S. 'Vorbasse: the development of a settlement through the first millennium AD', *Journ. Danish Arch.* 2 (1983), 127.

——*Hodde. Et vestjysk landsbysamfund fra aeldre jernalder* (Copenhagen 1985).

Ilkjaer, J. and Lønstrup, J. 'Interpretation of the great votive deposits of Iron Age weapons', *Journ. Danish Arch.* 1 (1982), 1.

James, E. *The Franks* (Oxford 1988).

Jensen, J. *The Prehistory of Denmark* (London 1982).

Kilian, L. *Zum Ursprung der Indogermanen* (Bonn 1983).

——*Zum Ursprung der Germanen* (Bonn 1988).

Klindt-Jensen, O. *Foreign Influences in Denmark's Early Iron Age* (Copenhagen 1950).

Kropotkin, V. V. *Rimskie importnye izdelija v Vostocnoj Europe* (Moscow 1970).

Krüger, B. (ed.). *Die Germanen* (2 vols; Berlin 1976, 1983).

Kunow, J. *Der römischer Import in der Germania libera bis zu den Marcomannenkriegen* (Neumünster 1983).

Lamm, J.-P. and Nordstrom, H.-A. (eds) *Vendel Period Studies* (Stockholm 1983).

Lebecq, S. *Marchands et navigateurs frisons du haut moyen age* (2 vols; Lille 1983).

Lemant, J.-P. *Le cimetière et la fortification du bas-empire de Vireux-Molhain, Dép. Ardennes* (Mainz 1985).

Liebeschuetz, J. H. W. G. *Barbarians and Bishops* (Oxford 1990).

Lind, L. *Roman Denarii Found in Sweden*, vol. 1 (Berlin 1979); vol. 2 (Stockholm 1981).

Lindenschmidt, W. and L. *Das germanische Todtenlager bei Selzen in der Provinz Rheinhessen* (Mainz 1848).

Lindqvist, S. *Gotlands Bildsteine* (2 vols; Stockholm 1941–2).

Mackeprang, M. B. *De nordiska guldbrakteater* (Aarhus 1952).

Majewski, K. *Importy rzymskie w Polsce* (Warsaw 1960).

Matthews, J. *The Roman Empire of Ammianus Marcellinus* (London 1988).

Menghin, W. *Die Langobarden* (Stuttgart 1985).

Mildenberger, G. *Germanische Burgen* (Münster 1978).

Musset, L. *The Germanic Invasions* (London 1975).

Näsman, U. *Eketorp: Fortification and Settlement on Öland/Sweden. The Monument* (Stockholm 1976).

Nierhaus, R. *Das swebische Gräberfeld von Diersheim* (Berlin 1966).

Norden, E. *Die germanische Urgeschichte in Tacitus' Germania* (4th edn; Darmstadt 1959).

Odobescu, A. *Le trésor de Petrossa* (Paris/Leipzig 1889–1900).

Ørsnes, M. 'The weapon find in Ejsbøl Moss at Haderslev', *Acta Arch.* 34 (1963), 232.

Périn, P. and Feffer, L.-C. *Les Francs* (2 vols; Paris 1987).

Pirling, R. *Das römisch-fränkische Gräberfeld von Krefeld-Gellep* (Berlin 1966, 1974, 1979).

Rouche, M. *L'Aquitaine des Wisigoths aux Arabes, 418–781* (Paris 1979).

Schlabow, K. *Der Thorsberger Prachtmantel* (Neumünster 1965).

Schönberger, H. 'The Roman frontier in Germany: an archaeological survey', *Journ. Roman Studies*, 69 (1969), 144.

——'Die römischen Truppenlager der frühen und mittleren Kaiserzeit zwischen Nordsee und Inn', *BRGK*, 66 (1985), 321–497.

Stenberger, M. *Det forntida Sverige* (Stockholm 1964).

——and Klindt-Jensen, O. *Vallhagar* (Stockholm 1955).

Thompson, E. A. *The Early Germans* (Oxford 1965).

——*The Visigoths in the Time of Ulfila* (Oxford 1966).

——*The Goths in Spain* (Oxford 1969).

——*Romans and Barbarians: The Decline of the Western Empire* (Madison, Wis. 1982).

Timpe, D. *Arminius-Studien* (Heidelberg 1970).

Todd, M. *The Northern Barbarians* (2nd edn; Oxford 1987).

Trier, B. *Das Haus im Nordwesten der Germania Libera* (Neumünster 1969).

Vana, Z. *The World of the Ancient Slavs* (London 1983).

van Es, W. A. 'Wijster: a native village beyond the Imperial frontier', *Palaeohistoria*, 11 (1965).

——'Friesland in Roman times', *BROB* 15–16 (1965–6), 37.

Waas, M. *Germanen im römischen Dienst* (2nd edn; Bonn 1969).

Wallace-Hadrill, J. M. *Early Germanic Kingship in England and on the Continent* (Oxford 1971).

——*The Barbarian West* (3rd edn; Oxford 1985).

Wells, C. M. *The German Policy of Augustus* (Oxford 1972).

Wenskus, R. *Stammesbildung und Verfassung* (2nd edn; Cologne/Graz 1977).

Werner, J. 'Zur Herkunft und Zeitstellung der Hemmoorer Eimer und der Eimer mit gewellten Kanneluren', *Bonner Jahrb.* 140–1 (1936), 395.

——*Die beiden Zierscheiben des Thorsberger Moorfundes* (Berlin 1941).

——*Die Langobarden in Pannonien* (Munich 1962).

Wheeler, R.E.M. *Rome beyond the Imperial Frontiers* (London 1954).

Wolfram, H. *History of the Goths* (Berkeley, Calif. 1988).

Zollner, E. *Geschichte der Franken bis zur Mitte des 6. Jahrhunderts* (Munich 1941).

Index